W9-ASE-684

CAMBRIDGE IBERIAN AND
LATIN AMERICAN STUDIES

GENERAL EDITOR
PROFESSOR P. E. RUSSELL, F.B.A.
PROFESSOR OF SPANISH STUDIES, THE UNIVERSITY OF OXFORD

The novels of Julio Cortázar

CAMBRIDGE IBERIAN AND LATIN AMERICAN STUDIES

already published

EVELYN S. PROCTER, *Curia and Cortes in León and Castile, 1072–1295*

future titles will include

JUAN LÓPEZ-MORILLAS, *The Krausist movement and ideological change in Spain, 1854–1874*

A. R. D. PAGDEN, *The fall of natural man: the American Indian and the growth of historical relativism*

FRANCISCO RICO, *The picaresque novel and the point of view*

A. C. de C. M. SAUNDERS, *A social history of black slaves and freedmen in Portugal, 1441–1555*

DIANE UREY, *Galdós and the irony of language*

The novels of
Julio Cortázar

STEVEN BOLDY

CAMBRIDGE UNIVERSITY PRESS

CAMBRIDGE

LONDON   NEW YORK   NEW ROCHELLE

MELBOURNE   SYDNEY

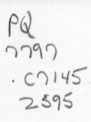

Published by the Press Syndicate of the University of Cambridge
The Pitt Building, Trumpington Street, Cambridge CB2 1RP
32 East 57th Street, New York, NY 10022, USA
296 Beaconsfield Parade, Middle Park, Melbourne 3206, Australia

First published 1980

Printed in Great Britain by
Western Printing Services Ltd, Bristol

British Library Cataloguing in Publication Data
Boldy, Steven
The novels of Julio Cortázar. – (Cambridge Iberian
and Latin American studies).
1. Cortázar, Julio – Criticism and interpretation
I. Title II. Series
863   PQ7797.C7145Z/   79-41579
ISBN 0 521 23097 7

For Isabel

Contents

Abbreviations

LR	*Los reyes*
B	*Bestiario*
AS	*Las armas secretas*
P	*Los premios*
H	*Historias de cronopios y de famas*
R	*Rayuela*
V	*La vuelta al día en ochenta mundos*
62	*62. Modelo para armar*
UR a, *UR* b	*Ultimo round* (top deck, bottom deck)
LR	*Literatura en la revolución y revolución en la literatura*
VM	*Viaje alrededor de una mesa*
PO	*Prosa del observatorio*
M	*Libro de Manuel*
C	'Corrección de pruebas en Alta Provenza'
F	*Fantomas contra los vampiros multinacionales*
OC	F. Hernández, *Obras completas*
Pa	Richard Wagner, *Parsifal*
Mo	M. Butor, *La modification*
CP	C. Fuentes, 'Documentos. El caso Padilla'

Introduction

The major geographical shifts in Julio Cortázar's life are emblematic of the nature of his writing. Though the youthfulness of his work would suggest a later date, he was born in Brussels in 1914[1] of Argentinian parents. In 1918 he 'returned' to Argentina, to live in Bánfield, a suburb of Buenos Aires, where, for our purposes, his main activities seem to have been reading, translating, and teaching English and French literature. In 1951, having published only one play and a collection of short stories, he returned to Europe and still lives in Paris. It was in Paris that the first of his four novels to date was produced: *Los premios* (*The Winners*), published in 1960. Here for the first time he wrote directly about Argentina, its people, its problems and (its) metaphysics. The very Latin American phenomenon of Peronism precipitated his departure from Argentina; he claims to have come to an understanding of its significance only by living in Europe.

Cortázar, then, is an expatriate Latin American writer, a central figure in the 'mafia' of writers in a similar position who participated in the editorial 'boom' of the sixties and seventies, 'commercially manipulated' from Barcelona. As such, he incurs the tedious, self-righteous wrath of many non-expatriate writers and critics. A reasonably balanced account of the reasons for the exodus of Latin American writers from their respective countries to Paris, Barcelona and London is given by the Chilean José Donoso in *Historia personal del boom*; a characteristic, if unusually venomous, exchange on the subject provoked by the remarks of José María Arguedas in *El zorro de abajo y el zorro de arriba* and answered by Cortázar completes the picture.[2]

Leaving aside prescriptive formulae, I believe one can safely say that cosmopolitanism is an important component in the best Latin American literature. Argentina, with its high percentage of relatively recent European immigrants and its lack of any real indigenous culture, is an extreme case. Ernesto Sabato puts it dramatically: 'Perplexed and anguished, we are the actors of an obscure tragedy, in that we neither have the backing of a great indigenous culture (like the Inca or the Aztec), nor can we claim as completely our own the tradition of Rome or Paris.'[3] Were Argentinian writers to obey the nationalist detractors of Europeanism, he adds in a different tone, they would be confined to writing about ostrich hunts in the language of the Pampa Indians.[4] Jorge Luis Borges is more concise: the Argentinian tradition is 'the whole of Western culture'.[5] Mario Vargas Llosa is positively jubilant about the cultural void of Latin America:

The lack of a cultural tradition implies a void which is also the ultimate freedom. Not only because the 'barbarian', that orphan, can plunder all the cultural reserves of the earth with equal ease (which is something the 'civilized' writer, limited towards other cultures by a view of them imposed by his own, cannot), but, especially, because his being a sort of Adam or pioneer in the field of creation is a strong incentive to his ambition.[6]

This Latin American dualism is probed in the shifting perspectives of Cortázar's second, most influential and best-known work, *Rayuela* (*Hopscotch*), published in 1963. Its tripartite structure is symbolic of the dilemma: one part takes place in Paris, another in Buenos Aires, and a third (optional!) section is generally devoted to the culture which links and separates the two main sections, the two continents.

Intertextuality and parody, an important element in all (modern) literature, becomes for Severo Sarduy the defining characteristic of the Latin American: 'Only in so far as a work of the Latin American baroque is a deformation of a previous work, which must be *read like a watermark* (*leer en filigrana*) for it to be fully enjoyed, will it belong to a major genre.'[7] Obsessive quotation from Chateaubriand's *Atala* and Bernardin de Saint-Pierre's *Paul et Virginie* gave Jorge Isaacs's *María* (1867) a very characteristic structure. Exactly the same tradition is followed in Fuentes's *Terra Nostra* (1975), in the extensive quotation and paraphrase of pieces by Poe, Kafka, Bernal Díaz del Castillo, and others. When combined, however, by writers like Borges, Carpentier, Fuentes, and Cortázar with an acute critical consciousness of their language, this tendency creates a literature which, far from being imitative or derivative, gains a special density and expressiveness. In Carpentier's *El recurso del método*, for example, the quotation of Proust in a phrase like 'in the shade of the flowering cannons'[8] concisely and ironically demonstrates the Latin American dependence on European discourse, and the frequent incongruity of the latter. The classical appeal to the idealism and spirituality of Latin American youth against the materialism of their Northern neighbours in Rodó's *Ariel* is similarly travestied and inverted by the account of the arms deals done in Washington by Ariel, the son of the dictator in the same novel.

62. Modelo para armar (62: A Model Kit), published in 1968, represents the furthest point of Cortázar's experimentation in this direction. The literal quotation of *Rayuela* goes underground. A set of European texts and myths, only summarily mentioned, dictate the course of the novel and the lives of the characters, whom they lead either to destruction or to liberation, according to the honesty or bad faith of the narrator towards his material.

Cortázar's interviewers have noted that more space is occupied on his bookshelves by French and English texts than by Spanish ones. On compiling a list of the influences on his own work, Cortázar's *alter ego* in *Rayuela*, Morelli, sensibly crosses out various names because they are too obvious (*R* 412, ch. 60). The names of Joyce, Beckett, Proust, etc. should clearly be treated in the same way. One general 'influence', however, might be noted: that of surrealism. The coincidence is more one of outlook and philosophy than of adherence to any Bretonian dogma: a preoccupation with the unconscious, a hope of reconciling the dualisms of modern man, an interest in causality, word play, and evil.

This filiation, which develops into a humanistic concern for the recovery of a unity of being threatened or destroyed by rationalism and technology, is shared by Cortázar with his Argentinian contemporary Ernesto Sabato, for whom art, and especially the novel, is 'the instrument which will recover the lost unity'.[9] Perhaps even more than Sabato, he claims to have bridged the gap between the two traditionally opposite tendencies in Argentinian literature, symbolically Florida and Boedo, i.e. between sophisticated, elitist writers such as Borges, Mallea, Macedonio Fernández, and more popular ones such as Roberto Arlt.[10] There are traces of all these writers in his work: the messianic madness of Arlt, the mysticism of Mallea, the humour and philosophical paradox of Macedonio; and of others: the macaronic combination of Buenos Aires *lunfardo* slang with the constant use of phrases from languages other than Spanish characteristic of the Cambaceres of *Silbidos de un vago*. But the father-figure is without doubt Borges, though the tone and purpose of their work is very different. From Borges, Cortázar learns the structural sophistication which culminates in the *figura*, and shares with him an initially similar treatment of the barbarous and violent.

The successful Cuban revolution of 1959 was a fundamental event in the life of Cortázar and of many other Latin American writers. He visited post-revolutionary Cuba for the first time in 1963. The Cuban experience, he claims, 'woke him up to Latin American reality'.[11] The 'events' of May 1968 in Paris constitute a second, lesser, but important landmark. Cortázar wrote enthusiastically of them in the essay 'Noticias del mes de mayo' from his collage work *Ultimo round*. So did Benedetti, and Carlos Fuentes dedicated a whole book to the subject: *París: la revolución de mayo*, which his enemies have claimed contributed to the tragic 1968 student revolts in Mexico.[12] For the first time, one senses, the wider aims of surrealism and Marxism finally coincide. The 'Padilla affair' in 1971 was a bucket of cold water. The Cuban poet Herberto Padilla was imprisoned for counter-revolutionary attitudes. Latin American and European writers wrote a letter of protest and talked of Stalinism, Castro made a vehement attack on them, and while they reaffirmed their adherence to the revolution, there was a second letter of protest which Cortázar, significantly, did not sign. Instead, he published an anguished piece entitled 'Policrítica a la hora de los chacales', asking to be let back into the fold, while insisting on his commitment to a wider, freer, more critical type of writing than that demanded by Castro, Portuondo and Haydée Santamaría.[13]

His fourth and latest novel, *Libro de Manuel*, published in 1973, two years after Padilla, takes a radically new direction from his earlier novels and stories. The result is not of the same literary standard, though the work is a brave and vital experiment in writing serious literature with an important component of experimentation, while at the same time reaching a wider public, communicating information of a political nature, and expressing an ideological commitment which his previous work tended to relativize and fragment. There is, however, no yielding in his expression of the importance of eroticism, play and fantasy in the revolutionary process.

Fantomas contra los vampiros multinacionales, published in 1975, follows the same synthesis of genres, combining the comic strip with political message, and gives little insight into where a next novel might go, only a guilty apprehension that the halcyon days of *Rayuela* and *62* are past.

Since the mid-sixties, Cortázar's work has attracted such a deluge of critical response that it is impractical to attempt to review (or read) it in its entirety. A few landmarks might be mentioned. The year 1968 brought two important studies. Graciela de Sola's *Julio Cortázar y el hombre nuevo* is a good, wide-ranging study which stresses Christian attitudes in Cortázar. García Canclini's *Cortázar: una antropología poética* is not a detailed work, but one of the most convincing, especially in its intuitive understanding of the monsters of Cortázar. David Viñas in *De Sarmiento a Cortázar* (1971) offers a radically politicized reading of Argentinian literature; his analysis of various escapist myths is extremely stimulating. The year 1973 was good. Davi Arriguci's *O Escorpião encalacrado* is one of the best-documented and most serious studies, but is seldom quoted, one assumes, because it is in Portuguese. Saúl Sosnowski's *Julio Cortázar: una búsqueda mítica* is a detailed and penetrating study of the mythical and primitive vision in Cortázar. In 1974 Joaquín Roy published *Julio Cortázar ante su sociedad*, informative and interesting both on Argentinian themes in general and on their presence in Cortázar. Marta Paley Francescato's 'Bibliography of Works By and About Cortázar' in *The Final Island*, edited by J. Alazraki and I. Ivask, is the most complete compiled to date.

What this book tries to do is, to define at least, simple: to understand the four novels of Cortázar, *Los premios*, *Rayuela*, *62. Modelo para armar*, and *Libro de Manuel*. Its methodology consists in laying hands on anything that will help. My starting point was one of incomprehension and perplexity at the whole phenomenon of the novels rather than a desire to prove a theory or analyse any one aspect of them. My presentation necessarily reflects this process of understanding, which was gradual and is almost impossible to formalize. I believe that any more formal or 'definitive' presentation would betray the nature of Cortázar's literary experiment, itself a living process rather than a series of finished and closed works of art. The space devoted to each novel has, unconsciously, expressed an evaluation of their relative literary worth. *Los premios* is used basically to introduce and illustrate the genesis of the principal themes and structures considered; *Rayuela* and *62* are dealt with in some detail;

Libro de Manuel, in less detail, as a continuation of previous structures and, one hopes, a prelude to a new direction rather than a coda.

The initial focal point has been the nerve centres of contradiction and tension in the texts. In this, I have tried to live up to the demands Cortázar explicitly makes on his reader, when he asks that the latter should be his 'accomplice' or 'lector cómplice' (*R* 454). The *lector cómplice* is that reader who does not avoid the complexity, obscurity and tension of the 'materia en gestación' (*R* 453) by focusing on one level of experience or reading – the human, intellectual, humorous or textual – in order to bypass the tension between them. This tension is perhaps the fundamental quality of Cortázar's prose. A combination of different modes of writing in one episode causes different possible readings to be cancelled out, or rather held in abeyance. Human tragedy, for instance, is insinuated in a basically humorous episode; symbolic readings of the same episode are suggested which clash with its human content; explicit meaning is contradicted by a system of meaning developed throughout the text. The writing creates, more than a meaning or a set of meanings, a 'space' in which the *lector cómplice* can fully and creatively internalize the issues, problems, aspirations and impossibilities posed. Thus the understanding, on the part of the critic, as to how this 'space' is created is of as great an importance as the enumeration of actual readings generated.

At a certain point when working on a series of texts of the same author there develops a swing or dialectic between an emergent general structural theory and the defining differences and particularity of the individual texts. The thorny question thus arises of whether the texts should be presented separately, as organisms which can only be seen to work with all their constituent parts, or together, thematically and structurally. I believe it would be possible, by starting with an almost abstract deep structure and a limited set of elements (situations, character types), to build a sort of Cortázarian grammar which, through a series of transformations, could account for or explain the production of the texts. But much immediacy and excitement would be lost in such an account which would, moreover, be difficult to follow and, no less importantly, to organize. Cortázar's statement that 'no hay mensaje, hay mensajeros y eso es el mensaje' (*R* 453) suggests that the text itself is both message and messenger. I have worked on the general premise that no reading is valid if, once it has been 'extracted', the text can be discarded. It is this all-important 'textuality' that decided me to present the texts individually.

The strong structural homogeneity of the texts has, nevertheless, been illustrated by the use of two myths which can be considered as the deep structures behind them, that is structures which are not necessarily conscious, or clearly actualized, but whose logic dictates the course of the action. These myths are introduced in the first chapter and their evolving utilization is followed from chapter to chapter. They centre around what seems to be of fundamental importance in the novels: the feeling of a lost presence or force, and the attempt to recover this presence. This loss and quest can be contained, without excessive arbitrariness or violence, in the myths of the imprisonment of the Minotaur in the Labyrinth (with the Minotaur seen as a natural but rebellious and dangerous force), and the descent of Orpheus (or any other similar figure) to Hades to recover a Eurydice which may be associated with the lost force of the Minotaur.

This pattern makes it possible to link together the basic elements of the work: monsters, doubles and dualism, *figuras*, the 'centre'. Very schematically at this point, these elements may be defined and linked in the following manner: An original presence, or unity of man with himself and his world (Eden), has been lost. This loss is represented and repeated in the novels in the repression by the individual of parallel forces in himself. Dualism is created by the splitting of the unity of man into, crudely, the represser and the repressed. The force, on being repressed, becomes taboo. The tabooed force is seen as a monster. The *figuras* are the patterns within the text and the lives of the characters through which the original presence returns, but which tend towards a repetition of its destruction as a monster. The laws (of society, language, superego, narrative, etc.) which are accomplices in this destruction must be transgressed if the repetitive pattern is to be broken or reversed, and the presence recovered. This transgression will be counterproductive if the guilt involved is not overcome. The 'centre' referred to (elsewhere 'rendez-vous', 'unity') would be achieved by the recovery of the lost presence, i.e. man's reconciliation with the monster within.

There is a strict coherence in the search for 'presence' between the various levels of the text, and I have endeavoured throughout to express this. The presence is embodied principally in certain female characters, of which la Maga in *Rayuela* is perhaps the prime example, themselves seen, in turn, as the lost or hidden part of the male protagonist; it is an elusive meaning which is fleetingly present in, yet escapes from, language; it is the origins of Argentina and the human race; the telluric force of the *pampa* and the Buenos Aires of Cortázar's youth; it is the force of many literary and mythological archetypes projected forward finally onto the freedom of a new socialist man. Similarly, on all these levels, there is a force antagonistic to those described above: a tendency in language to form rhyming patterns and phonetic analogies which negate the desired *signifié*; in the narrator to manipulate and censure facts and relationships; in officials to distort truth; in individuals to forget and repress; in the Argentinian to betray his 'destiny'.

This force and counterforce has been approached in three main ways, in three themes, some already mentioned. The first is that of the *doppelgänger*; the meaning, articulation and resolution of the relationship between double characters and sets of double characters. The clearest example is the relationship in *Rayuela* between Oliveira and Traveler, and between la Maga and Talita.

The second theme is ultimately a development from that of the double: the *figura*.[14] It might provisionally be defined as the structural relationship between episodes, between sets of characters in different places or times; the repetition of previous texts in the constellation of events or in the psychology of the characters.

The third manifestation of the opposition might be called the 'double text'. In all the novels, and in some of the stories, especially 'El perseguidor', there are two different discourses, two types of writing and logic: one critical, distanced and organized, the other more symbolic and irrational. There are often two opposed narrators, and thus this technique is closely connected with that of the double.

The single-minded search for 'presence' outlined above is paradoxically but characteristically articulated through a variety of cultural references and literary discourses difficult to equal in their eclectic range: Schopenhauer, Raymond Roussel and Sarmiento in *Los premios*; Merleau Ponty, Sheridan le Fanu and Wagner in *62*; Marcuse and St John of the Cross in *Libro de Manuel*. While such combinations, creating a multiplicity of readings and nuances, preclude uniformity of treatment and analysis, I have tried to bring out that within them which is orientated towards what I consider the central pursuit of the author. Determining the nature of the raw cultural material of the novels and the measure and significance of its transformation and utilization has been one of my main concerns. Such material has often proved the only way in which I have been able to approach certain problems posed by the texts and has not been introduced *a posteriori* in order to establish a respectable pedigree for any interpretation, nor, with a few exceptions, to point out influences for their own sake.

The translations from the Spanish are my own. They tend deliberately towards the literal rather than the interpretative. Simple page references in brackets in the text refer to the novel dealt with in the chapter in which they appear. The editions of works by Cortázar used are listed in the bibliography.

This study is based on a doctoral thesis (Cambridge, 1978). A research fellowship at the Centre for Latin-American Studies, Liverpool, provided the time and support for its actual writing. I am much indebted to the patience, attention, and generosity with which Mr J. T. Boorman of Corpus Christi College, Cambridge, supervised the original work. My thanks go too to Mrs L. Close, and to Professor D. Shaw for their encouragement and advice in later stages. I might also put out a *saludo* to the flesh-and-blood Julio Cortázar, who must exist somewhere beyond the pile of novels on my desk.

I

Los premios

INTRODUCTION

The qualities which most immediately make *Los premios* an enjoyable
and even gripping novel are not those for which Cortázar has come
to be admired. The latter elements are, however, present in an
embryonic or not totally satisfying manner, and it is on these more
basic aspects of the work that coherence obliges one to focus. *Los
premios* is a hybrid work, metaphysical and existentialist, romantic
and objectivist, with an exciting story of sinister happenings on
board an ocean cruiser, and a mutinous attempt by the passengers
to break through to the ship's telegraph. Its treatment of adolescence
is extremely sensitive, which rarely commends a novel, unless, as in
this case, it is an essential part of a wider framework. The sym-
pathetic and subtle satire of Argentinian class relationships and a
sharp ear for cliché in conversation make it fascinating reading, and
Cortázar already displays skill in depicting conformism, bad faith,
and rebellion compromised by the manipulations of authority.

The lack of integration, however, of its two principal components –
the main narrative and the monologues of Persio which are inserted
between chapters – make it a less successful novel than those which
follow. Even a committed reader is tempted to skip the monologues
in a way he would not with the 'dispensable chapters' of *Rayuela*.
They contain some excellent, experimental writing, but their
density does not gel with the very fluid narrative of the rest of the
novel, nor create the tension between different tones of writing which
is present even in early stories such as 'Las puertas del cielo', and
cleverly orchestrated in the novels from *Rayuela* onwards.

Like all Cortázar's novels, *Los premios* begins with an image of chaos
and chance. An extremely heterogeneous group of Argentinians
have won a national lottery prize and are gathered together to enjoy

that prize: a sea cruise, the destination of which is, throughout, a mystery. This initial image works on two main levels. It is a *coup de dés* on the part of the author, a creation of chaos from which a new order might arise, as is suggested in phrases such as 'The decomposition of the phenomenal should precede any attempt at building' (100). It also provides the framework for a questioning, in the spirit of Borges's 'La lotería en Babilonia', of the authority, in all the senses of the word, which has the individual accept as natural the arbitrary, partial or alienated nature of his reality: 'Who, but who could find the Lottery strange?' (97)

The characters soon come to perceive their lives on board as absurd and precarious: 'We are not the great rose-window of the Gothic cathedral, but the instantaneous and ephemeral petrification of the rose of the kaleidoscope' (44). Through this recognition of their acentricity, a desire develops in them for a central attitude and ontological foundation in relation to which their lives would become as justified as the elements of the rose-window or the spokes of a wheel:

Somehow to reach the central point from which every discordant element could come to be seen as a spoke of the wheel. To see oneself walking and know that it makes sense.[1]   (379)
[One character longs for] a time where duration, where being alive at the very centre of life, would be reborn in her and redeem her.   (394)

Perhaps the greatest value of the novel lies in the coherence which its structure allows between the different levels on which the search for a 'centre', for order and meaning, is pursued. The main levels to be distinguished are the following:

1. On the narrative level, there is an attempt to 'organize another equally possible and acceptable order' (64), over and above the traditional narrative order suggested by the first lines of the novel: ' "The marchioness went out at five o'clock", thought Carlos López. "Where the hell did I read that?" ' (11)[2]

2. On the level of national identity, there is an attempt to go beyond the empty nationalistic pomp and the rhetoric of official history, beyond the alternation in the Argentinian of stolid quietism and frenetic activity, to rediscover the origins and destiny of the country through a contact with the *pampa*.

3. On the personal and interpersonal level, there is a search for ontological foundation and authenticity. Before this is possible, the characters have to break down the barriers of taboo, frivolity and

escapism, personality and class which separate them from themselves and each other.

4. This search is paralleled on a metaphysical level by Persio. He attempts to go beyond the dualism of the Western mind, 'the thundering battle between yes and no' (227), beyond the dualism of subject and object, beyond plurality, time and space, to a state of mystical unity and harmony.

5. Persio's principal obstacle in this search is the nature of language: its tendency towards neutralization and vacuity through rhyme and echo, and its dualistic basis.

The prohibition

On boarding the *Malcolm*, the passengers learn of a disquieting prohibition: the stern is out of bounds to them. The unconvincing excuse of an outbreak of the mysterious 'typhus 224' among the crew is believed by only half the passengers, who become divided into two groups, those who are prepared to conform to the orders of the officers and those who find the prohibition humiliating and wish to reach the stern. The second group see the prohibition as a 'metaphysical swindle', and to go astern becomes an image of all the aspirations briefly enumerated above. The locked doors, bulwarks, hostile sailors and labyrinthine passages come to represent the barriers separating the characters and Persio from their goals. The divided vessel becomes an image of the dualism inherent in their lives.

THE DOUBLE TEXT AND ITS DEVELOPMENT

In all the novels of Cortázar, there are two separate discourses, often two 'authors'. In *Los premios* the main body of the narrative, the story of the passengers of the *Malcolm*, takes a largely traditional form. There are also nine chapters, in italics, of a fundamentally different type of writing, centred on the metaphysical and linguistic experiments of Persio, a passenger on the cruise and an eccentric amateur astronomer. His discourse is loosely based on the events on board, and forms a sort of structural and metaphysical commentary on them: 'Persio is the metaphysical vision of that everyday reality';[3] 'He has what one might call a structural vision of what is happening.'[4] He is looking for the *figuras* within reality, images which would point to a common process or direction within the plurality of the individual cases, trajectories and motivations. If, for example, he can make the image of the boat coincide with a painting by Picasso, this would be a sign that his own metaphysical constructs coincide with, order and ratify the individual quests of the characters. From the point of view of the economics of the novel, this preoccupation is redundant, since their individual searches have already been given a common image in their collective attempt to reach the stern, which probably explains why these chapters do not seem to have been successfully integrated in the novel.

It is perhaps this redundancy that moves Cortázar in later novels to modify the relation between the two discourses. In *Rayuela*, the main text is punctuated with the ('optional') 'dispensable chapters', which the reader has to jump through the text to find, thus playing himself the game of hopscotch and becoming the 'skipping reader' (*lector salteado*) referred to by Macedonio Fernández.[5] The 'dispensable chapters' are centred around the literary theorizings of the fictional Morelli, which suggest a different, more symbolic reading of the text, through the *figuras* mentioned above, but also incorporate passages from other authors which serve several purposes, but especially break the inertia of the surface reading of what Cortázar calls the 'female reader' (*lector hembra*) and Macedonio 'the orderly reader' (*lector seguido*). In *Rayuela*, there is greater tension between the two discourses than in *Los premios*, especially when the ending given in the 'dispensable chapters' apparently contradicts that of the main text. The seeds of this tension are, however, to be found in *Los premios*, but solely in the main text, when the passengers are forced by the authorities to sign a document giving the false, official version of the events on board.

This polarity between the true and official versions of reality is incorporated even more firmly in *62* and *Libro de Manuel* into the tension between the two discourses, which are no longer separated in the text, but interwoven, and where a symbolic causality and impersonal evolutionary process struggles against the censorship of a more traditional and authoritarian narrative represented by the collective doubles 'my paredros' and *el que te dije*.

ARGENTINA

Perhaps more than elsewhere in his work, in *Los premios* Cortázar explores the crisis of identity in Argentina in terms common to a wide group of writers. He sees national life as superficial and, more importantly, rootless, 'a blind, rootless happening' (403), in the same way as Marechal, who talks of 'the present-day Argentinians, without roots in anything',[6] and Mallea:

And these men had an adjectival, not a substantive function in our world, a function where acting a role, not being, was all-important. They were stripping themselves of their life-oriented humanity and were becoming a deliberate and artificial shadow of that humanity.[7]

In this context, the theatre played by Paula and López and the artistic *soirée* towards the end of the voyage, when the characters symbolically don masks, become significant.

The course Persio takes when confronted with this problem demands some explanation. Carlos Astrada[8] and Martínez Estrada agree that much of the responsibility for this situation is to be attributed to the Europeanist positivism of Sarmiento and those who followed him. In his now classical dichotomy, Sarmiento designated the life of the interior, the movement of Rosas, and the influence of Spain as *barbarie*, and the life of the city and Western culture as *civilización*. Everything associated with *barbarie* soon became taboo, explains Martínez Estrada, and as the most distinctive part of the country is banished, life becomes partial, partitioned, ghostlike:

Civilization was made into a programme and barbarism into a taboo, [...] ideas, values, issues, and real things began to be manipulated according to this mental rule. Large fragments of reality sank to the subconscious with outlawed words, and outlawed words dragged fragments of reality down to the subconscious. Eventually, they lost the link between the world to which they aspired and the other one they had before them and could not change. Ghosts ousted men and utopia devoured reality.[9]

This taboo zone can, I believe, be safely associated with the stern of the *Malcolm*.

The *barbarie* banished from the consciousness of the Argentinians takes the form, in the meditations of Persio, of the *pampa*. Sometime in his own personal or collective past, he talks of having betrayed his duty on rejecting the *pampa*, 'the plain where I betrayed my duty by withholding my embrace out there on the arable lands' (252). With Astrada then, who believes that the initial moment of the Argentinian destiny is situated in the *pampa*, and with Arlt, one of whose characters claimed that 'there was only one way out of the impasse of social reality [. . .] and that was to turn back',[10] Persio decides that he must try to return to the origins and renew his contact with the *pampa*: 'I'm running back, I'm returning! To return, yes, that's where the answers sleep their larval life, their first night' (249).

This return is, in many ways, a return to *barbarie*. Persio talks at various points of having himself sewn into a hide bag and abandoned on the *pampa*, a reference probably to the practice of Rosas, who would do the same thing to criminals and leave them to die.[11] He sees truth itself in the 'carcass of a cow which turns the air rotten from three hundred metres away, rotten with evidence, rotten with truth' (249).

That this search for a national identity should be accompanied by a metaphysical quest and the questioning of a whole system of epistemology is perhaps not devoid of significance. Moreno Durán makes the point that the European has always considered himself universal, indeed that 'the man *par excellence* was European'[12] – the opinion, of course, of thinkers such as Sarmiento. With the crisis of the European, rationalist, mode of thought, brought about through the rise of existentialism and historically oriented thought, the Latin American has been confronted with his own peculiar historical and cultural circumstances: 'This deep fissure in modern thought accentuated the Latin American's concern to define his mode of being, his genuine voice, his identity in the eyes of the world.'[13] Similarly, Jacques Derrida explains that the critique and end of European ethnocentrism coincides with the disappearance of metaphysics,[14] i.e. the system where the 'totalité *a son centre ailleurs*'.[15] The parallel searches for both a new national centre and an onto-logical centre with a strong irrationalist component are closely interwoven in Persio's discourse.

Even in the fiercely pro-European Sarmiento there is a great deal of love for the barbaric types of his own country, the *gauchos, baqueanos* and *payadores* of *Facundo*. This force has been neutralized in many ways in literature, for instance, as picturesque and poetical in Ricardo Güiraldes; in the vague populism of Cortázar's own 'Torito'. Elsewhere, it has been more ambiguously and complexly treated as in Borges's *Historia universal de la infamia*. In *Los premios*, great hope is placed by Persio on the forces of barbarism that will rise up and destroy the present moribund civilization. This rebellion is described in mythological terms which seem to have been inspired by a passage from Carpentier's *Los pasos perdidos*:[16]

Now they will be abandoned by the discontented gods, now the dogs and
the pots and even the grinding stones will rise up against the clumsy, condemned golems, will fall on them and tear them to pieces.   (358)
All is expectant rebellion and [...] the Latin American world is a sleight
of hand (*escamoteo*) but [...] the ants, the armadillos, the climate with
its humid suckers are working away underneath.   (358–9)

Yet the *pampa* described by Persio is empty. This barbaric force
must be associated with the sailors who guard the entrance to the
stern. They are described at various points as monsters or mythological characters: 'the dragons of Nordic tongue' (402); 'Charon
with snakes on his arms' (170); 'the only thing missing now is for us
to meet the Minotaur' (171); and, like the ants mentioned above,
often associated in Cortázar with monsters, are inhabitants of
subterranean passages. Their rebellion finds its main expression in
the rape of Felipe by Bob, which, significantly, breaks down the
main taboo in the boy's life.

This rebellion and destruction opens the way to the 'new man'
(*hombre nuevo*), a concept which occurs throughout the work of
Cortázar, but with different or evolving meanings until, in *Libro de
Manuel*, it takes on the meaning attributed to it by 'Che' Guevara and
with which it is used by explicitly left-wing writers such as Benedetti.
Here, it seems to be closer to Mallea's idea of the 'deep Argentinian',
which will begin to live when the ruling 'inauthentic Argentinian'
begins to die.[17] Persio sees the passengers in the artistic *soirée* as
wooden dolls where life and culture immediately coagulate and
become petrified: 'the insufficient wood of a grim and avaricious
creation [...], the sluggish hearts where nothing settles without
coagulating and clotting' (358). Yet these dolls will die, to be
replaced by monkeys and real men. Here and in Medrano's 'casting
away the old man [as opposed to the 'new man'] like a clay doll'
(382), there is a reference to the Guatemalan myth of evolution
reconstructed in Asturias's *Hombres de maíz*, where in fact, through a
series of rites, 'the real man' is rediscovered in the shell he had
deserted, in 'the outside, the doll, the dolls with duties of sedentary
folk'.[18]

A more pessimistic note is struck, however, when Persio describes
the life of South America in terms very reminiscent of Neruda's
Residencia en la tierra. The similarity may be due to a common
Schopenhauerian filiation.[19] Persio presents the frantic action of the
Argentinians – 'Something infinitely disconcerting in the yeast in

Argentinian bread [. . .] hurls us headlong into total drama' (253) –
in the same way as he does the strife of the 'Will' in nature: 'The joy
of disorder crushes and exalts and annihilates amidst screams and
mutations' (320). Through meditation and his experiments, Persio
goes beyond this strife, plurality and chaos (to an appreciation of the
'Idea'), becomes an 'immutable seat', 'indifferent witness', 'stable
eye': 'What can the silent procession of shadows, the destroyed and
renewed creation which rises up all around do to him now?' (319)[20]
But within the same philosophy, 'all creation is a failure' (320), and
ridiculous results are gained from these cosmic fireworks: 'What was
to remain of all that, only an abandoned shack on the *pampa*, a sly
storekeeper, a miserable outlaw *gaucho*, some little general in power?'
(320)[21]

THE INDIVIDUALS

A section of the passengers decide they would like to see the stern,
for a host of personal reasons subsumed in the collective impression of
having been submitted to a 'metaphysical swindle' (150). It is their
own cowardice and bad faith in not making the attempt earlier
(i.e. in accepting a partitioned boat by living unauthentic and
partitioned lives), and not the typhus 224 of the official version of
reality, that causes the illness of the young child Jorge. This illness,
however, lends the sort of verisimilitude to their attack (they have to
telegraph Buenos Aires for medical aid) that will not be required in
later novels. Oliveira in *Rayuela* will do similar things, but will be
proclaimed mad for his efforts. Nevertheless, the illness of the child
becomes in Cortázar the prototypal expression of the absurd, as in
Camus's *La peste*.

The absurdity of the voyage breaks up the faith the characters had
in the orderliness of their lives: 'How was he finally to order all that
which he had thought so ordered before embarking?' (379) The
attitude of the Argentinian is described as a carefully concealed fear
of the void: 'Oh, Argentina, why this fear of fear, this void to hide
the void?' (253) Claudia describes her own life as 'an assorted
collection of masks and behind [. . .], a black hole' (89). Their life
is an intranscendent chess game where anything is sacrificed in order
to assure the survival of the 'king':

We get back to the idea of the game. I suppose it's part of our present
concept of life, without illusions and without transcendence. One puts

up with being a good pawn or a good knight, moving diagonally or
castling in order to save the king.   (164)

This king is the false and repressive ego, as can be seen in the
symbolism of 'Lejana', a story from *Bestiario*, where Alina Reyes
discovers an anagram of her name which gives 'es la reina y...'
(*B* 36), 'she is the queen and...', suggesting the existence of a
double repressed or created by that part of her referred to as 'the
queen'. This ego is threatened by the surfacing of a truth pushed at
some point into the void, the 'black hole' of the individual, the
taboo zone in the consciousness of Argentina discussed in relation to
Sarmiento: 'We are so afraid of irruptions, of losing our precious
daily ego' (209); 'some moments when truth had fought to break
through' (393). Habit is seen as the great ally of the ego and ultimately of death: 'the solitary hopes which habit relegates to the
bottom of our dreams' (251); 'The passage from happiness to habit
is one of death's best weapons' (69).

Medrano

Medrano admits his life has been superficial and frivolous, describing
himself as an amateur at life: 'I became an *aficionado*. Don't ask me
what of, because I'd find it difficult to say. Of football, for example,
of Italian literature, of kaleidoscopes, of free women' (212). Just
before embarking, he had left Bettina, the last in a long series of
women he had abandoned in order not to commit himself and face
problems: 'seduce a virgin' as Claudia puts it. To reach the stern is,
for Medrano, to break out of this superficial way of life. He has a
dream or vision in which he is able to see beyond everyday reality,
seeing and accepting 'Bettina's true face' (382): 'He was seeing the
other side of things, he was seeing himself as he really was for the
first time' (326). On reaching the stern, this vision is confirmed, he
has the impression that he has destroyed 'the old selfish order' for
good, 'casting away the old man like a clay doll' (382).

It is interesting to note that Bettina is really himself, that 'he had
not dreamed about Bettina, but about himself' (326). Bettina is a
sort of double, the more conventional part of himself that he left
behind in Buenos Aires, while he travelled, i.e. explored his deeper
reality. This structure is expanded in *Rayuela*, in the relationship
between Oliveira and Traveler. There remains the problem of the
reconciliation of the two different visions of himself. He accepts the

'true face of Bettina' even though he knows that 'the Bettina who lives immersed in Buenos Aires', i.e. in reality, 'would never have that face, poor girl' (382). The problem is explored in the second part of *Rayuela*, but here, Medrano is shot dead before he can try to communicate his knowledge to anybody.

Paula and López

Paula Lavalle, a society girl forced into dissipation by her reaction against the strict values of her aristocratic parents, and López, an intellectual and democratic schoolteacher, find themselves pushed by habit into the ritual of seduced and seducer, 'an idiotic situation but with something inevitable about it, like Punch and Judy forced to give and take the ritual blows' (215).

Paula is travelling with the homosexual Raúl, with whom she has shared many years of her life intellectually, politically, and emotionally. López, of course, does not share this past with her and it becomes increasingly clear that the truth of the individual, like that of the nation, lies in his past. Time, as the relationship of Paula and López develops, becomes the bulwark separating them from their stern: 'the insurmountable space of the past', 'the invisible wall', 'the wall of air' (302), 'the doors' (346). Their conscious minds being accomplices of time, the only way for them to break the barrier, 'to meet in the origins, when she was not yet that woman who...' (346), is blind irrationality:

She reasoned that such incredibly stupid gestures might open the doors that all the malignity of intelligence was unable to cross. (346)
If only he could [...] run so blindly and so desperately that the invisible wall would smash to smithereens and let him through, take up all the past of Paula in a single embrace which would leave him for ever by her side, possess her as a virgin, an adolescent. (302)

The anti-rationalism of these characters, like that of Persio, is an essential part of Cortázar's philosophy, and is explored critically and in many contexts right up to *Libro de Manuel*.

Jorge

The importance of the origins is borne out by the role of children in the works of Cortázar. They are the bearers of a knowledge which will disappear with the development of the adult mind. Jorge, for example, 'knows things, he is the spokesman of a knowledge that later he will forget' (91). His illness is caused, in a sense, by the forgetting of this knowledge by those around him. It is interesting to note that he is the first to call the hostile sailors 'lipics' and 'glucics', pharmaceutical terms he has read on the instructions for use on some medicine. The 'lipics' are thus both the principal defenders of the dualism on board, the partitioned nature of reality, and representatives of medicine, i.e. science, the adult mind. It is ironically this medicine that produces the illness of the child. The identification of medicine with an anti-vital and falsifying rationality and classification will become a constant in the work of Cortázar.

Felipe

Felipe is perhaps the most finely drawn character of the novel. He is an adolescent Dionysus torn between masculinity and femininity: 'He's a man and a woman and both at once, and much more. There isn't the slightest fixation in him' (330). Though attracted by the homosexuality of Raúl, he lives 'contentedly within a scheme of things where everything was well lit up and in its proper place' (182), and which prevents him from taking this path. The consequence is that he, and those like him, 'are like statues, [...] really are statues, outside and inside' (278). Attracted by the life of the sailors and in an attempt to prove his masculinity by reaching the stern alone, he is raped by a sailor. The monstrous 'lipics' can thus be seen to represent both taboo and the tabooed activity. The status of the rape is made ambiguous by this distinction. It is an affirmation of the liberating nature of *la barbarie* but also illustrates how taboo converts the possible liberation into something monstrous. This ambiguity will, in later works, become increasingly complex and polarized and be finally resolved in *Libro de Manuel*.

El Pelusa

A similar ambiguity permeates the author's relationship with the working-class[22] figure el Pelusa, whom he did not like when starting the novel, but who takes on heroic dimensions as the action proceeds. Though the least mythified working-class character of Cortázar, he nevertheless is given all the attributes of the 'monster', a term covering fear, disgust and a basic incomprehension. He gives off 'an almost visible halo of oniony smells' (309), wears a brick-red jacket, and comes up to breakfast in his pyjamas. He turns out to be the purest of the characters in that his part in the sortie to the stern is the only one to be motivated exclusively by concern for the sick Jorge.

DEEP MYTHOLOGICAL STRUCTURES

The labyrinthine passages of the *Malcolm* through which the characters wander in search of a means of access to the stern are described simultaneously in two very different ways, introducing two themes[23] which may be taken as 'deep structures' present in all the novels of Cortázar – structures which are constantly virtual, even though they may be only partially actualized or greatly transformed. The passages are seen as the labyrinth of the Minotaur, the prototypal Cortazarian monster treated so sympathetically in *Los reyes*: 'The only thing missing is for us to meet the Minotaur.' But to visit the passages is also described as a 'trip to Hades' (279). One sailor is seen as Charon (170) and, significantly, another is called Orf, which suggests the descent of Orpheus to Hades to bring back to the world of the living the dead Eurydice.

Though no one is literally dead at this point in the novel, Jorge is seriously ill, and his recovery depends on the descent to the passages to reach the stern (to cable for medical aid which does not prove necessary). His illness is symbolically connected with the loss of certain vital forces and experience to the adult characters. These forces are in turn associated with the monstrous seamen, and the themes of the labyrinth and the recovery of Eurydice from Hades are also fused within the symbolism of the novel. In *Rayuela* they are brought even closer together: la Maga is Eurydice, recovered after her death by Oliveira's descent to the morgue of the lunatic asylum, but also the dead Minotaur, the force of *barbarie* to be recovered in a purified form for the world of the living.

FIGURAS

Cortázar has admitted that, on approaching the writing of a novel, his starting point has always been an almost abstract structure or geometrical pattern: 'When I write, I obey structures, mental or sensory polyhedra of which I have no actual *idea*.'[24] These structures are usually called *figuras*. The concept is deeply rooted in all the creation of Borges. The repetitive patterns in his work are presented as approximations to the real *figuras* in the world, which could only be understood by a divine (i.e. infinite) intelligence:

What is infinite intelligence? the reader may ask. There is not a theologian who does not define it; I prefer an example. The steps taken by a man, from the day of his birth to the day of his death, draw an inconceivable figure in time. Divine Intelligence intuits that figure immediately, as man's intelligence does a triangle. That figure (perhaps) has a specific function in the economy of the universe.[25]

This 'divine' nature, difficult but true, is also expressed by Persio, who talks of 'figures written and arranged by the angels' (44).

Persio is dismayed by the multiplicity and hence inadequacy of possible epistemological approaches to reality: 'His only anxiety is the enormity of the range of choice: should he guide himself by the stars, [...] by the principles of logic, [...] by the state of his gall-bladder?' (65) It is perhaps in order to stress the difficulty of any unified vision that, at various points (32–3, 265), scenes are described from different viewpoints, in a way reminiscent of *nouveau roman* techniques.

Persio illustrates his idea of the *figura* by reference to the stars. The stars are the reality produced by the lottery. This is clear intuitively and is perhaps suggested by his use of the word *pedrea* (318) – stones which fall from the heavens and also the lesser prizes in a lottery. He wonders whether the constellations, the patterns in this reality, are arbitrarily created by man's subjectivity or whether they are determined by something 'deeper, more substantial' (43). The discovery of a *figura* would imply that man and his society are not simply a product of chance: 'What I would like to ascertain [...] is whether the human centipede obeys anything more than chance in its constitution and dissolution; whether it is a figure in the magical sense' (43).

Though the basic idea of the *figura* is fundamental and constant in Cortázar's work, it varies greatly as emphasis is placed on different aspects of its functioning: the involuntary nature of a character's insertion in a pattern alien to his consciousness; the revolutionary nature of the *figura*; its connotations of guilt; its formal and philosophical connotations, and so on. Taken widely, however, the idea of repetition seems to be fundamental to the concept: only when repeated do patterns become significant, or even patterns. A metaphorical correspondence between two realities can be seen as a weaker form of repetition. This repetition can be seen both in those I take (perhaps arbitrarily) as the theorizers of Cortázar's *figuras* and throughout the novels themselves. In Auerbach, the *figura* is seen as a prefiguration or prophecy of a later event; in Jung, archetypal constellations are seen as a type of complex which is repeated indefinitely; Borges claims that 'the history of the universe is perhaps the history of the different intonations given to a few metaphors',[26] and bases some of his stories on the repetition of 'archetypal' acts such as the assassination of Julius Caesar: 'Tema del traidor y del héroe'. In Cortázar's own short stories, e.g. 'La noche boca arriba', a basic sequence of events in a prehistoric tribal war is repeated in a motorcycle accident in present-day Paris (not historically, but ambiguously in the consciousness of one character); in *Rayuela* a personal past (with mythological overtones) is partly repeated, partly fulfilled and completed in the present; in *62*, there is a symbolic repetition in the present of literary, historical and mythological archetypes; in *Libro de Manuel*, there is a strict correspondence between personal, general symbolic, and political discourses.

There come to be two separate but interrelated sides to the *figura*: what might be termed its meaning, usually a movement of liberation, increasingly impersonal and independent of the individual, and the more formal aspect of the repetition which confirms the *figura*. This aspect also has philosophical and metaphysical implications in that a repetition breaks the idea of linear time and associated concepts. Again, this is an idea favoured by Borges:

I suspect, however, that the number of circumstantial variations is not infinite: we can posit, in the mind of an individual (or of two individuals who know nothing of each other, but in whom the same process takes place), two identical moments. Once that identity has been posited, one may ask: Are not those identical moments the same one? Is not *one single repeated term* sufficient to undo and confound the series of time?[27]

The aim of the individual characters is to fulfil the possibilities offered by the *figura* to reach a personal 'centre', while a metaphysical centre is achieved by the author in destroying time. This in turn ratifies, metaphysically, the quest of the characters.

We have seen that the *figura* is often concerned with the repetition of a person's own acts, or those of others, in the past. This past denotes the unconscious or a collective unconscious as against the social ego, superego, the ideology of the status quo, etc. Hence, phylogenetically, the importance of children. The two terms of the *figura* often correspond to the alienating dualisms explored in the novels. The barrier between the two (in *Los premios*, the bulwarks, etc.) is increasingly seen as the mental censorship which prevents them from being confronted, fused, a unity formed and the liberating content of the *figura* incorporated into the totality.

The *figura* often contains rather barbaric acts. This barbarism has the function, especially when repeated in good faith by the characters on the primary plane (i.e. the present), of breaking down the censorship mentioned above. I will often use the terms 'barbaric', 'monsters', 'rape', 'invasion', in perhaps surprising contexts. There is a deep structural uniformity in Cortázar's texts, and certain very similar functions have always to be fulfilled. Thus, if in a particularly explicit text, one which might by its nature and chronology (e.g., a story from *Bestiario* or the early mythological play *Los reyes*) be called an archetypal text, this function is fulfilled by a character termed explicitly as monstrous, many aspects of a later character in a similar situation, though softened and sublimated (sodomy may be equivalent to rape; death under anaesthesia to murder; a startled reference to the smell of a character may constitute the latter's monstrosity), can best be expressed and synthesized by the use of such terms.

The *figura* formed by the characters of *Los premios* is of the least explicit type: their personal aims are expressed symbolically in the collective attack on the stern. There is no lack of consciousness in them of their aims (as from *Rayuela* onwards). Consciousness is seen rather as a barrier between them and the fulfilment of their search. More explicit repetition is, however, not absent from the novel: it is executed symbolically and poetically by Persio. If he can make two different things coincide, become equal, for instance the picture formed by joining the positions at any given time of the trains on a map of the Portuguese railway system and a fruit bowl designed by Petorutti, or his view of the boat with a painting of a guitarist by Picasso (i.e. reality and some other arbitrarily chosen figure), then, he believes, 'I will have a cipher, a module. In this way I will begin to embrace creation from its true analogical base, I will break up time and space, which are inventions fraught with defects' (94).

After long meditation and preparatory exercises, and, of course, through the action of the characters, this happens. The 'music of the spheres', using the stars (i.e. reality in the poetic mode) as a plectrum, is played on the rigging of the ship and translated into pictorial form – the guitarist (226). The idea is almost certainly taken from

Lugones's short story 'La metamúsica', where the 'music of the spheres' is projected through a specially adapted piano onto a screen.[28]

THE METAPHYSICAL EXPERIENCE OF PERSIO

Persio is searching for an archetype, a unity beyond plurality, time and space, beyond 'the incalculable kaleidoscope of life' (100), for a force akin to the 'Will' of Schopenhauer: 'For this plurality is directly conditioned by time and space, into which the will itself never enters. The will reveals itself just as completely and just as much in *one* oak as in millions.'[29] This archetype, closely associated with the *pampa*, is expressed in many different ways: 'radiant archetypes', 'weightless bodies where gravity is suspended and the germ of grace bubbles gently' (252); 'the absolutely ineffable cosmic "swing" of that first hair' (266); 'that third hand which is sometimes fulminatingly glimpsed in a poetic urge' (251); 'the image of the god of creation' (402); 'his ultimate blood' (228), etc.

Persio insinuates that man has at some time been in possession of this archetypal contact, but has been separated from it by what he calls the 'sinister ancestors', who 'have come between the Mothers and their distant children' (402), a reference to the falsifying path of (Argentinian) history and thought. They have the effect of 'killing the image of the god of creation, substituting it for a favourable commerce of ghosts' (402). 'Substitution' is a key word.[30] Society has substituted the vision described as 'the third hand' with Western classification and explanation: 'that third hand [...] which prestige and fame immediately substitute for impressive arguments, that leprous stonecutter's job called explaining and rationalizing' (251).

The elements are seen to be substituted in *Samsara*: 'Samsara, the solid ground sinks beneath my feet, Samsara, smoke and vapour replace the elements, Samsara, work of the great illusion, son and grandson of Mahamaya' (248). *Samsara* (the cycle of reincarnation, transmigration, and by extension the vicious circle of self-frustration caused by the attempt to grasp and control reality, to classify it: *maya*),[31] and 'the great illusion' ('the illusion which sees the ONE as two'),[32] refer to the introduction of plurality into the world. Schopenhauer himself used these terms, equivalent to his *principium individuationis*. The 'third hand' sought by Persio would thus be a vision beyond this duality, and is almost certainly related to the Buddhist 'third eye': 'But an eye is needed – a third eye. We have

two eyes to see two sides of things, but there must be a third eye
which will see everything at the same time and yet not see everything.
[...] Our two eyes see dualistically, and dualism is at the bottom of
all trouble.'[33]

It is this dualism and plurality that Persio refers to as 'the thundering battle between yes and no' (227), and 'what is happening and
what is not happening' (317). It is clearly Persio's own mind which
creates this plurality, which populates the empty stern with a
variegated menagerie: 'The stern, that there. Nothing to remind you
of anything [...]. But the stern, that there, that which is Persio
looking at the stern, the cages of monkeys to port [...] the lioness
[...] reflecting the full moon on the phosphorescent hide of her back'
(229). The word *phosphorescent* is a reference to the opacity of consciousness, as can also be seen in its application to the bridge windows,
where the officers can see and not be seen: 'the windows which
phosphoresce in the light river mist' (101). The function of this
barrier is to conceal the truth (of Argentina): 'my Argentina beyond
that phosphorescent curtain' (250).

It is only by destroying intelligence, 'the sedative channels and the
plastic and vinylite moulds of stupefied consciousness' (225), that
the dualism of subject and object can be broken, that the object of
knowledge becomes one's own self in harmony with totality: 'to
destroy oneself as consciousness in order to be both the game and the
hunter, the encounter which cancels out all opposition' (227). López,
similarly, is 'agent and patient of these visions provoked and suffered
under the blue sky' (226).[34]

Persio is finally (and momentarily) granted this vision and unity:
'There is a shift which splits him open like a ripe pomegranate,
offers him at last his own fruit, his ultimate blood which is one with
the forms of the sea and the sky, with the barriers of time and place'
(228). This communion with the essence of the sea is very similar to
that achieved by J. R. Jiménez in *Diario de un poeta recién casado*,
which allows the poet to go 'in a moment [...] from it to all of it, to
always and everywhere it'.[35] It is significant that this knowledge,
described as a 'head wind', 'is not even registered on the impressive
anemometer fitted on the bridge' (225), i.e. on his conscious mind.
In another, similar experience, Persio goes beyond his own senses, and
chaos is seen to be resolved in him, the kaleidoscope set into a pattern:

His senses cease little by little to be part of him, they extract him and
cast him onto the black plain; [...] straightening out like a tree, he

encompasses plurality in a single and enormous pain which is chaos resolving itself, the crystal coagulating, becoming ordered, the primordial night in American time.   (319)

Thus, Persio achieves a total simultaneity of vision. It is interesting to note, however, that he previously claimed that he personally would be destroyed by such a vision: 'Reality would cease to be successive, it would be petrified in an absolute vision in which the ego would be annihilated and disappear. But that annihilation, what a triumphant blaze, what an Answer' (92). We also saw that the destruction of mind was a prerequisite to this totalizing vision and abolition of dualism. This may have some bearing on the death of Medrano after breaking through to the stern. There may be in his death, which is seen as a failure in that he cannot communicate his vision, the seeds of a more positive, i.e. metaphorical, interpretation: the death of the 'old man', of the dualistic vision. This nascent ambiguity is taken up and expanded in *Rayuela*, where the possible death of Oliveira after a parallel experience clearly lends itself to both literal and symbolic readings.

THE DUAL NATURE OF LANGUAGE

Cortázar tells us that he 'wrote the first monologues of Persio in *Los premios* with the aid of a system of phonetic analogies inspired by that of Roussel' (*V* 1 123). Raymond Roussel, as explained in *Comment j'ai écrit certains de mes livres*, constructed his works by using a matrix phrase, sometimes included as the first sentence, and built episodes around words phonetically similar to elements of this phrase, i.e. by rhyme rather than a more metaphorical composition, by equivalence of *signifiants* rather than of *signifiés*.

There are two opposite ways of regarding this writing, that of Butor and that of Ricardou. Butor[36] sees his work as an attempt, through repetition, to recover the original or previous experience when Roussel believed he had a sun in him, i.e. to recover, in a sense, an ideal *signifié*. Ricardou, however, claims that this writing has the object of proclaiming 'je suis un écrit',[37] as against classical literature, which has little consciousness of language as such, which seeing it as a transparent medium between the reader and reality: 'L'art classique ne pouvait se sentir comme un langage, il *était* langage, c'est-à-dire transparence, circulation sans dépôt, concours idéal d'un esprit universel et d'un signe décoratif sans épaisseur et sans responsabilité.'[38] In Roussel's writing it is the very rules of language that produce the text: 'La "maudite" activité roussellienne s'efforce d'unir en constellations les improbables formations obtenues par l'aptitude productrice du langage.'[39] The perspective is thus opened up of what Foucault calls 'l'être du langage' – when language 'se rassemble',[40] the latter postulates, man will disappear, as one *signifiant* more. Any such recovery of a full presence as that described by Butor would thus become impossible.

The influence of Roussel is most interestingly obvious in monologue F. There is a constant insistence here on Persio's betrayal of his origins in the *pampa*: 'the plain where I betrayed my duty' (252). He is now on the 'Southern sea' (on board, separated from the stern, alienated from the *pampa*). Roussel's sun has been covered under a layer of language and erudition: 'the names and the dates which are gradually covering the sun' (251).

Yet Persio hopes that language, the nostalgic language of memory, will allow him to recover the lost experience of the *pampa*, bridge the distance between it and his present position, abolish the dualism it creates: 'Sweet, daft folklore words, the flimsy preface to everything sacred, [...] gradually give me access to the true Night, far from here and at hand, abolishing the distance between the *pampa* and the Southern sea' (250). Language is seen alternately in this optimistic manner and as an empty system of rhyme and echo, where memory cannot be distinguished from truth: 'Why such a confused agglomeration where I cannot distinguish truth from memory, names from presence? The horror of echolalia, of inane puns' (250). It is seen to share the same kaleidoscopic plurality as consciousness and time: 'My front of attack [...] is complicated by an overwhelming kaleidoscope of vocabulary' (248). The insoluble question of how he can go beyond language is thus posed, since what he seeks would be a languageless state: 'No, I don't want intelligible poetry on board, [...] something else [...] less copulatable [copula, copulation] by words, [...] because they would not be words, but pure rhythms' (252). His only tool is, however, language. This dilemma, in terms of intelligence, is very much present in *Rayuela*: 'the inexplicable suicide attempt of intelligence through intelligence itself' (*R* 189).

Thus, if language is to be meaningful, the 'sweet, daft folklore words' must produce the original experience of the *pampa*, *signifiant* produce *signifié*. Roussel shows the opposite, and Cortázar follows his example at significant points, as in the sequence,

The third hand, I would like to caress you with it, beautiful night, softly peel away the names and dates which are gradually covering the sun, the sun which once fell ill in Egypt and became blind, needing a god to cure (*curara*) it.   (251)

The sun is the vital *signifié* to be rediscovered, but language shows its opacity by developing on the level of the *signifiant*: the god who cured the sun was *Ra*, and this element is now symbolically seen to dictate the words chosen, the development of the discourse: 'cu-*ra-ra*'. It may be more than coincidence that the syllable *ra* is repeated forty-three times on the following page, the average in the monologues being about twenty.

Elsewhere, following the barrier symbolism, we see that original experience, 'the third hand', can break through the verbiage of alienating culture, the 'screen covered with painted stories', the 'sheet hung out to dry'. It is interesting to note, however, that language, the means of recovering this experience, dictates the latter's form, corrupts it, as can be seen in the following passage: 'so that finally that which all traditions mask might burst like a plutonium scimitar (*alfanje de plutonio*) through a screen covered with painted stories. Lying in the alfalfa, I could have (*en la alfalfa, pude*) entered that order' (252). The 'sweet folklore word' *alfalfa* is seen to rhyme (i.e. there is an equivalence of *signifiants*) with the ideal *signifié*, *alfanje*: '*alfa*nje de *plu*tonio', '*alfa*lfa *pu*de'. The idea is repeated in the following phrase: 'an encounter comparable with the impact of a St Elmo's fire against a blanket hung out to dry' (252). The meteor of truth and the barrier of the blanket it is to break through are made to rhyme: '*San Telmo*', '*sá*bana *te*ndida'. There is additional word-play here in that Persio's aspirations symbolized by the corposant, '*el fuego de San Telmo*', are homonymous with his everyday reality in the area where he lives: '*el barrio de San Telmo*'. The rhyme and suggested equivalence between *tradición* and *traición*, tradition and betrayal, may also be significant.

In a last, more obvious example, rhyme suggests language to be the accomplice of the conscious mind and of science in an exclusive monopoly of experience: 'appearances (*apariencia*), cushy ownership (*pertenencia*), dirty desire (*apetencia*), the sheer, infinite rhyme, where we must not forget science (*ciencia*) and consciousness (*conciencia*)' (253).

2
Rayuela

INTRODUCTION

The amount of general theorizing, eulogizing, criticizing, lyricizing, and condemnation around Cortázar's second and arguably best novel cows one into therapeutic but, alas perhaps, temporary silence on approaching it. Rhetoric is almost unavoidable: *Rayuela* is one of the great intellectual and human sagas of our time, the Argentinian *Ulysses*, etc. It is very much a book of the sixties, but has the quality of dating without losing any of its vitality. For what it is worth, the author of this study, having read the novel probably over ten times, can still re-read it with the same pleasure as initially.

Though often called an anti-novel, *Rayuela* has a more coherent and classical story than it is sometimes credited with. Anything novel about the form of a novel often decrees immediately that it is not a novel at all. *Rayuela*, unless one overindulges in the scholastic *vicio* of genre definition, is definitely a novel. What is most striking about its form are the 'dispensable chapters' and the 'table of instructions', which tells us in what order to interpolate the 'dispensable' chapters between those of the first two parts. One critic remarks that some future editor, out of concern for the spine of his books, will reorder the chapters to permit smooth reading.[1] This would be very sensible, but most probably a mistake.

The 'dispensable chapters' serve various functions. They form a constant commentary on the construction of the novel, the difficulties and contradictions inherent in it. They display the raw cultural material of the novel. They sometimes suggest to the reader the frame of mind in which the novel might be read, and at others intentionally catch him off his guard, jolt him out of his inertia. They are often inserted contrapuntally in order to subvert the causality of the main narrative, or to multiply its resonances.

The several different, seemingly contradictory endings to the novel have given rise to much discussion. Cortázar only recently let the cat out of the bag: Oliveira does not commit suicide.[2] *Rayuela* is not a totally open, aleatory novel, nor, as many detractors and enthusers agree, is everything left to the reader, whom they would have as a mysterious new animal recently invented by Cortázar. The reader is drawn into a bewildered but deep and critical commitment to his reading and involvement in the novel, by sometimes unconventional, but often conventional means, by the 'aesthetic ruses' (453:79), the misuse of which is decried by Morelli. As Borges comments in his peculiarly efficient manner on the stories of Herbert Quain: 'Each one of them prefigures or promises a good plot, intentionally spoiled by the author. Some, not the best, insinuate *two* plots. The reader, distracted by vanity, believes he has invented them himself.'[3]

The keynote of *Rayuela* is given in the first sentence: 'Would I find la Maga?' (15:1) The novel centres round a search: 'By that time I had realized that searching was my sign' (20:1). But this search is best characterized by the fact that its object cannot immediately be known: 'What are we looking for? What are we looking for? Repeat it fifteen thousand times, like hammering on the wall. What are we looking for?' (561:125) There is an intuitive, visceral certainty that something is very wrong in the world, but at the same time there is a refusal or inability to define what is wrong, because of the suspicion that it might be the very system of articulated thought which would allow that definition that is itself wrong: 'But everything is wrong, history is spelling it out, and the very act of thinking about it instead of living it proves that it is wrong' (562:125).

Oliveira is not looking for Truth in any absolute or scientific sense: 'But what use do we have for the truth which comforts the honest bourgeois?' (439:73) Even more importantly, he does not seek a transcendent truth: 'It has to be something immanent, without the sacrifice of lead for gold, cellophane for glass' (562). Reality is not sense and meaning, but discourse and myth, as can be seen from another character's attitude towards language: 'The creation of a whole language, even though it ends up betraying its meaning, irrefutably reveals human structures, be they those of a Chinaman or a redskin' (503:99). Transcendence would be bad faith, escapism and individualism. The problem is, provisionally, man's way of relating to his reality rather than that reality itself.

With this in mind, it is perhaps easier to grasp that the images used to express Oliveira's aims are almost synonymous with what he rejects. The whole novel is the transformation of these almost synonymous poles, the attempt to reconcile them, the space or trajectory between them.

Oliveira is looking for a 'centre', yet generally defines what he is rejecting as egocentrism or anthropocentrism. He is consequently wary of 'falling into an impoverished egocentrism (*criollo*-centrism, slumcentrism, culturecentrism, folklorecentrism)' (32-3:3). Such 'centrisms' are created principally by reason and language: 'Reason secretes through language a satisfactory architecture [...] and sticks us in the centre' (194:28).

He dissociates himself from the world with Rimbaud's assertion from *Une saison en enfer* that 'nous ne sommes pas au monde' (216:31), but at the same time demands 'citizenship', *derecho de ciudad* (215:31) (corresponding to Rimbaud's 'droit dans le monde réel',[4] from the same poem, 'Délires I'). There is a similar relationship between the epigraphs to the first and second parts of the novel: Vaché's statement that 'rien ne vous tue un homme comme d'être obligé de représenter un pays' (13), and Apollinaire's warning that 'il faut voyager loin en aimant sa maison' (255). The difference between 'pays' and 'maison', between 'country' and 'home', is the vital issue. This same point is stressed in the 'dispensable chapters' in a passage by Jean Tardieu, who lives in a house in every respect identical to his own, but nevertheless wants *his own* house back (621:152).

He claims to have 'refused collective lies from an early stage' (31:3), and rejects reality as 'an incredible mistake' (515:100), but will not accept the antinomical pair lie–truth: 'Why that Greek criterion of truth and error?' (515) He nevertheless stresses the importance of illusion, not of truth: 'Only illusions were capable of moving the faithful, illusions and not truths' (65:12).[5]

Something similar happens in the most dense writing of the novel, in chapter 73, a sort of microcosm of the whole, where the negative Paris of the 'Great Habit' is opposed to the positive Paris of the 'Great Screw' (*Gran Tornillo*). Oliveira wishes to make 'true' the *same thing* that he now senses as false: 'We could be *fundamentally* the same as on the surface' (120:22). But in order to achieve this, 'we would have to live in a different way' (120). Again, in the phrase, '[a world] where we would really shake hands instead of repeating the gesture of fear' (400:56), the basic reality is still the traditional value, the handshake, but this value would become realer, more justified: '*fundamentally*', 'really'.

Within this frame of reference, that is, a negative term and a near-synonym with a longed-for positive sign, there are indications that Oliveira's quest is successful. Many phrases and situations from the first part, 'That Side', are repeated in the second, 'This Side'. The shift in emphasis in the elements 'slipping an arm round her waist' and 'an arm hugging a waist' points to the fact that a measure of progress is made. In the first part, we read:

Oliveira, who was bored, slipped his arm round la Maga's waist. That too might be an explanation, an arm hugging a slender, warm waist [. . .]. If only la Maga could have understood how he was suddenly exasperated by obedience to desire.   (51:9)

And in the second:

He saw that Traveler was standing beside Talita and that he had slipped his arm round her waist. [. . .] but what beauty in the mistake and the five thousand years of false and precarious territory, [. . .] what love in that arm hugging a woman's waist.   (402:56)

It is the process which leads from the first statement at the beginning of the novel to the second in the final pages that will be analysed here.

BUENOS AIRES—PARIS

The novel is divided into two main parts, 'This Side' and 'That Side', the first recounting Oliveira's experiences in Paris, where he has arrived from Buenos Aires, and the second his subsequent return to Buenos Aires. *Rayuela*, as has already been suggested, is a novel of dualisms and there is a temptation to associate the two cities immediately with the two terms of the blank concept of dualism, to consider them in some way as opposites. It should be stressed that there are many different types of opposition at work in the novel, such as the simple good/bad, yes/no opposition of language and – for Cortázar – the Western mind in general; the type of opposition discussed above between two almost synonymous terms, one with a positive, the other with a negative load, which could be reduced to authentic/inauthentic, categorized/uncategorized, i.e. of the 'Great Habit'/'Great Screw' type; the opposition found between doubles, for instance between Oliveira and Traveler, *at one point*, more or less, primitive man/civilized man; and a more complex opposition between, for example, madness and sanity as an opposition, and madness and sanity as non-antagonistic, or even identical, i.e.

madness/sanity/ /madness = sanity. It is therefore necessary to consider carefully the meaning of the two sides of the Atlantic before Oliveira's experiences can be analysed.

As an introduction to this discussion, it will be useful to consider three points: a common objection to Cortázar's residence in Paris as escapism (which implies an analysis of his work), the strongest and most intelligent form of which is proposed by David Viñas in *De Sarmiento a Cortázar*; oppositions between Buenos Aires and other places in the short stories; the 'topology' of *Los premios* in relation to that of *Rayuela*.

Paris as escapism

David Viñas's critique of Cortázar is made in the context of his wider study of the schizophrenic attitude of many Argentinian writers towards Europe, and culture in general. His approach is in many ways valid, and certainly provides a useful analytical tool. His main point is that the traditional 'trip to Europe' (in the same way as the return to the *pampa* or to the *estancia*, and the condescending idealization of the *gaucho* and the 'favourite servant') is a means of avoiding contact with the 'body' of Argentina, in favour of the 'spirit' associated with Europe, with the idea of returning to purify and 'spiritualize' this 'body'. He consequently sees Oliveira–Cortázar's residence in Paris as a move from the 'earth' (body, Buenos Aires) of the hopscotch to its 'heaven' (spirit, Paris): 'All his work [up to *Rayuela*] can be read, half explicitly, half between the lines, as the plan, preparations, hesitations and premonitions up to the realization of and commentary on the trip to *Europe*: it is, in the final analysis, the distance between the "earth" and the "heaven" of the Hopscotch.'[6]

Oliveira is perfectly conscious, on arriving in Paris, that he is simply conforming with the time-honoured pattern of Argentinian intellectuals. When Perico comments, 'You've come here following the pattern of all your countrymen who go off to Paris for their *éducation sentimentale*,' Oliveira replies, 'You're not far wrong, kid' (69:13). Elsewhere, he makes the point himself: 'I only know that one day I arrived in Paris, [...] doing what others do and seeing what others see' (18:1). He is initially so fascinated by the prestige of European culture that he is incapable of 'seeing Gothic architecture without sticking labels on it, or walking by the river without seeing the Norman drakes sailing upstream' (486:93).

But this is only a starting point, and it is less surprising that Oliveira should fall into this pattern when, as we have seen, he is not sure what he finds wrong with reality and therefore cannot know what he is looking for. The pattern is gradually reversed, and this reversal can be expressed in the words of Cortázar on his own situation: 'A writer left my country for whom reality, as Mallarmé imagined it, ought to culminate in a book; in Paris a man was born for whom books should culminate in reality' (*UR* b 207). The reversal starts with Oliveira's contact with la Maga, a very uncerebral creature ('Her centre wasn't exactly in her head' (40:4)) whose intuitive contact with reality shows up the inauthenticity and limited reach of his intellectualism. La Maga is in many ways 'body': she is from Montevideo (and 'Montevideo was the same as Buenos Aires' (36:4)) and from a working-class or *lumpen* background. But in these terms, I believe that her real body is her sick child Rocamadour, denied by both la Maga and Oliveira in favour of culture: la Maga sends him off to the country *nourrice* whenever her penchant for singing Hugo Wolf is most active, and for Oliveira, he had been a 'bucket of cold water, he didn't know why' (37:4). There are constant references which relate Rocamadour to excrement and evil smells, to which Oliveira reacts with alternating rejection and repression (' "Please wash your hands properly," said Oliveira. "And get rid of all that filth" ' (100:20)), and acceptance, even hope: 'The only thing which is saving me is this kid's smell of pee' (97:19). Rocamadour dies, in one sense, as a result of this repression and neglect, but it is here that what might be termed scatological redemption begins.

The face and the anus have long been considered by psychoanalysis to represent respectively the reality principle and the pleasure principle. Octavio Paz relates the face to the soul and the anus to the body: 'By saying that our arse is like another face, we are denying the duality of body and soul.'[7] Juan Goytisolo in his marvellously outrageous *Juan sin Tierra* goes further along this road: defecation is a sign of the earth; the inhabitants of heaven, he 'proves', do not defecate.[8] After the death of Rocamadour, a reminder of the urgency of the situation, there is an increasing emphasis on excrement right up to the end of Oliveira's stay in Paris, corresponding to an increasing rejection of culture, which is insistently associated with Buenos Aires and the Argentinians, described as a 'race of full-time readers' (46:6). Morelli is hit by the car because he 'slipped on a pile of shit' (118:22). The account of Valentin, Berthe Trépat's husband, covering himself with cat excrement and painting patterns on his neighbours' doors with it makes Oliveira 'inconceivably happy' (143:123), and gives him the impression that he is progressing in his search: 'The mention of Valentin sitting in the bath daubed with cat muck had given him the feeling that he could as it were take a step forward, a true step' (144:23). The anus of Rocamadour, that of Morelli, and that of Valentin are linked with the image of the suppository, and an analogy is made between the anus and the mouth: 'That surprising upgrading of the anus, its rise to the status of a second mouth, should be analysed philosophically' (138:23). Thus, not surprisingly, Berthe Trépat's mouth is seen as the buttocks of Rocamadour (148:23).[9] The culmination of the process comes when Oliveira, following the example of Heraclitus, who is said to have buried himself in dung to cure his dropsy, (metaphorically) does the same in his long night with the *clocharde* Emmanuèle: 'So that might be the answer, being in the shit up to your neck' (247:36). This is seen as a prelude to a new, totally reversed vision,[10] as the eye is replaced by the anus: 'People got hold of the wrong end of the kaleidoscope, so you had to turn it back to front, [. . .] throw yourself onto the floor like Emmanuèle and then start looking at things from the mountain of dung, looking at the world through the eye in your arse' (253:36). Thus, Paris becomes for Oliveira the exact opposite of the 'heaven' of spirituality he had perhaps sought there. The initial dualism of his search is eliminated, Heaven and Earth placed firmly on the same level of human experience, and Oliveira's quest is 'no longer to ascend to Heaven (ascend, a hypocritical word, Heaven, a *flatus vocis*) but to walk with a man's stride through a land of men' (253). Heaven is situated 'on the same level as earth on the filthy pavement where games are played' (253).

Violación, *invasion, aggression*

The drawback of the wide critique Viñas applies to a whole group of writers (especially those associated with 'El Sur') is its blanket effect, its implications for any specific work. Cortázar's move to Paris in 1951 was certainly, in part at least, motivated by the rise of Peronism, and there is a clearly discernible group of works, including Borges's 'Tlön, Uqbar, Orbis Tertius', and Bioy Casares's *Diario de la guerra del cerdo*, which more or less explicitly refer to a similar 'invasion'. Cortázar's 'Casa tomada' (*Bestiario*) is a similar case, but to extrapolate too freely from this early short story does not do justice to *Rayuela*:

Among the immediate motives of that move [...] is Peronism: from the year of departure [...] to the transferred but permanent and unrevised allusions to the 'invasion' of the masses, everything confirms it. It now seems obvious to me: it is *the reappearance of the old metaphor of violation*. What is more, its specifically literary manifestations do not disguise the scorn for (or incomprehension of) the 'shapeless body' lurking outside [...]. It is the central key of the *bourgeois book* in that it uses symbolism as a device of seduction or distancing in order to 'spiritualize' matter and becomes not a mechanism of recognition but of defence against others. This is why the disquieting presence of the masses (the concrete, local, and numerous *cabecitas negras*) is seen as a possible 'aggression' permanently lurking in halls, behind screens, or is transferred onto the zoological forces which corrode his 'occupied houses' [a reference to 'Casa tomada'].[11]

The implication of this passage is that Paris is an escape from this 'invasion'. 'Invasion', *violación*, and aggression are certainly seminal elements in Cortázar's writing and can be considered as more or less synonymous. They are *barbarie* as discussed in relation to *Los premios*. The aggressive agent is seen in many guises: ants and insects, animals and monsters, Peronism, the people, masses, incest and other sexual taboos. The thread left running into the abandoned house in 'Casa tomada' suggests the presence there of the Minotaur. But the 'scorn', 'incomprehension' and 'defence' against these elements, ambiguous in 'Casa tomada', must be seriously qualified in the Cortázar of *Rayuela*. Viñas seems to suppose a greater identification between Cortázar and his later characters than is the case. Cortázar excels at the subtle depiction of bad faith in his characters and, indeed, it is on this aptitude that much of the density and ambiguity of his prose depends.

In 1971, Cortázar was well aware of his lack of understanding of Peronism before leaving Argentina in 1951, and talks with biting irony of his feeling of 'violation', clearly condemning his own elitist, intellectual stance:

Because of my petty bourgeois, anti-Peronist class, I belonged to a group which confused the phenomenon of Juan Domingo Perón, Evita Perón and a good part of their team of scoundrels with a fact that we should not have ignored and did ignore, i.e. that Perón had created the first big convulsion, the first big upheaval of the masses in the country: a whole new period had begun in the history of Argentina. That is obvious.

At that time, within Argentina, the confrontations, the frictions, the feeling of violation we felt daily at this popular upsurge, our situation of young bourgeois who read in several languages, prevented us from understanding the phenomenon. We were very annoyed by the loudspeakers on the corners shouting, 'Perón. Perón, how great you are', because they interrupted the latest Alban Berg concerto we were listening to. All that pushed us into a suicidal mistake, and we all cleared out.

But consider for a moment (history is very paradoxical) that the fact that we did leave has, in some cases, been very useful, because if I had stayed in Argentina I would probably never have come to understand Peronism.[12]

In 'Casa tomada', published in 1951, it is difficult to know how much irony there is in the presentation of the character's rejection of Peronism because he cannot get hold of the latest French literature (B 11), clearly equivalent to the latest Alban Berg concerto. The very heavy irony, however, of the last lines of 'El perseguidor' expresses a definite condemnation of the attitude of the critic Bruno, whose common sense, intellectualism, and commercial use of literature is threatened or 'invaded' by the anguished irrationalism of Johnny Carter:

Thus the biography was, so to speak, complete. It may not be right for me to say this myself, but naturally I speak on a purely aesthetic level. There is already talk of a new translation, into Swedish or Norwegian, I think. My wife is delighted with the news.   (AS 183)

When these lines are compared with the equally ironic last lines of Borges's 'Tiön, Uqbar, Orbis Tertius', where 'our' world is similarly invaded by another, the difference between the two authors becomes clear. The irony of Borges is based on his impish self-satisfaction in his *au dessus de la mêlée* aestheticism and common sense in ignoring the invasion:

I take no notice, in the calm days of my Androgué house, I carry on checking an indecisive translation after the style of Quevedo (which I do not intend to publish) of Browne's *Urn Burial*.[13]

Cortázar has taken from Borges many of the formal aspects of his writing, has learnt the 'interstices' where the 'monsters' are to be found and how they are conjured up. It is also fair to say that he has inherited the best part of Borges's humanism: his stand against dogmatism. But where the disciple differs is in his moral attitude towards his monsters.

There are two basic and paradoxically related thematic elements in Borges: barbaric literary types such as *gauchos* and gangsters, and stimulating patterns of philosophical thought – idealism, gnosticism, etc. There is also a constant insistence that the latter are human, provisional schemes to interpret a divine (i.e. incomprehensible), ineffable order, and cannot be extracted and applied in reality, since to do so would lead inevitably to totalitarianism, to the 'rigour of chess-players',[14] to Peronism, Nazism and communism, between which little distinction is made.

When applied, these ideas and forces become monsters, moral and intellectual *impossibilities* against the exclusive reality of Western culture, liberalism:

For Europeans and Americans, there is one, and only one possible order: that which once bore the name of Rome and which now is the culture of the West. To be a Nazi (to play at vigorous barbarism, to play at being a Viking, a Tartar, a sixteenth-century *conquistador*, a *gaucho*, a redskin) is, in the long run, a mental and moral impossibility.[15]

These monsters are rejected by the ego and themselves desire to be destroyed:

Nobody, in the central solitude of his ego, can desire it to triumph. I venture this conjecture: *Hitler wants to be defeated*. Blindly, Hitler collaborates with the inevitable armies which will annihilate him, as the metal vultures and the dragon (which could not have been unaware that they were monsters) mysteriously collaborated with Hercules.[16]

Cortázar, on the other hand, stands increasingly against the ego and Western Culture and on the side of his monsters. Cortázar's monsters do, incidentally, desire destruction too, as in the case of the Minotaur in *Los reyes*, but only to return, devoid of their monstrosity, as a redemptive force.

If Oliveira leaves Argentina to avoid contact with the invasion of the masses and *violación*, la Maga quickly brings him back into contact with them. Oliveira does at first not want to know about her origins in Montevideo and prefers an idealized, mental image of her: 'To see you the way I wanted, it was necessary to start by closing my eyes' (18:1). Gregovorius, however, rashly insists that Montevideo is her 'volume', i.e. body: ' "You are like a playing-card queen for me, viewed front on, but with no volume." [...] "And Montevideo is the volume..." ' (76:15). The theme of rape is now introduced, destroying the spiritualized image of la Maga in the same way as did the theme of excrement the perfection of fish in a tank: 'A transparent ribbon of excrement [. . .] strips them of their perfection of pure images' (50:8).

La Maga recounts how, as a child, she was raped in Montevideo by the negro Ireneo, and Paris becomes the place where the *violación* and invasion associated with America most clearly emerge and have to be faced. Though Oliveira's reaction to the story is mixed, his comment 'The negro was a hero, mate' (79:16) must be taken seriously into account as a factor in his later steeling himself to accept any method of combating the dead convention in *la piedad*, to 'have the courage to [. . .] witness without horror the revenge of the lackeys' (616:147).

The reading of rape as possibly a vital act within the novel becomes inevitable as a clear pattern begins to emerge. Both the 'lipic' Bob in *Los premios* and Ireneo are closely associated with ants.[17] The rape of the adolescent Felipe by Bob is followed by a description of how *escamoteo*, falsity and escapism, is undermined by the elements, animals and, characteristically, the ants, how 'the Latin American world is a sleight of hand, but [. . .] the ants, the armadillos, the climate with its humid suckers are working away underneath' (*P* 358–9). In the 'dispensable chapters', Ireneo is seen as a child feeding a live grub to an ant colony and an incipient association with ants is strongly suggested: 'Ireneo would have liked to be in the ant hill as well' (550:120).

Such rapes in all the novels except *Libro de Manuel* on the part of monstrous or barbaric characters – Bob–Felipe, Ireneo–la Maga, Frau Marta–the English girl (*62*) – are followed by similar rapes on the part of the main characters: the potential rape of Felipe by Raúl; Oliveira's played down rape of la Maga, his kissing Talita; in *62* that of Celia by Hélène; in *Libro de Manuel* (with no clear model in the novel) that of Francine by Andrés. These rapes are presented with increasing explicitness as acts of potential liberation, though their final positive or negative sign depends very much on the good faith of the character himself and on various other factors: the attitude of Traveler in *Rayuela*; the attitude and behaviour of Juan and Celia in *62*; that Andrés should combine his sexual liberation with political commitment in *Libro de Manuel*.

Paris then, rather than being escapism from rape and invasion, represents, somewhat like the *Malcolm*, the possibility of discovering the ambiguous, monstrous forces discussed above. Rather than a geographical site, it is a literary construct and an attitude, a bracketing off of the *escamoteo*, repression, ignoring and forgetting, involved in the attitude represented by Buenos Aires.

Buenos Aires and 'elsewhere' in the short stories

The link between *Rayuela* and the short stories is established by Cortázar himself. Whereas the latter are an intuitive and irrational form of writing about certain forces and presences, *Rayuela*, apart from being a wider orchestration of the same forces, is, as Cortázar admits in 'Volviendo a Eugenia Grandet', 'the philosophy of my short stories, an investigation of what for many years determined their subject matter or their impulse' (*V* 1 41).

The structure of the stories can be discussed with little regard to their chronology, as by their nature they seem to evolve less than the more self-conscious novel form. (One significative form of evolution is the greater consciousness in the characters of the forces which manipulate their conduct and thus of the possibility of disobeying these dictates. This can be seen most clearly in 'Instrucciones para John Howell' and 'Los pasos en las huellas'.) This discussion of the stories, orientated as it is towards something outside them, will be of necessity somewhat schematic due to their number and diversity.

Under the superficial opposition at work in the stories between the normal and the fantastic, there is for our purpose a more important, corresponding opposition between what might be loosely termed bourgeois civilization and what is repressed by it. The two terms of this opposition are often situated in different places: Buenos Aires is civilization in 'Lejana', 'El otro cielo', 'Reunión', the other term being situated in Budapest, Paris and Cuba. In other stories, civilization is in Paris: 'Cartas de mamá' and 'Las armas secretas'; the other term in Buenos Aires and Germany. The clear geographical distinction is however often replaced by a distance in time or a different location within the same city.

The attributes of the civilized 'place' are easily distinguished: present time, causality, culture, marriage and family, middle-class values. Those of the area repressed by it and which disrupts it are more varied: a primitive, prehistorical past ('La noche boca arriba', 'El ídolo de las Cícladas'); the world of prostitutes and the people, often seen as monstrous ('El otro cielo', 'Las puertas del cielo'); crime and violence ('El río', 'Los pasos en las huellas', 'El otro cielo'); a scene felt as absurd, often a concert ('La banda', 'Las

Ménades', 'Instrucciones para John Howell', 'Las babas del diablo'); revolution ('Reunión'); incest ('Casa tomada', 'Bestiario').

In 'Del sentimiento de lo fantástico' Cortázar makes a distinction between two types of relationship he has with the fantastic. When he was young, he tells us, he was a complete realist, and his first contacts with the fantastic were the fruits of a conscious effort. This provocation of the fantastic now alternates with a more passive experience of it: '[. . .] the fantastic pays me a visit (sometimes I am the visitor and my stories for the last twenty years have been born of these reciprocal good manners)' (*V* I 74). The distinction permits a useful classification of the stories:

1 (a). The area of the fantastic (the repressed), *lo otro*, is *consciously and intentionally* visited by a character dissatisfied with his primary reality. Here he comes into contact with monstrous characters and in some cases with a double who serves as an intermediary to this contact (a sort of Virgil figure). And, vice versa, the monster is also a medium to the contact with the double. This is the case in 'Las puertas del cielo', when the lawyer-writer Hardoy is introduced by the artisan class Mauro to his ex-semi-prostitute wife Celina, who, after her death, becomes a link between the two men. Similarly, in 'El otro cielo', the main character's 'double', the 'South American' Lau(t)r(éam)ent,[18] serves as his introduction to the world of Paris prostitution and crime.

1 (b). A variation on this first pattern of intentionally exposing oneself to *lo otro* is created by a character more or less unwittingly entering a concert or spectacle and coming into contact with what he (usually due to its unexpected nature, or contrast with his own medium) considers monstrous and absurd. This contact with the monstrous can be denied or ignored by the character as in 'Las Ménades' or lead to abandonment of profession and exile as in the case of Lucio Medina in 'La banda'.

2. The second type of relationship between the two areas, which is far more passive on the side of civilization, and received with hostility, is also much more fantastic in the traditional sense, involving metaphorical possession by incubi and succubi, the return of ghosts, eternity through metempsychosis, and the like. In 'Cartas de mamá', a dead brother, whose uncomfortable memory and death have been repressed, comes from Buenos Aires to Paris to take possession of his rightful bride. In 'Lejana', Alina Reyes is revealed the presence of her double by an automatic word-play – an anagram

of her name gives the suggestive 'she's the queen and...', after which, while living her normal life in Buenos Aires, she also becomes another, walking the cold streets of Budapest. In 'Las armas secretas', a French student is gradually possessed by a German soldier, who, years earlier, had been killed for raping the girl who is now the Frenchman's fiancée. His vengeance is suggested as he–they prepare to rape the girl anew.

These two types of contact with the fantastic are not normally mixed in one short story. The only exception, I believe, is 'Lejana', where Alina Reyes is first 'invaded' by the presence of her double and later travels to Budapest in search of her. The two types of contact, however, correspond to the two main parts of *Rayuela*. The first area of orderly, cultured, middle-class values is the Buenos Aires that Oliveira leaves. The Paris he sets out to visit is the secondary reality, where he will be exposed to the monsters and other forces repressed or disguised in the first.

At least two very important elements in the Paris section of *Rayuela* correspond to the models of the more intentional type of contact with 'the other', *lo otro*: the first is the exposure to la Maga, very close to the monsters of the short stories, Celina ('Las puertas del cielo') and Josiane ('El otro cielo'); the second, the concert given by Berthe Trépat and its sequence, analogous in effect to those of the stories, but possessing greater 'human vibration';[19] the third is the death of Rocamadour. Though the vigil is an important element in the stories, the death of a child seems to be a model evolved from the longer story 'El perseguidor' – the death of Bee, and continued in *Los premios* – the illness of Jorge. The episode with Emmanuèle, the *clocharde*, definitely belongs to the novels as it is the consequence of an attitude developed through meditation on the 'archetypal' episodes listed above. The philosophical discussion in the first part revolves basically around these three episodes. It can be seen as an attempt to understand and harness the forces only intuited vaguely in the stories. This force, as we have seen, has little to do with Paris *per se*, but rather with the subterranean aspects of what is represented by Buenos Aires.

In the second part, where the role of Buenos Aires as the primary reality is confirmed, the characters, as in the second class of stories, are subjected to a far more fantastic invasion or infiltration by the forces of the secondary reality discovered and provoked by Oliveira in Paris. The way in which Talita is possessed by la Maga, for example, is very similar to the way Alina Reyes discovered the presence of her double. Talita, trying out a tape-recorder, records 'Horacio at his desk, with a candle, reading' but when this is replayed, it becomes 'Horacio at his desk, with a green candle' (332:47). A new element is mysteriously introduced: the fact that the candle is green, which the reader knows, but Talita does not, is a sign of la Maga ('the flames of the green candles shone in her eyes' (57:11); 'you were holding two green candles' (17:1)).

In traditional terms, the two parts of the novel are in many ways separate entities, in that there is little continuity of characters, and those of the second part are kept in ignorance of the events of the first by Oliveira's refusal to talk about Paris. Throughout the first part, the narrative point of view seems to be from the end of that part or at least from after the death of Rocamadour. There is no knowledge evinced of what happens in Buenos Aires. At the beginning of the novel, for example, as in 62 and Libro de Manuel, there is a passage which refers forward to all the main episodes. No mention, however, is made of the second part: 'innumerable episodes where la Maga and Roland and Rocamadour, and the Club and the streets and my moral disorders and other pyorrhoeas and Berthe Trépat and sometimes an empty stomach [. . .]' (26:2).

This separateness has various functions. In the second part, for a certain time, it expresses the censorship applied by Oliveira to the memory of his Paris experience. It is also a narrative tactic to prepare the surprise nature of the 'invasion' of Buenos Aires from Paris. But more importantly it suggests that there is no traditional causal link between the two parts. As we shall see, there are several repetitions of elements from the first to the second parts, and it may be illuminating to consider the relationship between them in the light of the chronology of certain short stories. In 'La noche boca arriba', for example, different but formally and metaphorically analogous things happen simultaneously but in different historical periods to one character, who is involved in a motorcycle accident in Paris and a tribal war in America with the Aztecs. Such a comparison would suggest that the link between the two parts is not so much chronological as metaphorical. As Gregovorius explains, 'Paris is an enormous metaphor' (159). If this is true, the structure of Rayuela is a clear prefiguration of that of 62, and Paris an embryonic form of the 'city' in the following novel.

The topology of Los premios *in relation to that of* Rayuela

In *Los premios* there are four distinct places which connote different existential and ontological situations: the Buenos Aires which the *Malcolm* leaves at the beginning of the novel and where it arrives at the end, and which remains unchanged; the ship, the *Malcolm*, which (like Paris for Oliveira) quickly changes meaning from being an escape from Buenos Aires, a simple hiatus in the passengers' lives, to an area where a more authentic Argentina can be elaborated; the labyrinthine passages where the monstrous 'lipics' and 'glucics' lurk and which lead to the stern deck; the stern deck, the goal of the quest, a personal and metaphysical centre. In *Rayuela*, however, there are only two places: Paris and Buenos Aires, which have to fulfil the same roles. This leads to what might be called a 'recycling' of elements, i.e. they play different roles from different points of view, or from different points in the novel. The aggression and rape which is found in the labyrinthine passages in *Los premios* is presented in Paris as an unwanted memory from Montevideo. This labyrinth becomes the very streets of Paris where Oliveira and la Maga impose the rule that they should wander until they meet by chance, and the wasteland where the members of the Club de la Serpiente meet and wander. (All these elements later reappear in the 'city' in *62*.)

The stern in *Los premios* is reached after a completely linear passage through the previous three stages. It is an individual and transcendental goal. In *Rayuela* the stern corresponds to what Oliveira calls the 'centre' but this is no longer expressed in terms of a place. Moreover, for Oliveira, this centre can only be fully realized with others, i.e. in Buenos Aires, and can no longer be individual and transcendental. Many people may have reached this centre, but 'it is not enough, I feel that my salvation, supposing I could achieve it, has also to be the salvation of everybody, to a man' (507). Thus, even if Oliveira does reach some sort of centre in Paris, perhaps with Emmanuèle, it is meaningless until it is communicated to others, i.e. Traveler and Talita. This is presumably one reason for the existence of a second part in Buenos Aires, which would thus be a *structural* development from the simple disappointment expressed in *Los premios* that Medrano was not able to communicate his experience.

Oliveira suggests that it is this impossibility of personal salvation that prompts Morelli to publish 'the things he found or unfound' (491:95), and indeed to use the novel form. Such a preoccupation corresponds to the interest throughout *Rayuela* in the reader, referred to as the main character of the novel. Traveler and Talita, in this light, correspond to the reading public. They are 'persecuted' by Oliveira in much the same way as the reader is submitted to increasingly tense situations before the divergent readings proposed to him.

A very similar definition of 'centre' is given in both *Los premios* and *Rayuela*. In *Los premios*, as we have seen, the centre is reached if the ship becomes (is seen as) the painting by Picasso. In *Rayuela*, similarly, Oliveira talks of 'the exact point, [...] an anamorphic painting where you have to find the right angle [...] for a load of senseless lines to turn suddenly into the portrait of Francis I or the battle of Sinigaglia' (98:19). Concentrating for the moment on *Los premios*, it is clear that the image stems from the short stories, where one reality can be equivalent to another, as in 'La noche boca arriba'. But in *Los premios* the image is only a metaphor, as there are no two different realities which could become equivalent, whereas in the stories, it is a structural reality. (One symptom of this is the absence of properly developed doubles in *Los premios*.) If the image is realized in *Los premios* it must be in the reduction of the plurality of the individual psychological and existential problems and aims of the characters to the one, almost impersonal attempt to break through to the stern. Thus, in *Los premios*, Cortázar turns his back on what might be called the structuralism of the short stories, but in doing so, a teleology is discovered or introduced, an aim or movement towards something.

In *Rayuela* there is a return to 'structuralism' in that the characters in Buenos Aires are seen in terms of what happened to a different set of characters in Paris: Talita becomes la Maga; the dual and triangular structures are repeated. The dichotomy is still seen in terms of surface and deep or impersonal motivations (e.g. 'The visit to the *Cerro* had been fine, precisely because it had been based on reasons other than those he had supposed' (338:48)) but these deep motivations are given by and depend on the 'previous' actions of others. The important point is that the 'possession', 'invasion', in *Rayuela* maintains the *aims* established in *Los premios* and absent from the short stories. If Talita is possessed, it is because 'life is trying to change its key in and through and by them' (417:62).

A common objection to the argument that something is changed, or something achieved in *Rayuela* and elsewhere is that the end is so banal and anti-climactic: Talita tells her boss not to be stupid, Oliveira goes to the cinema with Gekrepken. It is the inner dynamics of the novel that confer meaning upon these episodes and, apart from the possible importance of their very 'suchness', the reader must be prepared to apply the principle of the possible equivalence between very different objects to his own reading:

Where there should be a farewell there is a picture on the wall; instead of a scream, a fishing rod; a death is resolved in a trio for mandolins. And that is a farewell, a scream and a death, but who is prepared to displace himself, to go beyond himself, to decentre himself, to uncover [or discover] himself? (497:97)

Banality is a central part of the humour of Cortázar – 'poor snack-bar Preadamite' (485:93), and it is up to the reader to discover an *imago mundi* in a group of women having tea and biscuits:

A crystallization where nothing would be subsumed, but where a lucid eye might peep into the kaleidoscope and understand the great multi-coloured rose-window, understand it like a figure, an *imago mundi* which outside the kaleidoscope would become a Provençal-style living room, or a concert of aunts sipping tea with Bagley biscuits. (533:109)

It is interesting to note that *Los premios* does give to *Rayuela* the seeds of the opposition between the characters and reality of Paris and those of Buenos Aires: the two groups on the boat, those in favour of direct action and those who are not. This opposition is, however, not exploited structurally in *Los premios*; the basic opposit-ions of meaning in the novel are not articulated through it. There is no complete formal return to the schemas of the short stories in the novels, however, until *62*, where the deep reality and transpersonal intentions of a group are expressed in a whole system of archetypal myths and separate literary texts.

In conclusion, the trip to Paris is not simply a search for 'spirit', it is the discovery of the 'body'. The violence, invasion, and the monstrous experienced in Paris is American (real), but repressed in America. Being in Paris is a putting into brackets of the attitudes which repress these forces.

Buenos Aires and Paris in Rayuela

Before dealing with more specific points, another aspect of the question suggested by Viñas's critique must be clarified. 'Spirit' can be opposed not only to 'body', but also to history. Cortázar's attitude to national politics, as defined in 'Acerca de la situación del intelectual latinoamericano', was the following: 'In the last analysis, you and I know full well that the present-day intellectual faces one single major problem, that of peace founded on social justice, and that the national allegiances of each one of us only subdivide the question without affecting its basic character' (*UR* b 201). There is a suggestion that national politics distract the writer from the basic issues. The position in *Rayuela* towards history is, however, more radical.

Oliveira rejects the whole world of history and politics, 'not because of Eden, not so much because of Eden itself, but just to leave behind the jet plane, the face of Nikita or Dwight or Charles or Francisco' (432–3:71). Thus he condemns oppressive Russian communism, American imperialism, French nationalism, Spanish fascism, not from any other political position, but for what they have in common, their negation of man. It is the whole system of thought in the West that he attacks: 'Since the Eleatics to the present day, dialectical thought has had plenty of time to yield its fruit. We are eating it, it's delicious, it is boiling with radioactivity' (453:79). Thus, until man's whole way of thinking is changed, any political action will simply be a perpetuation of the same state of affairs. Oliveira is 'not suitable to join the ranks of those who are struggling to destroy it [present reality, *la circunstancia*], since he believes that its destruction means no more than its substitution by another, equally partial and intolerable one' (441:74). Hence the conclusion that truth is not to be found in history: 'You may achieve historical results like Marxism or whatever you like, but the Yonder is not exactly history, the Yonder is like the finger-tips which emerge from the waters of history, looking for somewhere to get a hold' (509:99). This does not mean that truth must be transcendental, but that social organization does not automatically produce it.

Two points have been made here: that the search is obstructed, blurred, by national politics and values ('local values as against values pure and simple' (*UR* b 205)) and by a limited historical approach. These two ideas are brought together in Oliveira's

Argentinian nationality, his 'être obligé de représenter un pays':
'Apart from which he considered it dishonest and facile to mix
historical problems like being an Argentinian or an Eskimo, with
problems like that of action or abstention' (32:3, my italics).
Argentina, then, is history, *la circunstancia* (not, of course, solely that
of Argentina), and to go to Paris is to put historical judgements in
brackets (not to move into an ahistorical limbo as can be seen in the
references to the war in Algeria), just as was done with the *escamoteo*
and repression discussed above.

This does not mean that Oliveira automatically ceases to behave
like an Argentinian on his arrival in Paris. Indeed, there are two
reasons why it must be made clear what are the attributes of the
Argentinians for Cortázar: in order to understand what Oliveira is
rejecting, and also to understand why he behaves in the way he does
in so far as he is not true to the task he sets himself. It will become
clear that what Oliveira finds wrong with Argentina applies to
civilization in general.

One important point made about the Argentinians is their mistrust, illustrated by a quotation in the 'dispensable chapters' from
Cambaceres's *Música sentimental*. When a young *porteño* (someone
from Buenos Aires) is warned about the snares of France, he answers,
'I shall try to stay on my guard then' (662). Macedonio Fernández
illustrates the '*porteño*'s fear of being taken for a ride'[20] in a characteristically eloquent fashion: a man walks through Buenos Aires with a
lighted candle between his fingers and the passers-by let it burn him
rather than be taken in by a practical joke. Oliveira's stagnation and
inactivity in Paris springs from the same root, from 'the exercise of an
intelligence more intent on not letting itself be taken in than on
grasping the truth' (32).

As with the trait described above, most of the others mentioned
are seen as a defence. 'The reason which guides the actions of good
Argentinians' (371–2:54) is one of the most important defence
mechanisms. Its function, like that of culture, is often to disguise a
void: 'to defend oneself through a rapid, frantic accumulation of
"culture" [is] the trick *par excellence* of the Argentinian middle class
to dodge Argentinian and any other reality, and to believe themselves safe from the vacuum surrounding them' (31:3). Similarly,
the symmetrical classification of the world by Ceferino Piriz is
described as being inspired by *horror vacui* (571:129). This fear of
something, the existence of which is not even recognized, is seen as a

constant, and Buenos Aires described as the 'capital of fear' (444: 75).[21]

Another facet of the 'Argentinian' mind which will become very important in the novel is what might be called *naturalization* (as the term is used by Barthes in *Mythologies*). This involves the passing off of something which is arbitrary and historical as natural and thus true: *'their acceptance of the immediate as the true, the vicarious as the,* as the, as the [...]' (444). This is what Oliveira elsewhere calls the 'so typically Hispano-Italo-Argentine "You can take it from me!" ' (33) Language is seen as the coagulator of this false truth and unity: 'Loads of folk settled comfortably into a supposed unity of person which was no more than a linguistic unity and a premature sclero- ticization of character, [...] something which is not lived or analysed because *it is just like that* and forms us, completes us and strengthens us' (99:19). Indeed, Buenos Aires also seems to be the capital of words, a point made by the endless word-games played on Oliveira's return, as also in his answer in Paris to a phrase from Crevel's *Etes-vous fous?*: ' "*Tu étreins des mots* [...]". "No, my old friend, that's more like what they do on the other side of the sea" ' (115:21). Translated onto the plane of action, this attitude corre- sponds to Kant's categorical imperative: 'Act as if the maxim of your action were to become through your will a general natural law.'[22] Oliveira's inactivity in Paris, and his demand for a 'previous central attitude' (198:28), a certainty previous to, i.e. not conditioned by, language and convention, is a therapeutic reaction against this attitude.

In all these characteristics, Argentina has so far been seen simply as the repository of the most sclerotic aspects of Western culture. Argentinian culture is seen as limiting and coercive, but Argentina as a 'race' is only a metonym for the 'species', i.e. Western culture in general:

Later on he was amused to find how, in the higher forms of culture, the weight of authorities and influences [...] produced their own subtly disguised 'you can take it from me' [...]. As if the species were at watch in the individual to prevent him from advancing too far along the road of tolerance.   (33)

The move away from Argentina is thus the first step in the general 'decentring' (*descentrar*) proposed by the novel.

The last trait discussed is perhaps more specifically Argentinian, though it does have general resonances, especially in its reference to the attitude of the reader. This is the theme of the delegation of responsibility, and is best defined in an interview given by Cortázar in 1973:

I have no way of knowing what is the present situation of the Argentinian mentality, but I knew that of my generation twenty or thirty years ago, that famous 'mind your own business' (*no te metás*) which is so typical of us. That little phrase with which someone once defined us, that is, the tendency to delegate responsibility, not to assume it fully, can re-emerge at any time.[23]

Delegation is a seminal element in all Cortázar's writing and is perhaps the origin of the *dédoublement* of a hypothetical unitary character into Traveler and Oliveira. Traveler's name is an indication of this. He has never travelled, but Oliveira travels for him; Traveler delegates this 'travelling' onto Oliveira, his *doppelgänger*. The attitude of the passive 'female reader' is identical to that of Traveler:

Morelli considers that mere aesthetic writing [...] finishes up encouraging the female reader in one, the sort who does not want problems but solutions, or false problems belonging to someone else which will allow him to suffer comfortably sitting in his armchair, without committing himself to the drama which ought also to be his own. In Argentina [...] that sort of trick (*escamoteo*) has kept us as happy and as contented as can be for a century.
(500:99)

It is easy to trace this delegation through the novels. In *Los premios* and *Rayuela*, there is a *dédoublement* in two directions: between characters, Medrano–Bettina; Oliveira–Traveler; and between all the characters and a writer: Persio, Morelli.[24] In 'El perseguidor', Johnny delegates the explanation and purification of his own experience directly to his biographer, Bruno, hoping to 'recover' this experience at a later date: 'It is as if Johnny leaves these ghosts in pledge with me, puts them in my pocket like so many handkerchiefs until the time comes to retrieve them' (*AS* 152–3). In *Los premios* and *Rayuela*, repression and falsification is attributed to the doubles Bettina and Traveler, whereas the writers Persio and Morelli represent the authentic desires of Cortázar. In *62* and *Libro de Manuel*, however, the various versions of the delegation and *dédoublement* are unified, the double of the characters or groups of characters is also the (or a) writer of the novel: 'my paredros' and *el que te dije*. The falsifying effects of this delegation are incorporated into the texture of the writing and fully explored.

IN PARIS

Though there is a definite process and progression in this first part, it is very difficult to delimit its stages precisely. Attitudes, for example, which later prove to be valid, initially lead to *impasses* or to failure and retrogression, as in the case of Oliveira's dealings with Berthe Trépat. It is also difficult to determine how and exactly when certain ideas emerge, as they are often presented in the 'dispensable chapters', in quotes from other authors and in the theorizing of Morelli, to which most of the characters probably have access in their constant reading of the latter's work.

The world from which Oliveira starts, the Argentina I have discussed, could be described as an 'unthinking monism', a world which allows of no analysis because 'it's just like that', 'a satisfactory world for reasonable people' (436:71). What is desperately sought (and often occurs against the characters' will) to break the monopoly of this univocal order is a force or presence from outside its structures or *previous* to them, and which would suggest the possibility of another, new order. The three principal experiences of the first part (la Maga, Berthe Trépat, the death of Rocamadour), built on the models developed in the short stories, produce this effect both for Oliveira and for the reader. With Berthe Trépat, for example, Oliveira has the impression that the barriers of reality are yielding, 'the feeling that he could as it were take a step forward, [...] a step through the middle of a stone wall' (144:23).

The effect of these structural elements is strengthened by constant reference to Oliveira's more intimate proofs of the precariousness of the apparently iron laws of the reality he will not accept:

(a) The pure anguish which seizes him: 'this time I caught you, anguish, I felt you *previous* (*previo*) to any mental organization' (426:67).

(b) Dreams produce in him a 'feeling of the *precarious*, the false, especially the futile' (408:57, my italics), especially in that, on waking, he faces 'total forgetfulness of the *previous* marvel' (577:132, my italics).

(c) A similar effect is produced in Oliveira and la Maga, who have the experience of 'stumbling continually into exceptions, finding themselves in compartments different from those of normal people' (20:1). In *Historias de cronopios y de famas*, exceptions are seen to demonstrate 'the *precarious* nature of the existence within which we believe we exist' (*H* 64, my italics). They have much in common with the exceptions with which Jarry, one of Cortázar's favourite authors, had planned to discover and describe 'l'univers supplémentaire à celui-ci', 'un univers que l'on peut voir et que peut-être l'on doit voir à la place du traditionnel'.[25]

(d) The most insistently stressed 'proof' is the generalized nostalgia for a lost Eden, glimpsed in dreams, and a fundamental theme in modern literature: 'Everything written nowadays worth reading is orientated towards nostalgia' (432:71). This nostalgia is basic and inalienable: 'You can kill everything apart from the nostalgia for the kingdom' (436:71). Paris is the locus of this nostalgia, an existence centred round it, and created by it: 'Even this existence which I sometimes try to describe, this Paris where I move around like a dry leaf, would not be visible if behind there did not throb the axial anxiety, the reunion with the shaft' (28:2). It is this same anxiety that makes the 'zone' in *62* stand out from the cities, like Paris from Buenos Aires: 'The zone is an anxiety viscously insinuating itself' (*62* 16).

But more than anything else, the firmness of the world Oliveira comes from (its 'comforting categories' and 'hierarchies of values' (29:2)) is swept away by la Maga: 'When embracing that concretion of nebulose, la Maga, I believe that it makes as much sense to make a doll out of breadcrumbs as it does to write the novel I will never write or defend with one's life the ideas which redeem nations' (28–9). La Maga is a primitive and lives a life of what Oliveira describes as disorder. Oliveira in a sense emulates the disorder of la Maga, but soon comes to realize that the disorder he *chooses* is too deliberate, is simply the *opposite* of order: 'All that ABC of my life was a lamentable piece of stupidity because it did not go beyond a mere dialectical swing, the choice of a non-behaviour instead of any sort of behaviour, moderate indecency instead of gregarious decency' (25:2). It thus becomes clear that the monism discussed is firmly based in dualism, whereas the disorder of la Maga has no opposite: 'You couldn't pose reality to la Maga in methodical terms, the praise of disorder would have scandalized her as much as its condemnation' (25). The cause of the dualism he is condemned to, he realizes, is the distance between subject and object ('It was always me and my life, me with my life facing the lives of others' (26:2)); between life and thought ('as always, I found it much less difficult to think than to be' (26)). The whole ideal of *Rayuela* is to reach a state with no opposite, a non-dualistic state, such as 'a sanity (razón) other than that sanity the failure of which is madness' (94:18). The two terms 'madness' and 'sanity' will become increasingly important in the second part.

The subject–object dualism prevents Oliveira from really participating in life: 'There are metaphysical rivers. [...] I describe and define and desire those rivers, she swims them' (116:21). It is this same dichotomy which imposes a constant choice between alternatives: 'the choice of a non-behaviour'. Oliveira rejects this choice: 'It would seem that a choice cannot be dialectical, that just by posing it one impoverishes it, that is, one falsifies it, that is, one transforms it into something else' (439:73). He gives various reasons for this refusal. The very fact that there are so many possible remedies to humanity's ills suggests to him that they are partial:

Believing in what they call matter, believing in what they call spirit, living in Emmanuel or following courses in Zen, [...] the list is long, the choice multiple. But the very fact that there can be a choice and that the list is long suffices to prove that we are living in prehistory and prehumanity.[26]   (507:99)

The 'Judaeo-Christian dialectic' is the 'falsest of freedoms' (616:147), he says elsewhere, as it cannot ask the right questions. He equates choice with language, as against the spontaneity of action sought by Zen. Love, for example, he claims, cannot involve choice: 'From the word to acts, mate; in general there is no *res* without *verba*. What a lot of people call loving consists in choosing a woman and marrying her. [...] As if you could choose in love, as if it wasn't a streak of lightning which breaks your bones and leaves you flat out in the middle of the patio' (484:93).

Oliveira's ideal here is rather hard to grasp. He demands a choice which will necessarily be right: 'Genius lies in choosing to be a genius and *being right*' (463:84). Or rather, that the terms 'invention' and 'choice' should become synonymous, but not in the sense here expressed by Sartre: 'Vous êtes libre, choisissez, c'est-à-dire inventer. Aucune morale générale ne peut vous indiquer ce qu'il y a à faire; il n'a pas de signe dans le monde.'[27] Oliveira definitely demands a *signe*, something that will justify his choice and make it inevitable. There is a rather beautiful passage at the beginning of the novel that well expresses this mysterious adequation of free choice and a reality: 'A mouth chosen among all possible mouths, chosen by me with sovereign freedom to draw it with my hand on your face and which by a chance process which I do not seek to understand, coincides exactly with your mouth which smiles under the one my hand is drawing you' (48:7). This perfection must be taken to have occurred in a state of grace which is soon dispelled, as Oliveira and la Maga begin to 'unfind each other minutely' (18:1). An important term in this cluster of ideas is coercion: 'être *obligé* de représenter un pays' (my italics). In the terms of Lezama Lima that Cortázar makes his own in the 'dispensable chapters' ('true belief lies between superstition and licentiousness' (457:81)), one's freedom should coincide with the unfreedom of superstition, invention becomes a renovation of the anchylosed fundamentals: 'Let us try to invent new passions, or to reproduce the old ones with equal intensity' (457). But at this point and for many reasons, this possibility is not open to Oliveira and before any choice can be made, any action undertaken, he demands a point of central certainty outside the given, 'a previous central attitude' (198:28).

Oliveira's moral position at this point is complex and leads him into a vicious circle. We have seen that the basis of the monism represented by Buenos Aires is dualism, but Oliveira in an attempt to escape from its arbitrary dogmatism exacerbates the dualism by placing himself at the centre of all alternatives, renouncing all action and choice: 'The trouble was that by dint of fearing an excessive polarization of points of view, he had become too given to weighing and even accepting the yes and the no in everything, viewing the scales from the pointer. In Paris everything was Buenos Aires to him, and vice versa' (32:3). The problem is that this position, which is in principle provisional, can become hardened into a reflex. It makes him suspect that his possible salvation with la Maga is a trap. This new dualism is incorporated into the novel mainly in the presence of the two women Oliveira moves between, la Maga and Pola. (A similar pair is present in all the novels: Bettina–Claudia, Tell–Hélène, Francine–Ludmilla.) His relationship with Pola, though on the one hand the fruit of a valid decision to abstain from commitment to any order, is also a sign of his bad faith. Pola or Pola París represents the Paris traditionally sought by the Argentinian. She represents order and bourgeois culture as can be seen in the description of her room. Just like Yolande, La Ville, in Crevel's *Etes-vous fous?*, she is a splendid incarnation of the city: 'the naked city with its [or her] sex attuned to the throbbing of the curtain' (482:92). Pola has cancer and is associated with the pavement drawings which are erased every evening to be repeated in exactly the same form on the next day for the money given by tourists, that is, with a dying order artificially perpetuated. This too she has in common with Crevel's Yolande, who has to rub herself every twelve hours against a fakir in order to stay alive!

La Maga's love offers Oliveira the salvation he is seeking, but because of the very position he has taken to escape from what he considers a false life, he has been unable to take advantage of this love: 'Giver of infinity, I don't know how to receive, forgive me' (484:93). Love is similarly described elsewhere as a 'giver of being' (339:48). But through his frustrated relationship with la Maga, his quest comes to be framed in increasingly human terms; to reach the *centro* becomes union with another. *El otro* becomes *lo otro* – another person becomes otherness. This can be seen in the passage describing Morelli's accident: 'in the arms of another' – 'possession of otherness' – 'on the verge of otherness' – 'another hand from outside, from the other (*lo otro*)' (120–1:22).

The absurd, that is, what is wrong with things, is now also seen principally in social and personal terms: 'The most absurd thing about these lives we claim to be living is their false contact' (450:78). This is most clearly focused upon when Oliveira sees an old man knocked over by a car, and a large crowd forms only to be dispersed immediately by a shower of rain:

The slightest grade of objectivity was an opening onto the absurdity of Paris, of gregarious life. [...] Only biological and sexual objectivity could hide some people's insularity from them, whatever John Donne might have liked to think. Contacts in action and race and profession and in bed and in the stadium were contacts between leaves and branches, criss-crossing and caressing each other from tree to tree, while the trunks scornfully raise their irreconcilable parallels. (120)

Motivated by this first revelation of the absurd, Oliveira makes his first attempt to break out of inactivity and marginality. It occurs to him that 'only by living absurdly could one ever break this infinite absurdity' (123:23). This paradox is inserted within a more generalized philosophical discussion within the novel and demands some clarification.

The absurd. Two emphases, two conflicting paths

The first emphasis is couched in Wittgensteinian terms, what Oliveira calls an 'anthropological circumscription' (510:99). It stems from a basic perception: 'The mistake lies precisely in the fact that it is impossible to say that it is a mistake' (516:100). Wittgenstein makes the point that language and logic (Oliveira extrapolates to the whole cultural system) can represent things, make propositions, but can say nothing about how they do so, about the logic or being of language itself:

Propositions can represent the whole of reality, but they cannot represent what they must have in common with reality in order to be able to represent it – logical form.
[. . .] What finds its reflection in language, language cannot represent. What expresses *itself* in language, *we* cannot express by means of language.[28]

There is thus no point within the world whence one could make a statement on logic and language: 'In order to be able to represent logical form, we should have to be able to station ourselves with propositions somewhere outside logic, that is to say outside the world.'[29] As Morelli puts it, 'one cannot denounce anything unless one does so within the system to which what one is denouncing belongs' (509:99).

But within Cortázar's literature, as we have seen, the 'fantastic' in certain situations can produce an *extrañamiento* (surprise, feeling of strangeness) which shows up the absurd, carries the subject outside the structures of the real (*descentrar*):

I will call it paravisions / that is to say (the trouble is just that, saying it) / an instantaneous aptitude for going out of myself, for suddenly grasping myself from outside.   (461:84)
An instantaneous slip to one side shows him for a second, without unfortunately giving him time to *know what*, shows him his partitioned being.   (463:84)

But these experiences are only momentary, and can only serve Oliveira as a stimulus to find a more solid position. The way he goes about this is perhaps partially suggested by the ideas of Klages, who believed that humanity at some stage took a wrong turning (193:28, 507:99), which leads to the idea that one could return to that point and start again. Oliveira thus believes that 'a man should be capable of isolating himself from the species within the species itself' (560:125),

and hence the 'notion of being a dog among men' (560). This he
attempts by painstakingly destroying all human traits in himself,
especially by a denial of such cardinal human values as *la piedad*,
pity. (Morelli follows a parallel course in language.) He aims at
reaching a sort of zero point of humanity, 'a sort of meeting *ab ovo*, a
maximum shrinking back to that point where the last spark of
(false) humanity is about to die' (558–9:124). He talks of this destruction and the consequent ill-treatment of people, especially la Maga,
in terms of digging a hole: 'I renounce nothing, but simply do
everything I can for things to renounce me. Didn't you know that to
dig a hole, you've got to get the earth out and throw it well away?'
(216:31) The emphasis on pity, rather than on any other value, is
most probably of Nietzschean origin: 'Nothing in our unhealthy
modernity is more unhealthy than Christian pity.'[30]

The second view of the absurd is more optimistic. As Oliveira puts
it, 'It is not things that are absurd, what is absurd is the way things
are there and we feel they are absurd' (194:28). It is man's link with
things, his intelligence, that makes them seem absurd. This link is
seen in two lights. In a very clever passage where love and philosophy
are firmly united, the link is seen as an inescapable coercion: 'Not
explanation: pure verb, to-love, to-love. "And afterwards always the
copula", mused Oliveira, grammatically. If la Maga could only
know how obedience to desire suddenly exasperated him' (51:9).
Elsewhere intelligence, Kantian categories, are seen as a reflex
defence that Oliveira (as an 'Argentinian') uses to ward off the
fantastic, 'invasion', *lo otro*: 'a grotesque collage which one had to
regulate with vodka and Kantian categories, those tranquillizers
against any excessively abrupt coagulation of reality' (72:14). In
either case, these categories are seen to be at the source of the
problem: 'If we continue to rely on Kantian categories [...] we will
never get out of this mess' (507–8:99).

What Oliveira is doing then, when he says that by living absurdly
he can abolish the absurd, is to deny the categories that decree life
absurd.[31] This leads to the fusion or at least the reversal of the
antithetical pair so dear to Ortega, *surface–depth*: 'We could be *fundamentally* as we are on the surface' (120:22). This is exactly the
reversal that Nietzsche effects on his arch-scapegoat Kant, by
taking his categories, antithetical values, not as the base to reality,
but as 'foreground valuations', 'provisional perspectives',[32] whereas
life itself with all its contradictions becomes the prime reality. Such

irrationalist vitalism would, claims Nietzsche, transcend dualism, good and evil:

The falseness of a judgement is to us not necessarily an objection to a judgement. [...] The question is to what extent it is life-advancing [...]. To recognize untruth as a condition of life: that, to be sure, means to resist customary value-sentiments in a dangerous fashion; and a philosophy which ventures to do so places itself, by that act alone, beyond good and evil.[33]

This new irrational acceptance in Oliveira of the purely human leads to his desperate attempt to communicate with the grotesque Berthe Trépat. It returns with greater urgency after the death of Rocamadour, when Oliveira suddenly thinks of the line from Valéry's 'Le cimetière marin', 'il faut tenter de vivre' (189:28). It only finally comes into its own, however, at the conclusion of the second part, in Oliveira's reconciliation with Traveler and Talita: 'but what beauty in the mistake and the five thousand years of false and precarious territory' (402:56).

The conflict

Oliveira's two ways of seeing the absurd thus present him with two conflicting modes of behaviour. A corollary of the first view is that civilization is moribund and must be destroyed before it can be reborn: 'Morelli wants to save something that is dying, but in order to save it, it has previously to be killed or at least given such a blood transfusion that it would be like a resurrection' (506:99). Oliveira must deny and destroy his own humanity. The second suggests an urgent need for direct human contact, an acceptance which would itself break the absurd. It is this contradiction in Oliveira that leads to the painful and paralysing tension which characterizes the first part of the novel.

Berthe Trépat, a premature exploration of the second path

Oliveira's sitting through Berthe Trépat's absurd concert and accompanying her home through the wet and cold Paris streets, the pity he allows himself to feel for her, is an attempt to destroy the absurd by conniving with it, becoming it. The presence of Onetti in the writing of this episode is very strong. Rodríguez Monegal suggests that it is inspired by 'Un sueño realizado'.[34] It also has much in common with the sense of inside and outside in *El astillero*. Oliveira longs to be admitted to the pianist-composer's house to escape from the cold and rain[35] of his inhuman intellectual exile, 'to go in there and advance and be saved from the other (*lo otro*), from the rain in his face and the water in his shoes' (144:23). Larsen in *El astillero* has a similar choice between the rain, lucidity, sanity, and the collective madness[36] of his absurd job in the decrepit ship-repair yard: 'Larsen felt the horror of lucidity. Beyond the farce he had accepted literally as a job, there was only winter, old age, nowhere to go.'[37]

There is a point when Oliveira seems to have reached his goal, feels 'inconceivably happy' (143:23) and senses that he can 'take a step forward, a true step' (144), but everything falls to the ground when Berthe Trépat interprets his offer of finding her a hotel room as an indecent proposition and slaps his face. The conventionality of his pity backfires on him, the rain mingles with his tears and puts his cigarette out.

One must ask why this attempt fails. To put the onus completely on the reaction of Berthe Trépat ('The outstretched hand had to be answered by another hand from outside' (121:22)) would be altogether too aleatory. In the second part there is a parallel episode, Oliveira's approaching Talita and Traveler in a similar way, almost a repetition (forming a *figura*), where the attempt is far more successful. The initial decision to 'live absurdly in order to abolish the absurd' (120:22) is repeated in only slightly different terms: 'The only possible way of escape from the territory was to immerse himself in it to the hilt' (402:56). Oliveira himself is reminded of the Berthe Trépat experience and wonders whether it could in fact have worked: 'He knew that as soon as he hinted at that (once again, that) he would glimpse the picture of a man walking arm in arm with an old woman along rainy, bitterly cold streets. "I wonder", he mused. "I wonder whether I stopped at the edge, and there might have been a passage" ' (402–3).

The vital difference between the first attempt and its repetition is that prior to his communion with Traveler and Talita, Oliveira has completed the process of *despojamiento*, of destruction and self-destruction which culminates in the ultimate sacrifice of la Maga, who is resurrected and recovered, through Talita, as a redemptive force. One must thus come to the conclusion that his approaching Berthe Trépat was, though vitally urgent, premature.

The death of Rocamadour

After leaving Berthe Trépat, Oliveira returns to his room and discovers that la Maga's baby son Rocamadour has died without her noticing. This chapter, mainly composed of a long conversation on the absurd, in the presence of the child's corpse and the inadvertent mother, is one of Cortázar's most impressive.

The death can be seen as a consequence of the failure of the affirmation of life, of human values and contact with Berthe Trépat. We have already seen how the illness of Jorge in *Los premios* is due to the acceptance by the passengers of the anti-vital situation (on board). At least the first three novels of Cortázar are rather like time-bombs in that once the ontological contradictions and falsity of the characters' lives becomes clear, if the latter fail to remedy the situation quickly, a child or youth's life is at risk. Children, as we saw in relation to *Los premios*, are an expression of the origins, of innocence and intuition. The insistence on a long process of purifying destruction prior to a rebirth of human values in *Rayuela* causes a postponement[38] of human concern, a negation of it which has tragic consequences, and almost invalidates the process *a priori*.

It is the strict adherence to formal, adult rules of behaviour and relationships that causes the death of Pablo in 'La señorita Cora'; the orderly and repressive routine of Hélène that of the 'dead lad' in *62*. It is only in *Libro de Manuel* that the time factor is relaxed. Andrés is, like Oliveira, faced with two necessary paths of action (to break taboo with Francine, to join the revolutionary group in Verrières), neither of which can be successful without the other; but (to put it simplistically for our purposes here) the relation between the two is more dialectic, the failure of the first ceases to be a failure on the accomplishment of the second, and has no ill effects (though concern is shown) on baby Manuel, to whom Lonstein and Andrés are acting as baby-sitters.

Onetti, more than any other, has appreciated the importance of children to Cortázar, as is eloquently shown in María Esther Gillio's account of his reaction to 'El perseguidor':

Dolly [Onetti's wife] took me to the bathroom, where she showed me a cabinet with the mirror torn off. On the wood which had supported it, it said in red pencil: 'Charlie, brother. The problem is Bee.' [...] He broke that mirror with his fist, early one morning, after reading the story.[39]

Though responsibility in Cortázar is always very hard to define, and never straightforward, Oliveira does feel responsible for Rocamadour's death: 'We are guilty of his death. Guilty, that is to say the accomplices of a state of affairs...' (185:28). Johnny's relation to the death of his daughter is very similar. When living with Bee and his wife Lan, he felt that they were a trap, the object of which was to make him conform, yet when he abandons them, and Bee dies, he realizes that the deepest meaning of his musical pursuit was to express the life in her: 'It's the difference between Bee having died and being alive. What I play is the dead Bee, you know, whilst what I want, what I want...' (*AS* 174). There is a tragic paradox in that he feels that he must distance himself from what he really wants to express, but that in doing so, the latter dies, is killed: ' "I think I've been wanting to swim without water", murmured Johnny. "I think I've wanted to have Lan's red dress but without Lan. And Bee is dead, Bruno" ' (*AS* 176). Likewise Oliveira, in destroying what he considers the false, moribund aspects of his humanity, has destroyed its very base. To use a somewhat flippant expression, he has thrown out the baby with the bathwater.

It is perhaps to this tragic paradox that Oliveira refers when he quotes Cernuda's 'Of what use was the summer to you, oh nightingale in the snow?' (204:28), which continues, in the original, 'Of what use was the summer to us,/oh nightingale in the snow,/if only so brief a world/surrounds the dreamer in vain?'[40] When Oliveira had been confronted by Wong with photographs of a man tortured to death, he muses that man was created for something better, yet despairs at the inadequacy of the arms available to man to change his reality: 'I stubbornly hold on to the weird idea that man was created for something else. And so, of course... What feeble tools to find a way out of this hole' (73:15). The question thus seems to ask whether the reality of his attempt, the price he has paid, is justifiable. The same lines are repeated in the second part of the novel in the context of the life of Buenos Aires (280:41).

The tragedy of the death is made all the more poignant by the theorizing of the Club over the body before the mother realizes her child is dead. The death itself is totally irreducible. There is no way of extrapolating from it. This effect has been carefully prepared: Oliveira had earlier come to the conclusion when faced with death and suffering that 'there are no general ideas' (78:15), after reflecting on his indignation at his mother's grief at the death of a neighbour and indifference at thousands of deaths in natural disasters and in wars. To reach that position, he muses, one has to have read all Plato, the Church Fathers and 'every single last classic', at which point one falls into 'such a state of cretinism that one is capable of grabbing one's poor illiterate mother by the point of her shawl and getting annoyed because [...]' (74:15). A large number of views on death are accumulated in the novel before this episode: Wong's view of torture as an art, reports on capital punishment in the 'dispensable chapters' 114 and 117, a Buddhist view of death (188:28). This is characteristic of the general working of the novel. Morelli's work is described as 'the deep-biting corrosion of a world denounced as false, an attack based on accumulation and not destruction' (604: 141). The effect of this accumulation is not an 'addition' but an 'implacable subtraction' (595:137), and one is left with the stark reality of death. Hence, statistics do not help Oliveira to come to terms with what has happened, they 'did not stop his cigarette tasting greasy' (181:28). 'The whole of communications theory' is, in the process, 'annihilated' (183:28).

The death thus takes on the status of an absolute scandal reminiscent of a similar death in Camus's *La peste*. But Oliveira is not permitted the outlet of action as is Rieux in the French novel. The whole structure of thought and life must be modified before anything can be done. Action would be futile and irrelevant, or else in bad faith as suggested in Ronald's reaction: ' "How absurd this all is", he thought. The idea of everything being absurd made him feel uneasy, but he did not realize why. He turned to helping Babs, making himself, useful, soaking compresses' (205:28).

All these considerations are set against a real distress on Oliveira's part, a desire to react 'normally', and a constant reminder of the urgency of some solution in the repetition of Valéry's 'il faut tenter de vivre', forming a counterpoint to the knocking of the madman upstairs. His failure with Berthe Trépat has shown him that he has not freed human relationships of conventionality and sclerosis, which leads him to repress his impulsive feeling of pity for la Maga: ' "I could conform to the pattern", thought Horacio. "Scream, turn on the light, kick up the normal and obligatory rumpus. But what's the point? [...] If I scream it's Berthe Trépat again, a repetition of the stupid attempt, pity" ' (176:28). While the others mill round to console la Maga, Oliveira turns his back on them to leave, apparently unperturbed, though, as Etienne asks: 'I'd like to know why your mouth is twitching so much' (204:28).

After the death of Rocamadour, the path of destruction is intensified by Oliveira. He leaves his friends in the Club de la Serpiente, abandons la Maga and completes the process of washing himself of civilization, his 'de-education of the senses' (246:36), in his night 'up to the neck in shit' with the *clocharde* Emmanuèle and, presumably, during the time subsequently spent in prison. Meanwhile, la Maga disappears, leaves Paris or commits suicide as she had threatened. There are reasons to believe that this 'death' can be taken as her 'murder' by Oliveira.

THE DEATH OF LA MAGA

Literary derivations

La Maga has many of the characteristics of the archetypal literary heroine. It is hardly surprising, then, that other figures are suggested by her. Perhaps the most obvious is Breton's *Nadja*, the surrealist heroine *par excellence* (the chance meetings in the streets of Paris, her mystery and intuition, her idealization of her lover). Oliveira's attitude towards la Maga is paralleled by the incapacity of Breton to live up to the ideals of his lover when, for example, Nadja wants to crash the car he is driving at speed by kissing him.[41] This incapacity seems to have been a common surrealist theme. It is explored by Crevel, and becomes very important in *Rayuela*:

[Breton:] Je n'ai peut-être pas été à la hauteur de ce qu'elle me proposait.[42]
[Cortázar:] She chose me like a burning bush, and all I turn out to be is a jug of cold water down her neck. (226:33)
[Crevel:] Approfondis et avoue que tu étais bien doué pour la rhétorique. Tes négligences, ton désordre, ils étaient encore appliqués, organisés.[43]
[Cortázar:] No, we haven't lived like that, she would have liked to but once again I established the false order which disguises chaos, pretended to throw myself into a deep life, when I was only touching its waters with the tips of my toes. (116:21)
[Crevel:] Homme mort, ferais-tu pousser une plante entre les lattes de ce parquet? – Mais non, cabotin. Tu vas encore temporiser.[44]
[Cortázar:] Hypocrite, perfect hypocrite bastard. (177:28)

Another very similar figure is Solveig Amundsen in Leopoldo Marechal's *Adán Buenosayres*. The hero of the novel, Adán, whom

Cortázar describes as 'the exile from perfection, unity, what they call heaven',[45] is also a similar figure to Oliveira. Solveig inspires Adán's search for his lost unity, but this ideal side of her becomes dissociated in his mind from the real woman, whom he resolves to kill that the purified idea of her should better direct his search.[46] Oliveira too, like Adán and Breton, is infuriated by the real Maga, by her ignorance and disorder, and conceives the idea of destroying her: 'Killing the object of one's love, that old suspicion of man, was the price to be paid for not interrupting one's ascent of the ladder' (339:48).

This same idea of destroying or leaving the loved one, and searching for her outside her real presence is also at the centre of another work: Pedro Salinas's *La voz a ti debida*. The poet searches for his lover 'behind her';[47] has to go far away to search for her.[48] Like la Maga ('Babylonia, root of time, previous thing, terror and delight of the beginnings' (486:93)), Salinas's lover offers the poet a 'return / to the first stirring, / without light, before the world, / total, without form, chaos'.[49]

There is perhaps a certain Proustian element in the recovery of la Maga by Oliveira on kissing Talita. The syncretism of the two women unites Paris and Buenos Aires, 'This Side' and 'That Side', for Oliveira as does Mlle de Saint Loup the *côtés* of Guermantes and 'chez Swann' in *Le temps retrouvé*.

Such speculations, however, only add nuances to any reading of the text, and la Maga's death can be considered more fruitfully in the light of patterns established in Cortázar's own works.

The archetype of Los reyes and its development

Carl Jung makes some very illuminating remarks on monsters in dreams. Phylogenetically, he argues, man is both human and reptile and can never reach a complete unity of body and soul without a recognition of this fact. Any life-style of purely intellectual attraction, or which goes against human nature, will wake the reptile, the monster in us, in protest.[50] Cortázar's monsters likewise appear in a neurotic society to protest at its inauthenticity, as does the illness of children.

The archetypal appearance of the monster is to be found in Cortázar's treatment of the Minotaur myth in his early play *Los reyes*. It is the origin of much later exploration of the theme. Despite its rather pompous language, *Los reyes* is a splendid example of

Cortázar's inversion of traditionally immutable patterns. The Minotaur itself is the positive figure in the play, Ariadne gives Theseus the thread so that the Minotaur will kill him and escape. Theseus is mediocre and rather stupid, acting out of fear and simply on orders, without understanding his actions: 'I am a hero. I think it is sufficient' (*LR* 35). Born from a beautifully described and joyful relation between Pasiphae and a bull, a joy inherited by Ariadne, the Minotaur is a symbol of freedom and play: 'master of the games', and 'leader of the ritual' (*LR* 73).

Above all, the Minotaur is seen as a threat to the power and authority of the king, Minos. The meaning of *rey*, *king* as order, super-ego, power, is carried over to later works. Alina Reyes in 'Lejana' 'is the queen and...'. In 'Jack the Ripper Blues', Jack is a sort of double of the 'barbarous' Juan Manuel de Rosas, born to kill Queen Victoria, and 'when I say Jack, when I say queen, perhaps you now understand me' (*V* II 103). The image is also present in the chess symbolism of *Rayuela* and *Los premios*. The labyrinth and the Minotaur are thus ultimately the unconscious of Minos: 'Oh dreams over which I am no longer lord!' (*LR* 11); 'To reign over myself, oh that last task of a king, oh impossibility!' (*LR* 12) The king paradoxically comes to see himself as the prisoner of the Minotaur: 'I am your prisoner, you I can tell. [...] Knossos became for me this hard cell' (*LR* 36).

Monsters, which are ultimately only made monsters through 'the fear of what is different, not immediate and possible and permitted' (*LR* 50), can only really be made inoffensive, killed, de-monsterized, by accepting them, as the Minotaur explains to Theseus: '[M:] Look, there is only one way to kill monsters: accept them. [T:] Yes, and for them to gore your throne. [M:] They would not have horns' (*LR* 64–5). But this is not possible and when the Minotaur mistakenly believes that Ariadne is in league with Theseus, he realizes that the only course of action left open to him is to die. It makes no difference how he dies, whether he allows himself to be killed or is defeated by Theseus. Once dead, he will lose his monstrousness and become far more powerful, will enter his kingdom and heaven, the unconscious of man (of Ariadne and her stock) as a vital and guiding force:

I will reach Ariadne before you. [...] I will go down to inhabit the dreams of her nights, of her sons, the inevitable time of her stock. From there I will gore your throne, the insecure sceptre of your race [...] (*LR* 66).

In that way I intend to gain access to the dreams of man, their secret heaven and remote stars, those stars which are invoked when dawn and destiny are at stake (*LR* 75).

The Minotaur expresses himself in the classical oxymoron of the mystics: 'Don't you understand that I'm asking you to kill me, that I'm asking you for life?' (*LR* 65) The importance of this will be seen in our subsequent discussion.

The recovery of the monsters

In *Los reyes*, then, we have the promise that after their death, the monsters become a mythical force in the subconscious of man to be invoked when 'dawn and destiny are at stake'. It will perhaps be useful at this point briefly to sketch out a general theory of the deep structure of the novels which will link three capital aspects of them: the monsters, the *figuras*, and the descent to Hades. Though it may not be totally comprehensible in the context of *Rayuela*, where all its connotations are not explicitly realized, it should become clearer and will be expanded in our discussion of the far more self-conscious and formal *62*.

The monster survives and is reproposed to man in the *figuras*. The *figura* is the story of the monster's denunciation by an established moral code and its destruction. To decree something a monster is to taboo and repress it, the *figura* is thus a repetition of this repression. It is up to the individual to reverse the pattern of the *figura*, 'demonsterize' the monster and release the force it represents. This inversion demands some form of transgression, which usually corresponds to that for which the monster was originally decreed a monster. Its recovery, its being brought back to life after its destruction, involves, as was glimpsed in relation to *Los premios*, the myth of the descent to Hades (by Orpheus, to recover Eurydice). This structure is, significantly, inseparable from the transgression referred to above. It additionally permits the transgression to be seen as an initiation, purification or trial before the descent can be effected, the monster faced.[51]

The conjunction of transgression and descent can be clearly seen in all the novels: Felipe is raped in a cabin in the depths of the *Malcolm* and Jorge recovers; Oliveira kisses his friend's wife in the morgue of the lunatic asylum and la Maga is recovered; Hélène rapes Celia, which is symbolically seen as going down to the hospital

morgue to transfuse her blood into the veins of the 'dead lad';
Andrés in *Libro de Manuel* rapes Francine by a graveyard, which is
also seen as a descent to a cellar, presumably to the morgue where
Lonstein symbolically brings back to life the corpses by washing and
loving them.

The link between the Minotaur and the Orpheus myths, between
monsters and the descent to Hades, is first made in 'Las puertas del
cielo'. Dr Hardoy and Mauro descend to the heaven–hell of the
milonga ('hell and its circles, a Japanese park hell at two-fifty the
ticket' (*B* 127–8)), where the dead Celina, once a whore and thus a
monster (Hardoy 'used to go to that *milonga* because of the monsters'
(*B* 129), and remembers Celina as 'closer to the monsters' (*B* 131))
is seen alive again. She offers the couple a salvation, 'the gates of
heaven' (*B* 138), that they are incapable of taking from her.

The descent to Hades by Orpheus is, of course, only taken as an
example of the archetypal idea of the descent. Many other descents
and other religious and anthropological archetypes are suggested
throughout the works. The descent of Gilgamesh is suggested in
Libro de Manuel (*M* 218), that of Dante in 'Las puertas del cielo'
(*B* 128), that of Goethe's Faust in *Los premios*.[52] Oliveira's turning
the world upside-down with Emmanuèle ('looking at the world
through the eye in your arse') suggests the recreation of the original
chaos in primitive societies at the end of a cycle before a new one
can be born. His idea of climbing the circus tent pole in Buenos
Aires suggests the ascent of the Siberian shaman up the pole or birch
tree with nine notches (the nine heavens – the squares of the hopscotch) in order to enter, on behalf of his people, the sacred time,
the spirit world above.[53] This ascent on the part of Oliveira is seen
as being symmetrical to his descent to the morgue, the 'Eleusinian
pit' (367:54), whence Kore returned to her mother Demeter to
bring spring and renovation.

La Maga as a monster: four aspects of her 'death'

As was hinted in our discussion of *Los premios*, characters are sometimes explicitly referred to as monsters: Celina, for example, and the
procuress of 'La babas del diablo' (*AS* 89). Others, however, such as
whores, rapists, vampires, though far less obviously so than the
Minotaur, fulfil the same roles, have the same force behind them, and
in general can be recognized by the way in which they disrupt the

structures of order and reason. La Maga falls very much into this category, especially in the way her life denounces the 'false perfection of others' (369:54). Her 'death' is posed in terms of the possibility of a phoenix-type resurrection after her 'murder' by Oliveira: 'the resurrection of the phoenix after he had strangled her' (45:5).

Oliveira's position as regards her death is contradictory and complex in the extreme. The deaths of monsters can be placed in two main categories. These are reflected in the attitudes of Oliveira, but are further complicated by another two positions in the latter.

(a) The first attitude corresponds to that of Theseus, who simply wishes to silence the disturbing message of the Minotaur: 'At least die in silence!' (*LR* 68) Just as in 'El perseguidor' Bruno wishes Johnny dead (*AS* 169), some characters go even further in first declaring another character a 'monster' in order then to 'kill' it. The clearest example of this is in 'Los pasos en las huellas', where the writer Claudio Romero forces his lover to become a whore and thus is justified in abandoning her, after which she eventually disappears and dies. Something similar happens in *62* where Marrast declares Nicole a whore, whereupon she is carried off by Frau Marta, probably to become a vampire.

(b) The second corresponds to the death-wish, to the suicide of the Minotaur himself. 'Las puertas del cielo' is a good model of how this idea works in the stories. Though the monster, Celina, dies of illness, it is suggested that she had chosen to die: 'a little as if she herself had chosen the moment when it should all end' (*B* 117). She decides to die not because she has been made into a monster but, more insidiously, because she has been assimilated, 'tamed', by the *petit-bourgeois* order of her husband Mauro. She had paid back his kindness 'with a few years of cooking and *mate* with sugar in the patio. She had given up her *milonga* heaven, her warm vocation of anisette and *criollo* waltzes' (*B* 133). On dying, she re-enters this heaven. Exactly how she dies, however, is, in a sense, irrelevant. It is the pattern that counts, as in *Los reyes*.

(c) Oliveira adds a third position to the two described above: the consciousness on the part of the killer of his role in the ritual.

(d) At times, however, he shows great incomprehension of the process he is involved in, and even tries to block it by tergiversation and cynicism.

All these attitudes coexist in Oliveira. Though in *Rayuela* they do not affect the actual development of the textual action nearly so

much as in *62*, they are to a large extent responsible for the quality
and tension of the text, and Cortázar–Morelli's concept of the
'reader-accomplice' suggests that such tensions should not be
ironed out for the sake of a linear, mechanistic analysis:

> Make an accomplice of the reader, a fellow traveller. Make him simul-
> taneous, since this sort of reading would abolish the time of the reader
> and transfer him to that of the author. In this way the reader could
> become a co-participant and co-sufferer of the experience undergone by
> the novelist, *at the same instant* and in the same form.[54]   (453:79)

1. It will be accepted here for the purposes of this discussion that
for Oliveira to abandon la Maga is symbolically to kill her, that is,
to deprive his love for her of its corporeal object. Just as Theseus
wishes to silence the Minotaur, Gregovorius explains that la Maga
has destroyed Oliveira's faith in the intellect and that if he leaves her,
it is because he will never forgive her for so disrupting his world:
'[Oliveira] is looking for the black light, the key, and is beginning to
realize that things like that are not to be found in libraries. It was
really you who taught him that, and if he is going to leave, it's
because he will never forgive you' (161:26). His other motives for
leaving her would thus be excuses and in bad faith. This would be
the case with his exasperation at her ignorance ('of the sort which
ruined any pleasure' (228:34)) and at her readiness to recount the
least decent passages of her life (like Nadja), qualities which have
been of great importance in the novel. But perhaps the most important pointer to his bad faith is the appearance of and insistence on his
jealousy at her imagined unfaithfulness with Gregovorius: ' "I
always suspected you would end up going to bed with Ossip", said
Oliveira' (97:19). This jealousy is equivalent to declaring la Maga
a whore, and thus a monster. The importance of jealousy in the
novels of Cortázar should not be underestimated: Traveler's
jealousy precipitates the dénouement of the second part; Marrast's
jealousy of Nicole, and Andrés's of Ludmilla, are determining factors
in *62* and *Libro de Manuel*.

2. La Maga, at one point, wishes to be killed by Oliveira, on a
mythical plane, and be reborn: 'La Maga really expected Horacio
to kill her and her death to be that of the phoenix' (45:5). Her
suicidal threats on a more superficial plane ('and to think that an
hour ago it occurred to me that the best thing was to go and throw
myself into the river' (109:20)), which may be carried out, must be
read with these connotations. Like Celina, la Maga has been

partially assimilated by a more orderly world. Whereas she is by
nature intuitive and natural, she has come to seek, against that
nature, her realization in culture: 'La Maga wanted to learn, she
wanted to get e-du-ca-ted' (45). The heaven she aspires to, like
Celina's '*milonga* heaven' is 'the heaven of hotel rooms', where, in
love, she can commune with Oliveira, whereas she cannot on a
cultural level. Her death and resurrection would thus, logically, undo
this assimilation.

3. On the same occasion, Oliveira talks of killing la Maga
explicitly in terms of the Minotaur myth, of liberating the mythical
forces in her:

Oliveira felt that la Maga expected him to kill her, something in her
which was not her conscious ego, an obscure form demanding annihilation, the slow knife thrust face upwards which breaks the stars and
returns space to questions and terror. Only that once, outside himself
(*excentrado*) like a mythical *matador* for whom to kill is to return the bull
to the sea and the sea to the sky, he abused la Maga in a long night
about which they spoke little later, he made her Pasiphae, doubled her
and used her like an adolescent. (44:5)

This line of action is paralleled by a far less mythological desire
to kill la Maga, which derives towards the general theme of destruction and subtraction, of which this ritual murder is, ultimately, an
aspect. Love is seen as falsifying its function when realized:

Love was perhaps the highest achievement, a giver of being; but only by
spoiling it could one avoid its boomerang effect, by letting it fall into
oblivion and sustain itself, alone again, on that new rung of open, porous
reality. Killing the object of one's love, that old suspicion of man, was the
price to pay for not interrupting one's ascent of the ladder. (339:48)

4. Almost simultaneously, there is an opposite movement in
Oliveira, an attempt to block the process described. This is presumably due to a certain extent to the idea of mistrust discussed earlier,
and his fear of being limited by the relationship. Oliveira describes
himself as being 'fearful of perfect moments' (43:5), but he also
fears that the games might 'seek to rise to the level of sacrifice'
(44) – surely the sacrifice he refers to a few lines before – and insists
on bringing the experience back onto a banal level: 'His first words
on this side had to lash her like whips, and her return to the side of
the bed, the image of her increasing consternation [...] satisfied
Oliveira particularly' (44). There is much in this attitude of Oliveira
confronted with a 'mythical and terrible (*atroz*)' (43) Maga of that

of Doctor Hardoy in 'Las puertas del cielo', who refuses to recognize and accept with Mauro the image of Celina they see in the *milonga* after her death, and whom he describes in the following way: 'Happiness transformed her terribly (*atroz*), I would not have been able to bear Celina the way I saw her at that moment in that tango, [...] her enraptured, stupid face in the paradise she had finally reached' (*B* 137). The behaviour of Hardoy, who cannot face up to what he has sought, and who tries to convince Mauro that they have not seen anything, is identical to that of Oliveira: 'My notorious cynicism piled pose upon pose at full steam. I kept calm, nonchalantly smoking a Virginia cigarette' (*B* 138). It is also the same fear which prevents the hero of 'El otro cielo' from approaching Lautréamont.

Oliveira also misrepresents what is happening in what would seem total bad faith. As elsewhere, for example in the final lines of 'El perseguidor', Cortázar gives no explicit indication as to the sincerity of his character, which produces very dense reading. His night with la Maga is at one point seen as a 'challenge to the Logos' (44), as a violent rejection of intellectualism, yet he almost immediately suggests that la Maga's resurrection would mean her full participation in the intellectual group of friends, the Club de la Serpiente, to which they belong: 'Her death was to be that of the phoenix, her admission into the council of philosophers, to the conversations of the Club de la Serpiente' (45). It might be argued here (the narrative point of view hovers between those of the author, la Maga and Oliveira) that such is the aspiration of la Maga, but this could not be reconciled with a subsequent definition of her desire, that 'Horacio should kill her in love, which was where she could succeed in meeting him. Facing each other in their hotel room heaven they were equal and naked and it was there that the resurrection of the phoenix could be consummated' (45).

An impersonal, mythical force

Despite these divergent motivations, however, the pattern is consummated and la Maga returns to life in Buenos Aires. They may, nevertheless, determine the one note of ambiguity in her return: Oliveira and Talita are described as 'paying or collecting something for somebody else' (373:54), either recovering something or paying for a fault. It is the same difference as exists in the short stories between a character being 'haunted' by another or being possessed by a liberating force, between unfreedom or predetermination, and mythically guided action. The dualism, however, loses its importance when confronted with the force of the new causality.

The very fact that Oliveira's motivations become less important points to the existence of an impersonal force. Indeed, as Oliveira gradually and painfully strips himself of his ego and its allies civilization and culture, a process which culminates in his night with the *clocharde*, his ideals and desires become increasingly impersonal and almost independent of him. When he conceives his 'kibbutz of desire', this 'desire' replaces the arms of the Western mind: it is a kibbutz 'of desire, not of the soul, not of the spirit' (240:36). He goes on to define his kibbutz further: 'It was his desire just as he was his desire and the world or the representation of the world were desire, were his desire or [the] desire, it did not matter too much at that stage' (241:36). *His* desire becomes *the* desire (as *el otro* had become *lo otro*). The Schopenhauerian vocabulary, 'the world or the representation of the world', reminiscent of *The World as Will and Representation*, suggests that 'desire' has much in common with 'Will' as defined in that work, that is, it is a common, cosmic force. At this point (by the Seine, just before encountering Emmanuèle), 'desire' is seen as 'a vague definition of incomprehensible forces' (240), but it is later given greater content: 'A love which could forgo its object, which found its food in nothingness, perhaps joined with other forces, articulated them and fused them into an impulse which one day would destroy that visceral contentedness which comes from a body blown up with beer and chips' (338:48). 'Desire' is related to love without an object, with an object in abeyance or an object like la Maga which has been destroyed to purify and universalize it. It is either equivalent to, or gives access to and directs the 'other forces', which will break down the structures of the self-satisfied culture Oliveira has been fighting.

Oliveira's general destruction of civilization in himself, Morelli and Cortázar's parallel destruction of language and traditional literary structures,[55] and Oliveira's 'ritual murder' of la Maga should, by now, be coming into focus together. In this destruction, Oliveira follows the pattern of primitive ritual, a repetition of archetypal acts, as described by Mircea Eliade, and it is only after destroying himself as ego that he can find himself in what he has in common with humanity: 'En d'autres mots, il ne se reconnaît comme *réel*, c'est à dire comme "véritablement lui-même", que dans la mesure où il cesse précisément de l'être.'[56]

In a manner splendidly characteristic of Cortázar's eclecticism, such mythical patterns are combined with theories on the chemical functioning of the brain. Thus, chemical reactions among a group of people, evocative of the notion of manna, could take place independently of their consciousnesses, creating a 'drama which is *impersonal* in so far as the conscious minds and the passions of the characters are committed only *a posteriori*' (416:62). This process constitutes a force superior to the individual and separate from him, and is basically the same force as described above in very different terms. It is moving towards a goal which would change the whole nature of man, and is described as 'inhabiting, foreign forces, advancing in search of their citizen's rights; a search which is superior to us as individuals and which uses us for its ends, an obscure need to escape from the state of homo sapiens towards... what homo?' (417:62). All the action of the second part of *Rayuela* is determined by this type of psychology, as Oliveira suspects: 'It occurs to me that our relationship is almost chemical, a phenomenon outside ourselves' (328:46). The configurations of characters created, and unconsciously motivated by this force, closely related to that of the monsters, form the *figura*. Such a reduction of behaviour to a material and transindividual process seriously questions the dualism of body and soul, as Morelli suggests: 'The old dualism had cracked before evidence of a general reduction of matter and spirit to notions of energy' (558).[57]

The possibility of action

As we have seen, historical and political action has been excluded from *Rayuela*, and, indeed, there is little action of any sort in the novel. Yet the kind of dramatic action expected from the wide discussion of the problem in the novel is replaced by totally ludicrous acts – entering a concert and escorting an old woman home, straightening out bent nails, and barricading a room with lengths of coloured string. Such acts, however, must be taken seriously.

There have been many different ways throughout the novel of thinking about the possibility of action, but it is only as the process described above, that is, a force outside man's everyday structures, begins to make itself felt, that the possibility becomes real. The type of action that Oliveira 'leaves' in Buenos Aires is that defined by the categorical imperative: to take as a natural law one's own personal motives derived from a historical circumstance. To this, Oliveira objects that 'reflection must precede action' (34:3). A stronger form of this demand evolves as Oliveira loses faith in thought. He demands a certainty *previous* to any action, outside the structures of history, personality and ethics: 'Won't you realize that action, like inaction, must be deserved? How can one act without a previous central attitude, a sort of agreement on what we believe right and true?' (198:28) There follows a type of vitalist irrationalism, the idea of acting in the name of some vaguely intuited certainty: 'We are left with the amiable possibility of living and working *as if*, choosing working hypotheses, attacking, like Morelli, what seems to us most false in the name of some obscure sensation of certainty' (512:99).

Oliveira's final attitude, however, is more complex, but rather interesting. One day in Buenos Aires, he sets about straightening bent nails and feels that he will only know what he needs them for, once he has finished the action: 'I have the impression that as soon as I have nice straight nails I will know what I need them for' (278:41). Thus, action comes first and its purpose afterwards: 'First the nails and then the purpose of the nails' (278). This constitutes a complete reversal of his earlier demand for a 'previous central attitude'. His hope is more or less justified when Traveler suggests they build a plank bridge between the windows of their rooms. The nails would then represent the possibility of bridging the dualism of their two positions: '[The bridge] would come in handy to start using the nails, you on your side, me on mine' (282:41).

This idea on action becomes the central one in the second part, and is of prime importance in later novels, especially *Libro de Manuel*, where Andrés can only find out what the Cuban's orders are after having carried them out. A later chapter confirms the meaning of this reversal. Before reaching Buenos Aires, Oliveira stops off at Montevideo. He believes that he has stopped there to find la Maga, if she is still alive, and definitively terminate their relationship: 'that tendency of man's to finish what he does cleanly, without leaving any loose threads' (337:48). Anyone with a knowledge of Cortázar's vocabulary knows that threads are what he most appreciates: 'At the end there was always a thread stretching beyond, protruding from the volume' (602:141). He soon realizes that he had not gone there for that reason, but to renew his contact with la

Maga. This is the first of the acts dictated by motives alien to the consciousness of the characters and, though Oliveira is at first annoyed, he is soon consoled by the idea: 'The visit to the *Cerro* had been fine, precisely because it had been based on reasons other than those he had supposed. To know that he was in love with la Maga was not a failure' (338:48). Implicit, then, in the reversal of the mechanics of action must be a trust in the forces which direct that action and which are represented by the influence of the purified la Maga. He thus asks the question, 'What is the point of knowing or thinking that we know that every path is false if we do not take it with a purpose which is no longer the path itself?' (340:48) Such a purpose cannot be conscious, but must be provided by the impersonal forces discussed above.

This new attitude in Oliveira is basically of a religious or mystical character, involving a faith in forces (though in a sense set in motion by him) 'beyond' him. There may be some analogies to be drawn between this attitude and that expounded in the *Bhagavad Gita*, the Sanskrit dialogue between King Arjuna, who does not wish to enter battle and kill members of his own family, and Krishna, who gives him the religious reasons why he should do so. Arjuna is mentioned by Oliveira at various points when the question of action arises: 'Shouldn't I go back and put the boot into him? Advise me, oh Arjuna' (531:108); 'Are you going to give battle, Arjuna?' (34:3) Man must act, according to Krishna, but his action must involve a renunciation of self and of desire: 'The world is in the bonds of action, unless the action is consecration. Let thy actions then be pure, free from the bonds of desire.'[58] No man can truly act unless he liberates himself from the forces of the outside world: 'All actions take place in time by the interweaving of the forces of Nature; but the man lost in selfish delusion thinks that he himself is the actor.'[59] Selfless work and action places man beyond plurality and dualism ('beyond what is done and beyond what is not done'),[60] beyond the three *Gunas*, the intertwined constituents and changing conditions of nature: 'And he who with never-failing love adores me and works for me, he passes beyond the three powers and can be one with Brahman, the ONE.'[61]

We noted earlier the oxymoron often associated with the Spanish mystics. The presence of St John of the Cross is explicitly recognized in *Libro de Manuel* ('Let's turn left, even though it is night, my beloved Juan de la Cruz' (*M* 352)), and the position he represents is not absent here: an emptying oneself (as in Oliveira's 'subtraction', and destruction of la Maga), an abandonment of intelligence (Oliveira: 'Along that path of not understanding, we were drawing closer to them, who do not understand themselves' (49:8); San Juan: 'no entender entendiendo, toda ciencia transcendiendo'),[62] and a waiting in the dark (Oliveira's long night with Emmanuèle) that the void created be filled with another presence.

THE RETURN TO BUENOS AIRES

When Oliveira returns to Buenos Aires, the reader is surprised that so little seems to have been achieved. He lives with a well-meaning but rather stupid former girlfriend, Gekrepken, and in close contact with his friend Manuel Traveler and his wife Talita, sells cloth from door to door, and later works in a circus. Yet, though living the life of Buenos Aires, 'he could not reconcile himself hypocritically with Buenos Aires, and [...] he was now further away from his country than when he had been in Europe' (268:40). It becomes clear that Oliveira has achieved a total destruction in himself of civilization, intellect, and intelligibility: 'So, we are no longer with others, we have ceased to be a citizen' (561:125). He has reached a state previous to 'humanity', and has become an animal, a dog, 'a sort of monkey among men' (358:52).

To become a dog was simply a healthy step backwards, a spring-board from which to rejoin his fellow man, but this he has not yet done: 'But even so, we haven't been able to leave the dog to reach that which hasn't got a name, let's call it that conciliation, that reconciliation' (561). This reconciliation with the world of Traveler and Talita, and the transformation of that world through the forces Oliveira has discovered and set in motion is his task in the second part. In a sense, he has found what he was looking for, but this is not sufficient: 'It is not a search because it has already been found. It's just that the find does not coagulate' (561). Oliveira believes that the Travelers are the 'coagulant' needed (328:46), but much must happen before they can fully play their roles.

There are various different types of *dédoublement* of characters in this part, and different relations between them, but perhaps the most important and traditional is the double 'character' composed by Oliveira and Traveler, who represent two sides of one person, in the way of Stevenson's *The Strange Case of Dr Jekyll and Mr Hyde*, Poe's

'William Wilson', Hoffmann's *The Devil's Elixirs*, and Dostoyevsky's *The Double*. Other models, however, are also involved in their reconciliation. Oliveira is that part of Traveler which would have liked to travel, i.e. to explore reality, while Traveler is the 'form' left behind by Oliveira in his trips beyond custom and conventionality, i.e. Buenos Aires. He is the present, and civilization:

That's why I feel you are my *doppelgänger*, because I spend all my time coming and going from your territory to mine, if I ever actually reach mine, and it seems to me that in those pitiful passages you are my form which stays there looking at me with pity, you are the five thousand years of man piled up in one metre seventy, looking at this clown who wants to escape from his pigeon-hole.   (400:56)

Their relationship is described as a see-saw: ' "But always in symmetrical positions", said Oliveira. "Like two twins playing on a see-saw" ' (393:56). According to a similar phrase earlier in the novel, Oliveira would loosely represent intuition, and Traveler intellect:

Ergo, Madras and Heidelberg console themselves fabricating positions, some with a discursive base, others with an intuitive base. [...] Madras and Heidelberg are two different doses of the same prescription, [...] but on the two ends of the see-saw there are two equally unexplained homo sapiens, kicking away at the ground to go up at the other's expense.   (190:28)

An element of vampirism is also introduced, which clearly foreshadows that of *62*: 'As if we were vampires, as if we were united, that's to say disunited, by the same circulatory system' (355:51).

Many of the polarities and alienating dualisms of the novel are finally confronted in these two characters. As in the first part, Oliveira sees the absurd in terms of the superficiality of human relationships: 'The most absurd thing about these lives we claim to be living is their false contact' (450:78). Oliveira and Traveler wish to talk, to understand each other: 'I too would like to come to understand you, and *you* means much more than you yourself' (326:46). Their attempts to do so, however, are vitiated by what they call *pudor* (327:46), which leads, in their conversations, to a series of substitutions of irrelevancies for important sentiments, which Cortázar, here as elsewhere, handles admirably. This substitution is only a particular case of a wider spectrum of substitution by Traveler, man in society, of his deeper aspirations (delegated onto Oliveira) for evasion, the circus. In *62*, the substitution of one character for another in the person of 'my paredros' is also seen as 'a form of *pudor*' (*62* 27). Thus, affection is usually a substitute for a deeper hatred and fear: 'How we all hate each other, without realizing that affection is the present form of that hatred' (450). This hatred originates in a basic ontological gap between individuals: 'The reason behind this deep hatred is this "being off centre" (*excentración*), the insurmountable gap between I and you, between this and that' (450). That the gap is described as *excentración*, separation from the centre, suggests that the centre that Oliveira has sought to define throughout the novel would now mean unity with Traveler, 'the unity that he used to call the centre' (384:56).

The ontological gap between people is extended to things ('the insurmountable gap [...] between this and that'), to the separateness and impermeability of phenomena that Oliveira and Cortázar would unite in the moving, symbolic causal clusters of the *figuras*. This can be seen in relation to time in Oliveira's dismay at the separateness of '*mate* time' and 'milk-coffee time', at what he calls the 'vertiginous discontinuity of existence' (300:41); and in relation to words and their reference, in the games that Oliveira plays with Talita, where dictionary definitions are confronted in all their irreconcilability. All this is expressionistically represented by the 'thin slice of air' (449:78) which separates Oliveira's room from that of the Travelers, and in the episode where the two face each other across a bridge they build with planks from one room to the other.

Just as in the first part la Maga is seen as a 'giver of infinity', here, affection is seen as an 'ontological swipe' (450). Hence the ontological importance of Oliveira's relationship with the Travelers. But this affection, if it is to be effective, must not be the superficial affection which is only a substitute for something else. Thus, Oliveira's affection is not devoid of aggression, as he is determined to avoid the false pity of the first part: 'In that case, feeling pity would have been as idiotic as the first time: rain, rain' (341:458). He is once more called an inquisitor. 'An affectionate inquisitor, at the most', he muses (451:78).

Traveler and Talita

These characters, like most of Cortázar's, do not represent one clear-cut attitude. Their general life-style is open and seemingly untrammelled by convention, yet strongly marked and determined by definition and classification, culture and arbitrary action. The contrasts in their attitude clearly show up the nature of both sides of it. This is the case with their fascination with the ludicrous system of Ceferino Piriz, who classifies the whole world according to colours and extravagant corporations. The effect of this classification is to show, of course, as Borges does with a similar Chinese encyclopaedia, that 'there is no classification of the universe which is not arbitrary and conjectural'.[63]

In this context, the main attribute of Talita, apart from being defined as an 'encyclopaedia reader' (257:37), is that of pharmacist. 'A shame', exclaims Oliveira (270:40). Pharmacists figure very low on Cortázar's private anthropological scale, as can be seen in *Historias de cronopios y de famas*, where his favourite type of humans, the *cronopios*, fire on a crowd 'with such good aim that they brought down six naval officers and a pharmacist' (*H* 122). Pharmacy has to do with classification and labels: 'With greater neutrality, Talita sticks labels on things or consults the *Index Pharmacorum Gottinga*' (600:140). Similarly, when Traveler refuses to understand what Oliveira is trying to do, the latter says, 'You get right to the edge of things and one would think you were going to understand, but it's useless, you start turning them upside down, reading the labels. You don't get beyond the directions for use, mate' (291:41).

The negative connotations of medicine are clear throughout Cortázar's work. Oliveira associates it with the mind as against the body: 'Coquille, cunt, concha, con, coño, millennium, Armageddon, terramycin, oh shut up, don't start it up there with your despicable images, your facile mirrors' (613:144). In the short story 'Cefalea' it is clearly medical diagnosis and science that creates the illness of the hypochondriacal keepers of the monstrous *mancuspias* and the slow deaths of the latter. Similarly, in *Prosa del observatorio*, the eels are seen to be forced to retire to the Sargasso Sea to escape from classification. As we have seen, it is significant in *Los premios* that Jorge should call the monstrous seamen 'lipics' and 'glucics' after reading the instructions supplied with some medicine, and that later they should be seen as partially responsible for his illness, by blocking the way to the stern. The most repressive aspects of Hélène in *62* are associated with her profession as an anaesthetist.

The basis of Traveler's life is negative as his name suggests: he has hardly ever left Buenos Aires. 'To travel', of course, is only a metaphor: 'Talita knows that his concerns are deeper' (260:37). To

travel would be to visit the 'primordial depths' (261:37). Traveler
is contemporary man living in society, 'the man of the territory'
(402:56),[64] a man of action and culture: 'The warp of his action is a
well-stocked mental library, two languages, a facility for writing'
(261). But his action is based only on the absence of any ontological
foundation to his life: 'For want of anything else (*lo otro*), Traveler
is a man of action' (261). It is this escapist or distorting action that
Oliveira has avoided throughout. The plurality of Traveler's
occupations is as great as that of Medrano. His life, 'to give it its most
outward and inevitable name' (261), is the circus, which Oliveira
would like to join. The role of Talita in their marriage is to stifle
the metaphysical urges in him: 'She does all she can to get such
ideas out of his head. So she takes him to see Marilyn Monroe'
(262:37).

Traveler, Talita and Oliveira

In Oliveira's relationship with the Travelers, a distinction must be
made between his conscious conduct and his insertion in unconscious
patterns in which all three are involved. In general, Oliveira has
come, after his life in Paris, to represent all that the Travelers have
repressed.

In a far more active and conscious way, Oliveira plays the same
role towards the Travelers as la Maga towards him, by denouncing
the superficiality of their lives: 'I don't hate you either, brother, but
I denounce you, and that's what you call pushing you against the
wall' (394:56). 'Live and let live', Traveler repeats (302:41).
Paradoxically, at the same time as Oliveira tries to convince Traveler
that reality might not be what he would like it to be ('Aren't you
capable of intuiting just for one second that things can't be like
this?' (399:56)), he also wishes to become (like) the Travelers, to
join the circus: 'You break yourself literally in two to get into the
hintimity of the Travelers, to be the Travelers, to hinstal yourself in
the Travelers, circus and hall' (450:78). This desire gradually takes
on overtones of vampirism which can be associated with the invading
forces of the short stories. He wishes to 'take possession of the manna
of Manú, the spirit (*duende*) of Talita' (450). At this point, Oliveira
is simply a virtuality, 'as if disembodied' (394), and the fusion of this
virtuality with the circus would create a truer, non-dualistic form of
being, realizing the aspirations of Oliveira, who 'was dying to gain
access, to mix in, to be' (310:43).

Oliveira's presence soon makes itself felt on the Travelers. Talita describes him as the 'inhabitor', and feels indeed that she is both herself and him: *'I'm me, I'm him*, she had said it without thinking, which means that it was more than thought, it came from a territory where words were like the madmen at the asylum' (334:47). Traveler too experiences a similar feeling: 'As soon as I'm on my own, it feels as if you were exerting pressure on me, from your room for example' (355:51). Oliveira's presence makes him want to live differently: 'I never thought [. . .] that you would make me want so much to be different' (328:46).

The emergence and articulation of the impersonal force through the figuras

Oliveira increasingly comes to realize that his experiences in Paris are not a closed episode. In a sense, he is still there, and is 'quite happy to feel that way, not to have returned, to be still on his way, even though he did not know where to' (338:48). His behaviour in Buenos Aires is not totally willed, he is 'a sort of messenger' (318:44) of a message of which he himself is unaware. This lack of consciousness is a large step forward and indicates the disappearance of the dualism which had distinguished him from la Maga: 'I describe and define and desire those rivers, she swims them.' As Morelli says of his own narrative: 'There is no message, there are messengers and that is the message' (453:79). Analogously, he no longer consciously searches for harmony; the search happens through him or, more radically, he is the search: 'No idea. I'm not even looking for it. It all just happens to me' (328:46).

Traveler senses the presence of a new consciousness which, through Oliveira, is demanding access to their lives, 'a stammering like an untranslatable announcement, [. . .] demanding recognition and acceptance' (590:133). Oliveira too feels the 'call of something wanting to become incarnate' (338:48). The recognition of this force is combined in Oliveira and Traveler with an awareness of their whole relationship as a series of chemical reactions alien to their consciousness: 'It occurs to me that our relationship is almost chemical, a phenomenon outside ourselves' (328). It was this chemistry which opened up the possibility of the 'foreign forces' which would create a new *homo*, the force that we associated with the monsters, that which has been destroyed, repressed or lost to man. Our notion that this force is articulated and reproposed to man through the *figuras* becomes clearer as the relationship of Oliveira and Traveler is seen as 'a sort of picture gradually taking shape' (328). Both of them and Talita are 'dancing a slow, interminable figure' (335:47). Morelli too brings out the teleological nature of the *figuras*. He is interested in them as a means of description 'on the margin of superficial time', which would point to a new humanism: 'Ultimately it orientates them towards a transcendence at the end of which man stands waiting' (545:116).

The use of *figuras*, Morelli points out, is a parallel with the art of the Middle Ages. Thus, Cortázar's *figuras* seem to be connected with the use of the term in Auerbach's essay 'Figura'.[65] Figural interpretation was taken up and developed by Christian biblical exegetes to demonstrate how the Old Testament, besides a history of the Jewish people, was also a prefiguration of the New Testament. The important point for the purposes of our discussion is that the *figura* is formed by a repetition and demands at least two terms: a prefiguration (*umbra, imago*),[66] and a repetition or fulfilment (*veritas*). As the presence of la Maga in Buenos Aires makes itself felt, and Talita becomes la Maga in the same way as Traveler is Oliveira ('I know it's Talita, but a second ago it was la Maga. It's both of them, like us' (401:56)), we see that the *figura* forming in Buenos Aires is the repetition of what happened in Paris, a reproposing to the characters of the force which could not be utilized there, but which, through the purification of Oliveira and the death of la Maga, has been released.

Some of the repetitions have already been pointed out. Perhaps the clearest one is the repetition of the triangular structure: Pola–Oliveira–Maga (–Gregovorius) and Traveler–Talita–Oliveira (–Gekrepken). Another rather ingenious one, though contrived by Oliveira, and one which reintroduces the theme of human contact, occurs when Traveler puts his foot in a basin of water, and gets his foot and shoe wet in the same way as Oliveira did in the streets of Paris with Berthe Trépat.

All this produces in the characters a feeling that they are not free: 'It almost seems as if something is talking, as if something is using us to talk' (323:45). They have the sensation that they are pieces in a chess game: 'There are other things using us to play, the white pawn and the black pawn' (394:56). The aim of the game, as seen by Oliveira, is to abolish the dualism formed by the two friends, thus re-establishing the lost totality of man, as seen by Jung: 'two modes, so to speak, in need of one being abolished in the other, and vice versa' (394).

Oliveira, Talita: the return of la Maga

Much of the play in the second part revolves around Talita. She is at the cross-roads of various processes and her role evolves as the plot develops. She is, as we have seen, the guardian of the values of Traveler's world and, in a way, an attribute of him, a symbol of his prevalence. Thus, if Oliveira can win her from him, this would be a sign that his own values, causality, etc. are beginning at least to make themselves felt. In the bridge episode, when she is made to cross with the pretext of taking Oliveira some *mate* and nails, and both wonder whether she will return, Talita feels that some sort of trial is being held: ' "It's like a trial", thought Talita. "Like a ceremony." [. . .] But it was not Manú who was being tried, but her. And through her, who knows what' (292:41). What is at stake is the whole system of thought and values that she represents.

But, as Oliveira points out, the three of them form 'a highly Trismegistic triangle' (328–9:46). Talita is a bridge between the two men, a medium, their 'nymph Egeria' (311:43). Just as Oliveira was seen in the first part as the fulcrum of the scales (between action and inaction, Pola and la Maga), Talita is now described in the same way. The decisive difference is the subterranean influence of what happened in Paris inclining her to one side: 'And you [. . .] have accomplices. [. . .] Me [Oliveira] to start with, and somebody who is not here. You think you are the pointer of the scales, to use your pretty figure of speech, but you don't know that you are throwing your weight on one side' (312:43). The accomplice Oliveira is referring to is la Maga. Oliveira had noted the likeness between the two women on disembarking, 'as if there suddenly sprang from his apparently so well compartmented memory an ectoplasm capable of inhabiting and completing another body and another face' (337:48). The presence of la Maga makes itself felt in Talita, in the recording session discussed earlier, etc., to the point of her feeling herself to be a zombie (a corpse revived by witchcraft) of la Maga: 'I'm nobody's zombie, Manú, I don't want to be anybody's zombie' (589:133).

Talita's life is described as a 'time which was like a waste land covered with twisted tin cans' (333:47), the same waste lands where

Oliveira walks the performing cat, and, more importantly, where he would meet Maga and the Club in Paris (19, 367, 344). Even Talita, puzzled by the paradox that Oliveira should 'at the same time be interested and not interested' (335:47) in her, realizes that out of this dualism and choice of opposites, comes a third, unitary possibility, corresponding to the 'inhabiting forces in search of their citizen's rights', which harmonizes superficial and unconscious motivations in a search for a new form of living: 'From the combination of the two things a third one should be born, something which had nothing to do with love, [...] something on the side of the chase, the search' (335).

Things come to a head when the Travelers and Oliveira start working in a lunatic asylum (a place where the bonds of logic are relaxed, while the dualism mad/sane, normal/abnormal is exacerbated). One night, Oliveira sees Talita in the patio from the window and believes she is la Maga. He sees her dressed in pink (like the inmates), and playing hopscotch (a game he had watched with la Maga in Paris (36:4), and the last square of which he has always taken for his spiritual goal). She rather enigmatically wets her finger in the fountain playing there (the inner spring defended by the monsters? the tap from which la Maga drinks as a girl before being raped by Ireneo?).

Oliveira is contemplating suicide by throwing himself down the lift-shaft which leads to the morgue, when Talita brings him a glass of lemonade. With her, he goes down into the morgue, from which a madman with a dove which had once been white has just emerged. They descend, in other words, to Hades, but Oliveira altogether too pessimistically declares that he has no Eurydice to recover (372:54). For the first time, he speaks freely to Talita about Paris and la Maga, and for the first time enjoys being felt sorry for: 'Pity was not disappearing' (372). He feels he is renouncing his rebellion. Yet when Talita touches him in a gesture of consolation, something changes in Oliveira, who looks at her as if she were la Maga, 'through eyes which came from somewhere else' (373:54). He recovers the presence of la Maga and accepts the force which comes from the river where she died: 'accepting something else which must have been coming to him from the centre of life, from that other pit (with cockroaches, with coloured rags, with a face floating in dirty water?)' (373). He kisses Talita and they both feel that they are golems consummating a union not possible to their masters: 'It was as if they were reaching each other from somewhere else, with another part of themselves, and it wasn't anything to do with them, as if they were paying or collecting something for someone else, as if they were the golems of an impossible meeting between their masters' (373).

It is perhaps significant that they should be referred to as golems. A very similar process takes place in Gustav Meyrink's novel *The Golem*. (A 'golem' is a type of homunculus created by a rabbi which periodically comes to life in others.) In this way, the hero of the story becomes the long-dead Athanasius Pernath and seemingly facilitates the latter's union with the mysterious Miriam. He learns that a superior spiritual state, 'the miracle of resurrection',[67] can only be reached when two lives are grafted into one.

Oliveira, then, wins Talita over to his side, recovers the force of la Maga, and reaches the 'centre'. Yet this is only the first of two crises. The pattern followed at the end of the novel is that of 'Las puertas del cielo', where Celina, the wife of Mauro, dies and later returns (in her own form, not in that of another) to create a possible union between the intellectual Hardoy and the 'natural' Mauro: 'I think it was then that we both reached each other on the deepest level' (*B* 134). Oliveira's recovery of la Maga is meaningless unless it results in his fusion with the world of Traveler.

In the syncretism operated in this episode, a state has been reached where the deep symbolic and the superficial causalities have become one, where one can be (superficially – *estar*) in grey (Talita's skirt) and really be (*ser*) pink (the colour of the inmates' pyjamas; mad; la Maga): 'Somehow they had entered another order, that order where it was possible to be in (*estar de*) grey and be (*ser de*) pink, to have drowned in a river [...] and turn up in the Buenos Aires night' (374). Though this is the 'centre' sought by Oliveira, 'the last square, the centre of the mandala, the vertiginous Yggdrasil' (374:54), Talita points out that it is such a piece of madness that it would be totally alien and meaningless to the world of Traveler, 'such absolute foolishness (*insensatez*) that Manú and everything that Manú was and was on Manú's level could not participate in the ceremony' (373). It is part of Traveler's world to keep grey and pink firmly apart: ' "Well", said Traveler, "there is one difference: they dress in pink" ' (354:51).

Traveler

Much of the success of the process Oliveira introduces into Buenos Aires depends on the acceptance of it, or resistance to it of Traveler. As we have seen, one important piece of progress from *Los premios* is the return to Buenos Aires after reaching the stern, and the insistence on communication, on the necessarily collective nature of any salvation. This corresponds to the importance of the reader for Morelli: 'I wonder if I will ever get it across that the only real character I am interested in is the reader' (497:97). Throughout the chapter it has become clear that the motivations of the characters are alien to them, that what they believe to be their motives are simply a substitute for the real ones: 'I don't think we've come here just because the Boss has brought us' (355:51); 'You think you got up to come and calm me down, reassure me' (393:56); 'you don't know you are throwing your weight on one side' (312:43), etc. Thus, if Traveler insists on reading their situation on the superficial, deterministic plane, he will misunderstand and frustrate the quest of Oliveira as much as the *lector hembra* that of Morelli:

He provides him with a sort of façade, with doors and windows behind which a mystery is taking place which the accomplice reader must look for [...]. As for the female reader, she will stick with the façade, and it is a well known fact that there are some very pretty ones, very *trompe l'œil*, and that one can still play the comedies and tragedies of the *honnête homme* satisfactorily in front of them. (454:79)

Traveler's attitude towards the changes which began on the arrival of Oliveira is mixed, and fluctuates greatly. Oliveira repeats that Traveler's basic position has been to demand conformity: 'And you are the standard-bearer, the herald of surrender, of the return home and back into line' (397:56). Nevertheless, Traveler takes his arrival as a challenge even though it would have been easy for him to tell Oliveira to go away. He does not do this, and even finds him a job in the circus. His position is similar to that of Alina Reyes in that he refuses to avoid confrontation: 'I feel that I must not defend myself with a lightning conductor, and that I must go abroad bareheaded until it is twelve on some clock' (317–18:44). The real test of his openness is his understanding of Oliveira's relation with his wife, as jealousy is a very strong force in Cortázar's work. At one point, he admits that it would be irrelevant to talk of jealousy: 'It's something bloody well different, damn it!' (318)

Traveler at times participates in Oliveira's word games, which have the aim of breaking down the order of Western thought, and which culminate in the *preguntas balanzas*, reminiscent of the Zen Buddhist *koan*, which are answers given to questions by the master in a Zen monastery aimed at breaking down the dualistic structures of the rational mind,[68] or the questions and answers devised by Breton, where the answer is given without knowing the question.[69] Yet at other times, he refuses to play Oliveira's games: 'Why should I play your game, brother?' Oliveira replies that 'games play themselves, it's you who's putting a spanner in the works' (291:41). Characteristically, after the break in logic of the bridge episode, the first thing Traveler notices and puts right is the disorder in his room.

The instability of his position is brought out when he learns that Oliveira has kissed Talita. It is accentuated by reading the 'dispensable chapters', where an episode is repeated almost verbatim (the only occurrence of the sort), with the difference that Traveler is seen reading and meditating on the work of Ceferino Piriz. He is enjoying himself greatly and decides that Piriz 'breaks up the hard mental crust, [...] and begins to see the world from a different angle', but adds significantly that 'that's what they call being round the bend (*piantado*)' (581:133). He nevertheless suggests trying a world like that of Ceferino (584:133), and, when Talita returns, decides that she is a *pampa*, a double, 'formed by two or more colours' (588:133). He enjoys the coincidence that la Maga, like Piriz, should be Uruguayan, but his attitude soon changes to moral indignation and incomprehension as Talita continues with her story: ' "So you went down", said Traveler. "Great!" ' (589:133) La Maga was not drowned, he snaps. Talita tries to convince him that the episode cannot be discussed in these terms, insisting that 'it was different' (589), 'it was something else' (590:133). Yet at the same time, 'struggling against a spongey wall of smoke and cork', Traveler feels 'an explanation that [he] was incapable of rejecting, a contagion which came from beyond, from somewhere deep down or high up or anywhere different from that night and that room, a contagion which, through Talita, possessed him in turn, a stammering like an untranslatable announcement' (590).

But he is able to reject this message and return to a more obvious, superficial explanation of the facts, as a 'communicable system gradually came back into his ears' (377–8:55). He also convinces Talita of his logic, and realizes, not without regret, that 'she was on his side again', that she had not drowned with la Maga, and that they are once again the people they always had been: 'the same old satisfied sadness at becoming his everyday self again, carrying on, keeping afloat against wind and tide, against the call and the fall' (378).

THE FINAL CONFRONTATION AND RECONCILIATION

Three possible endings

Cortázar provides the reader with three possible endings to the novel:
(a) Oliveira goes mad.
(b) He commits suicide by throwing himself out of a window.
(c) He plans to see a film with Gekrepken. This last possibility is only suggested in the 'dispensable chapters'.
I believe that these possibilities are not mutually exclusive – indeed, that they may be reconciled in one reading. The very disparity of critical judgement on the final pages negatively suggests this.

Brody accepts that Oliveira 'becomes totally insane at the end of the novel'.[70] Aronne Amestoy believes that Oliveira commits suicide in order to avoid the death of Traveler: 'Only suicide, throwing oneself literally down again to the territory of the beautiful mistake, renouncing lucidity for the sake of the misguided species can avert the death of Manú.'[71] Joaquín Roy, backed up by the author's own avowed ignorance of what actually happens,[72] says, while excluding the possibility of suicide, that the reader, within the spirit of the novel as a whole and taking into account the theories of Morelli, must decide himself.[73] This is undoubtedly the case. Sosnowski notes Cortázar's assertion in the interview with Harss that Oliveira's quest may be a failure in that it is not at all easy to cease living according to the rationality of the West: '*Rayuela* proves how a large part of that search may end in failure, in so far as one cannot stop being a Westerner just like that, with all the Judaeo-Christian tradition we have inherited, and which has made us what we are.'[74] He sees Oliveira failing in his absolute aspirations where la Maga had succeeded, but, rejecting the temptation of suicide, finding a lesser goal in the love of his fellow man, in 'the human meaning of reality'.[75] Graciela de Sola, without going into the final episode in any detail, also insists on the human dimension of Oliveira's whole adventure, on his 'pure *act of love*, surrender to other

human beings, deep participation in their fallen and pitiful condition'.[76] The reading proposed here most closely follows that of
García Canclini, as on other points, such as the importance of
monsters. He says that it is possible that Oliveira is both mad and
commits suicide,[77] but prefers a third possibility, that he is
'redeemed'[78] by the kindness and humanity of Traveler.

Madness

As suggested by Roy, the possibilities must be judged according to
the logic, symbolism and vocabulary of the novel. Perhaps the most
crucial point is that of Oliveira's madness. The final episodes are
played out in a lunatic asylum.[79] It may be significant that the
inmates are often far more perspicacious than their guardians. To
the astonishment of the latter, they continually demand the death of
a non-existent dog: the dog of the 'city' in 62, the dogs which
destroy Actaeon in *Prosa del observatorio*. Like the office-worker in
'Tema para San Jorge', they are the only ones to see the monster,
which is 'a living nothingness, a sort of void which encompasses
and possesses' (*V* I 43). They thus share Oliveira's conviction that
reality cannot be as it is. Talita significantly associates the logic of
the presence of la Maga in her with insanity: it came from 'a
territory where words were like the madmen at the asylum'.

It should be stressed that madness is just one term in yet another
dualism in the novel: madness/sanity. Earlier, Oliveira expressed the
hope that through madness he might reach a non-dualistic 'reason'
which would dissolve the opposition, a 'sanity' not so fragile that on
breaking down it would immediately become its opposite: 'Through
madness one could perhaps achieve a sanity other than that sanity
the failure of which is madness' (93–4:18). A *cronopio* or *piantado*
(nut-case?) has, by definition, reached this state:

> To understand a madman it is advisable to be a psychiatrist, though it is
> never enough; to understand a nut-case (*piantado*) a sense of humour is
> sufficient. All nut-cases are *cronopios* [amusing, semi-fantastic individuals
> of Cortázar's invention], i.e. humour replaces a large part of those mental
> faculties which constitute the pride of a prof. or a doc., whose only outlet
> in the event of their malfunctioning is madness; whilst being a *piantado*
> is not an outlet but an inlet.   (*V* II 127–8)

The opposition between madness and sanity is the opposition
between Oliveira and Traveler. Madness is closely associated with

sleep and dreams (and it is in dreams that one glimpses the lost unity): 'While dreaming, we are allowed to exercise our aptitude for madness free of charge. We suspect at the same time that all madness is a dream which sticks' (456:80). It is thus significant that the dualism of the two characters becomes that between dreaming and waking life: 'But to talk of dreaming against waking life was already to return to the dialectic, to corroborate once again that there was not the slightest hope of unity' (384:56). To break this dualism, the dearest aspiration of the surrealists, for Oliveira and Traveler to become one, would also be to break the opposition between madness and sanity, and thus to reach the 'unity' or 'centre' sought throughout.

The syncretism of Talita and la Maga has in itself broken down the dualism madness/sanity: 'They had entered another order, an order where it was possible to be in (*estar de*) grey and be (*ser*) pink' (374:54). A level has been reached where 'grey' (the colour of the skirt of Talita, an official of the asylum, hence sanity) is simply a superficial level (*estar*) of the more fundamental (*ser*) 'pink' (the colour of the pyjamas of the inmates, hence madness, and of the dress Oliveira imagines la Maga to be wearing).

Such syncretism or equivalence is, however, described as madness. Oliveira's earlier hope that one thing be equivalent to another is described as foolishness (*insensatez*): 'Foolishness demands that gold should be worth the same as lead, that more should be contained in less' (562:125). Talita herself, on realizing and accepting her identity with la Maga, describes it as an *insensatez* (373:54) which would be incomprehensible on Traveler's level. It thus very much depends on the reaction of Oliveira's social ego Traveler (his jealousy, etc.) whether this 'madness' is seen as the liberation of the non-dualistic *cronopio* or the conventional condemnation of the *loco*. By declaring Oliveira *loco*, he would get rid of the threat posed to his way of life and values in much the same way as if he were to declare him a monster. Before (to a certain extent) coming round to Oliveira's point of view, this is in fact the path taken by Traveler: 'That is called madness' (401:56).

We have seen then that to accept the subterranean causality which has slowly imposed itself throughout the second part of the novel, i.e. the presence of la Maga, is, from the point of view of Traveler 'madness', and from that of Oliveira an abolition of the dualism madness/sanity. Madness also has a second, very different, meaning within the novel. It is this double meaning which allows the seemingly divergent endings of the novel to be encompassed by one reading.

Just as Oliveira arrives, through madness, at a non-dualistic form of sanity, with Berthe Trépat he had aimed to break the absurd by living absurdly: 'Only by living absurdly could one hope to break this infinite absurdity' (123:23). This paradox is paralleled now by a similar decision: 'The only possible way of escaping from the territory was to immerse oneself in it to the hilt' (402:56). This can be paraphrased as: the only way to cease to be mad (or sane with reference to the arbitrariness, madness, of society, i.e. exiled from it) is to become mad by accepting madness. This is confirmed by a phrase from the first part: 'join the world, the Great Madness' (239:36). Note that Oliveira had believed he was 'going mad' with Berthe Trépat: ' "I'm going mad", he thought. "And arm in arm with this crackpot it must be contagious" ' (142:23). If he does not 'go mad' before this point, it is due to his pride and mistrust: 'If he had been so lucky as to go mad that night, the liquidation of the Traveler territory would have been absolute. But such a solution was totally unacceptable to his pride and his intention of resisting any form of surrender' (389:56). As in *62*, madness is a privilege attained but by few: 'Not everybody can go mad, such things have to be deserved' (*62* 141).

With all this in mind, a more general interpretation of the lunatic asylum may be attempted. Talita sees the move from the circus to the asylum as a 'sort of step forward' (342:49). The asylum is the final step in the process of undoing falsification and substitution. In the morgue scene, the substitution of la Maga by Talita (deep 'madness' substituted and repressed by a vicarious veneer of civilized sanity) is uncovered and undone. This corresponds to the removal of *pudor*, which for Cortázar always leads to falsity and substitution, in the final conversation between Oliveira and Traveler. A world without substitution would, for Oliveira, be a definition of Arcadia: 'We would all like the millenary kingdom, a sort of Arcadia where [...] we would no longer have to play this rotten game of substitutions which takes up fifty or sixty years of our lives' (399–400:56). The move from the circus is thus a move from a feigned or superficial madness, a false ontological state, to one made real, fully accepted and justified, where surface and depth ('We could be *fundamentally* the same as on the surface') finally become one.

The fortification of Oliveira's room

Much of the ambiguity of the final chapters depends on the play between different levels of understanding. Oliveira himself moves between these two levels. He is afraid that Traveler is out to kill him (out of jealousy; for 'denouncing' him; to rid himself of the 'invasion'; to fulfil unwittingly the necessity that one side should be predominant) and fortifies his room against attack. This fortification is the main base to the claim that Oliveira is mad, but contains important symbolism which has been developed through the novel. The fortification consists of numerous pieces of string attached to pieces of furniture. These strings, the same that he uses in his mobiles, are an image of the open logic of the novel, of the mysterious relations between disparate objects and people: 'Threads seemed to Oliveira to be the only justifiable material for his inventions [...]. He especially liked everything he made to be as full as possible of free space, and the air to come in and out' (379:56). It also comes to symbolize, not only a defensive system, but the 'hard mental crust' of Traveler, the barrier of logic between them, 'a spongey wall of smoke and cork'. The basins of water have the purpose of making Traveler repeat Oliveira's experience of getting his feet wet with Berthe Trépat, an image of human suffering and solidarity. There is much humour in the repeated mentioning by an inmate of the necessity of a *Heftpistole* for Oliveira's defence. The reader immediately thinks of a pistol, whereas the artefact turns out to be a stapler for attaching the strings to the wall.

Traveler enters the room, steps in the basins of water, and brings down the furniture with a din which wakes the rest of the institution. There follows a long and sincere confrontation, the content of which is contained in earlier discussion of the characters. Oliveira sits by an open window, through which it is believed he will throw himself if approached. Talita, whom Oliveira will not distinguish from la Maga, stands in the patio below. Though afraid that their meeting might be an 'incalculable disencounter', his hope is that a final unity will be achieved, that it will prove 'an extreme point from which once more to attempt the leap from the one into the other and at the same time from the other into the one' (388–9:56). Traveler is increasingly disarmed and open, but nevertheless still clings to his primary logic and to his jealousy: 'You can talk as much as you like about la Maga, but my wife is clothed and fed by me' (401:56);

' "It's not la Maga", said Traveler. "You know perfectly well it's not la Maga" ' (397:56); 'And all because he gets reality and memory mixed up in a supremely non-Euclidean fashion' (394:56).

Self-defenestration

Oliveira refuses to give the same meaning of suicide to his throwing himself out of the window as does Traveler on the other side of the strings. 'Do you mean to say that if somebody tries to get hold of you, you will jump?' asks Traveler. 'It may mean that from your side', answers Oliveira (398:56). In the same way, he refuses Traveler's definition of madness: ' "That's what they call madness", said Traveler. "Everything is called something, you just choose, and there you are" ' (401:56).

His own fear that Traveler is out to kill him for kissing his wife gives us a clue to the possible meaning of his throwing himself out of the window. Talita had earlier described this fear as a *defence* against throwing himself from a height: 'His fear is like a last refuge, the bar he's holding on to before he jumps' (378:55). This implies that the belief that Traveler is going to kill him out of jealousy (which he does not believe: 'What's the kiss to you?' (395:56)) is his last defence against believing in the real presence of la Maga, and the process she represents. Before the arrival of Traveler, he feels the fear receding, which means being at peace with himself, and the disappearance of the 'territory', that is, the difference between himself and the world of Traveler (390:56).

'To jump' is equivalent to the final abandonment of Western rationality and the recognition of a possible *novum organum*, as can be seen in the following passage from the 'dispensable chapters': 'We need a real Novum Organum, we have to open the windows wide and throw everything out into the street, but above all we have to throw the window out as well, and ourselves with it' (616:147). Cortázar's own tentative interpretation of the final episode of *Rayuela* would seem to support this theory: 'I think it was an attempt to show from a Western point of view, with all the concomitant limitations and impossibilities, a jump into the absolute like that of the Zen monk or the Vedanta master.'[80]

Such a jump into the absolute does not contradict the final possibility of Oliveira having *tortas* with Gekrepken and going to see a 'musical in colour' with her (437). The mention of the Zen monk confirms the many parallels with Zen Buddhism throughout the novel. As the *Zenrin* says, 'To save life it must be destroyed. / When utterly destroyed, one dwells for the first time in peace.'[81] The jump into the courtyard is not a falling into the awful nothingness of Western existentialism, but an abandoning oneself to the 'marvellous void' of Buddhism. The object of Zen is to destroy the distance between the subject and his experience that reality be seen in its 'suchness'. When asked 'What is Buddha?' Y'ung-shan answered, 'Three pounds of flax!'[82] The 'musical in colour' and the *tortas* are Oliveira's 'three pounds of flax'.

Reconciliation

As the hubbub increases and attempts are made to enter the room, Traveler, before leaving to join Talita, warns the rest to let them talk in peace: 'Stop being such a bloody nuisance' (400:56). He advises Oliveira to bolt the door, as he does not trust them (402:56). Oliveira is moved by this kindness and tacit complicity with him, and through this human comprehension is reconciled with the other side, the world of Traveler and the beauty of the 'incurable mistake of the misguided species': 'After what Traveler had just done, everything was like a marvellous feeling of reconciliation and that foolish (*insensata*) but living and present harmony was inviolable' (402). He is now able to accept as true and real the love in the arm around Talita's waist that in the first part he had found so false and coercive: 'what beauty in those eyes which had filled with tears, [...] what love in that arm hugging a woman's waist' (402). The feeling of harmony is increased when Talita also firmly sides with Oliveira against the staff who try to tempt him down, presumably to put him in a straight jacket: 'Don't be stupid' (403:56). Oliveira's eyes meet Traveler's and it is as though they fall like two birds, firmly entangled, onto square nine of the hopscotch, the threshold of 'heaven': 'Traveler and Oliveira's eyes met like two birds colliding in mid-air and falling tangled together onto square nine, or at least that is how the interested parties experienced it' (403).

It is at this point that Oliveira's self-defenestration is pointed to with the preterite indicative 'it was all over' (*se acabó*) and questioned with the pluperfect subjunctive 'would have been' (*hubiera sido*):

That was how it was, the harmony was lasting incredibly long, there were no words to answer the goodness of those two down there [...]

after all there was some sort of meeting (*encuentro*), even though it could not last longer than that terribly sweet moment when without doubt the best thing would have been to lean slightly further out and let oneself go, bang it was all over.   (404:56)

I hope it has become clear that only with a superficial view of the logic of the novel can one see this and the other endings as contradictory.

3

62. Modelo para armar

62. Modelo para armar is a difficult work, the most complex and radical of Cortázar's writing, which perhaps explains why it has not received the critical attention it deserves. The first twenty pages are of such density that one imagines they must have discouraged many potential *62* readers. Though they are among his most fascinating pages, and are an integral part of the novel, they risk giving the impression of being a prologue or introduction. *62* is not, nor can it be, so spectacular and flamboyant a novel as *Rayuela*. The nature of its psychology, mapped out in chapter 62 of *Rayuela*, does not allow the intense introspection, and anguished treatment of the big questions of death, commitment and community of the previous novel.

The tone of its writing is perhaps not sufficiently homogeneous, in that the humour sometimes gives the impression of being 'light relief'. Nevertheless, the humorous episodes, which are often very funny indeed, do add much to our understanding of the whole and, if not absolutely necessary, are structurally coherent with it.

There are three main areas of the novel which contribute to its difficulty and originality. The first is the dualistic creation of two levels of existence, which perhaps develop from the dualism Paris–Buenos Aires in *Rayuela*, but do not retain the geographical dimension: the 'city' and the 'zone'. The second is the semi-character or collective double 'my paredros', who is a synthesis of the existential double like that formed by Oliveira and Traveler, and the literary double composed of Oliveira and Morelli. The third area is the psychological causality of the novel, its distance from more traditional concepts of responsibility. It is indirect to an extreme, and further mediated by the presence in the text of what I have called 'codes', other literary texts which dictate the course of the action.

97

They produce a very atmospheric impression of vague manipulation by mysterious forces, which is very effective, but which has prompted critics to suggest that not even Cortázar really knew what he was doing. The tools of *62* are those of *Rayuela*, but considerably sharper and more sophisticated. A commensurate increase in analytical flexibility makes this Cortázar's most demanding and rewarding work.

In his essay 'La muñeca rota', Cortázar discusses several works parallel in intention to *62*, which serve as a good introduction to its functioning and nature. He quotes a passage from Aragon's *La mise à mort*, where the incoherence of life is seen in terms of an almost illegible novel:

Cette vie débrochée, en charpie, où le texte ne se suit plus, les pages n'importe comment, dans tous les sens. Un roman dont on n'a pas la clef. On ne sait même pas qui est le héros, positif ou pas. C'est une suite de rencontres, de gens à peine vus qu'on les oublie, d'autres sans intérêt qui tout le temps reviennent. Ah, que c'est mal foutu, la vie. On essaie de lui donner une signification générale. On essaie. Pauvre petit. (*UR* a 105)

La mise à mort, like *62*, begins with a scene in a restaurant, in front of a mirror. The hero, Alfred-Anthoine, can no longer see himself in the mirror. He has, like the vampire, lost his reflection. The suggestion is that the Western world no longer corresponds to the idea that it has of itself. A gap has opened up between its morality and ideology and its actual reality: 'Quel désordre, mon Dieu, quel désordre! Il n'y a pas que moi qui ai perdu mon image. Tout un siècle ne peut plus comparer son âme à ce qu'il voit. Et nous nous comptons par millions qui sommes les enfants égarés de l'immense divorce.'[1] Whereas Alfred ends in madness, hurling himself at the mirror, Cortázar's mirror is far richer in possibilities. Nevertheless, Cortázar shares Aragon's dismay and consequently refuses to 'construct' a novel according to models which are no longer valid or relevant to what they aim to describe, rejects 'literature conceived as a humanistic, architectonic project', accepting 'no clear idea, no formal plan' (*C* 18).[2]

Octavio Paz points out the lack of legibility, i.e. predictability, in twentieth-century social revolutions: 'Both events and actors contradict the text of the play. They write another text – they invent it. History becomes improvisation. It is the end of discourse and rational legibility.'[3] Likewise, Cortázar announces in *Rayuela* that the characters of *62* will conform to no traditional psychological norms: 'Standard types of behaviour (even the most unusual, their de luxe category) would be inexplicable with current psychological apparatus. The actors would seem insane or totally idiotic' (*R* 417). Thus, as always in Cortázar, there is strict cohesion between the formal and psychological planes. There is, however, a level on which the unconventionality of the characters is psychologically coherent in that they 'co-operate' with Cortázar in consciously reacting against any traditional code of action: their lives are a 'cheerful and obstinate trampling of decalogues' (83); their actions always directed against the 'well-thinking and well-acting masses' (50). It is this conscious attitude which creates the 'open', i.e. causally porous, zone in which a different, new psychological causality operates, is discovered and improvised.

Most of the elements and episodes of the novel are present in the first few pages, linked by a series of acausal and atemporal 'there is', 'while', 'and' (16). One must be very careful not to make any *a priori* judgements about the nature of these elements: though there is no whole, original reality or 'story' outside the text, its presence or at least its potentiality is suggested, and must at times be posited for a comprehension of the functioning of the narrative. Thus, no distinction is made in this initial presentation between 'straight-forward' episodes, ones which can be understood as symbolic, such as the happenings in the 'city', and those created by the narrative process itself.

These elements are seen by 'my paredros' as insects flying around a light, forming an almost infinite number of patterns, naturally resistant to any ordering (16, 268). When this image is compared with a description by Cortázar of his creative process, it becomes clear that the light is equivalent to the interrogative void of the emergent text: 'In my case, what has always happened is that I have gone through cycles when what was really significant revolved around a central hole which was paradoxically the text about to be written or in the process of being written' (*UR* a 104). The elements are attracted by and tend towards a meaning, yet this meaning is absent. Paz's notion of the poem is very similar: 'The poem is a set of signs in search of a *signifié*. We revolve around an absence and all our *signifiés* are annulled in the face of that absence.'[4] This 'deferred', imminent meaning is the hollow centre of the doll which passes through the novel, like the soldier's box in Robbe-Grillet's *Dans le labyrinthe*. *62* is to a great extent a psychological novel and, parallel to the rather abstract absence of meaning discussed here, there is the sense of a more ontological absence ('la vraie vie est absente'), a constant search for what might be called ontological wholeness, for the *hombre entero*. This void is most clearly felt in the self-mutilation of Hélène, her 'absence': 'a meeting of vague signals [. . .] around the blue shadow, the absence of Hélène' (96). The characters revolve, like the insects round the light, round this absence/imminence. Celia, for example, wishes to tell Hélène that 'she was dead, [. . .] and above all [. . .] that we would never understand and accept that scandal because at the same time we were so to speak dancing around her, the Hélène light, a sort of Hélène reason' (158-9). Thus, the first line of *62*, looking back to *Rayuela*, could well have been 'Would I find Hélène?'

The lamp image is obviously one of randomness and senselessness. This intuition, however, cannot be applied too literally to the main body of the text, since, as we shall see, several distinct ordering forces have operated on its (original) randomness. Nevertheless, the aleatory intent is clear. As in *Los premios*, the lottery theme is all-important here: the presence of the Heliogabalus figure, M. Ochs, followed by the experiments of various characters (Marrast, Tell) are all images of the author's own *coup de dés*. There is a deeply felt mystique which leads to the belief that, in relinquishing authorial initiative, in 'céder l'initiative aux mots', the text will produce a new order and meaning. This trust in language, still seriously qualified in *62*, will become increasingly explicit in Cortázar's work. In *Prosa del observatorio*, for example, a slightly later work which, from clear lexical similarities,[5] was present in Cortázar's mind at the same time as *62*, we read of a force which 'is already flowing in a disorientated, liberated word, which seeks independently, which is also setting out from the sargassos of time and aleatory semantics, the migration of a language' (*PO* 12). Cortázar thus claims that *62* 'wrote itself', creating its own logic:

Do you imagine I knew what would happen after Marrast sent the anonymous letter to the Neurotics Anonymous? I knew some things, that the bureaucratic and aesthetic order of the Courtauld Institute would be disturbed by that foolish (*insensata*) action which at the same time was necessary and almost inevitable within the mechanism of the story ('a web of sense'!); but on the other hand I did not know that Nicole would give herself to Austin a hundred pages later, and that formed part of 'the other' (*lo otro*) which was biding its time beyond the 'known' (*lo sabido*).   (*UR* a 108)

Carlos Fuentes, in an essay on Paz, asserts that language alone can discover the truth of man, but that this personal truth can only be impersonal, that one must understand, 'once one has accepted the sovereignty of language over the author, that the only personal truth is an opening onto the impersonal and that every poem is collective: it is the semantic intention (*el querer decir*) of language itself'.[6] Though the logic of *62* is not purely linguistic, this idea, close to that of Lacan,[7] throws some light onto Cortázar's description of *62* as a 'drama which is *impersonal* in so far as the conscious minds and passions of the characters are committed only *a posteriori*' (*R* 416).

In the context of the exploratory nature of language, Cortázar quotes the following passage by Merleau Ponty:

Le nombre et la richesse des significations dont dispose l'homme excèdent toujours le cercle des objets définis qui méritent le nom de signifiés [...]. La fonction symbolique doit toujours être en avance sur son objet et ne trouve le réel qu'en le devançant dans l'imaginaire.   (*UR* a 109)

These perceptions can be sharpened by a brief examination of other passages from the same collection of essays: *Signes*. Merleau Ponty characteristically sees expression in terms of intentionality, but the 'intention significative' is sensed as originally empty, void (the 'absence' referred to by Cortázar). Only *a posteriori*, after the mediation of *la parole*, does the subject become conscious of the meaning of the void:

Exprimer, pour le sujet parlant, c'est prendre conscience; il n'exprime pas seulement pour les autres, il exprime pour savoir lui-même ce qu'il vise. Si la parole veut incarner une intention significative qui n'est qu'un certain vide, ce n'est pas pour recréer en autrui le même manque, la même privation, mais encore pour savoir *de quoi* il y a manque et privation.[8]

In Cortázar, language reveals the unknown in much the same way, with the significant difference that it works against the intention and resistance of the speaker, so that the intention is truly trans-individual. Juan realizes that 'the trouble with explanations was that, as usual, as they developed, they became a sort of second explanation for the person who was doing the explaining, which annulled or perverted the superficial explanation' (226).

Language in Merleau Ponty, however, is not seen as in Foucault[9] as something apart from man, foreign to him and potentially able to destroy him, and as suggested by the use of the techniques of

Roussel in *Los premios*, but the living process of humanity itself, its roots and history:

Les mots, même dans l'art de la prose, transportent celui qui parle et celui qui les entend dans un univers commun en les entraînant vers une signification nouvelle par une puissance de désignation qui excède leur définition reçue [...]. Cette spontanéité du langage qui nous unit n'est pas une consigne, l'histoire qu'elle fonde n'est pas une idole extérieure: elle est nous-mêmes avec nos racines, notre poussée et comme on dit, les fruits de notre travail.[10]

In so far as Cortázar accepts this means of discovery, it is ultimately to exorcize what is discovered about man, and free him from his subjection to it. Language reveals the subjection within the *figuras*, the 'patterns which were fulfilled from outside', but Juan's ambition is to 'leave one of those patterns behind' (233). 'La parole' is 'parlée par les préjugés',[11] but the uncovering of these basic *préjugés* serves as a negative indication of what lies behind them, 'de quoi il y a manque'.

MY PAREDROS

62 is a dialectic between the exploratory nature of language and experience, and forces which counter the liberation offered by this exploration: the conscious mind and its manipulation of the narrative. In this, it is a continuation of the double text of the earlier novels: the main narrative of *Los premios* and the monologues of Persio; the main text of *Rayuela* and the 'dispensable chapters'. A large part of *62* is narrated by the characters themselves or perhaps by that part of them which corresponds to the semi-character 'my paredros'.[12] Any character can be the *paredros* of another, though there are times when he becomes independent of all of them. 'My paredros' is thus a collective double and indicates a synthesis of the two previously separate factors of the double text and the double characters.

The role of 'my paredros' is complex, and I have found it helpful to approach it through the works of the Uruguayan Felisberto Hernández, quoted in 'La muñeca rota'. Cortázar quotes the following sentence from the story 'Por los tiempos de Clemente Colling': 'I do not believe that I should only write what I know, but also the other things (*lo otro*)' (*UR* a 103). *Lo otro* in Hernández's stories is usually the mystery of his childhood memories, from which he has become estranged, or the mystery of another person, often from his childhood. The sensibility of the language used when approaching the brilliant but seedy and ruined pianist Colling places this story on the level of 'El perseguidor'. It will be useful to reproduce the opening paragraphs of the story:

I do not really know why certain memories want to enter the story of Colling. They do not seem to have much to do with him. The relation with that period of my childhood and the family through which I got to know Colling is not so important in this affair as to justify their intervention. The logic of the link would be very weak. For reasons that I do not understand, those memories are attracted to this story. And as they are insistent, I have preferred to attend to them.

Moreover, I will have to write about many things about which I know little; and it even seems to me that impenetrability is an intrinsic quality of theirs; perhaps when we think we know them, we simply stop knowing that we do not know them; because their existence is inevitably obscure: and that must be one of their qualities.

But I do not believe that I should only write what I know, but also the other things.[13]

In 'Explicación falsa de mis cuentos', Hernández describes his fantastic short stories as plants with a life of their own, which totally subordinates intelligence: 'And it will teach the conscious mind to be disinterested' (*OC* IV 103). In his longer, less metaphorical investigations of his 'mystery', however, the relation between intelligence and spontaneity is more complex.

Like Cortázar, who talks of 'the breaking of all logical and especially psychological bridges' (*UR* a 108), he rejects all conscious ordering of his work: 'The logic of the link would be very weak.' He does this in favour of elements which seem to be spontaneously attracted to the narrative intention: 'For reasons which I do not understand, those memories are attracted to this story. And as they are insistent, I have preferred to attend to them.' In a similar vein, Cortázar asserts that 'it suffices to concentrate on a certain area: frequent analogies are attracted and jump over the wall of our specific subject' (*UR* a 104).

The elements of Hernández's stories, his memories, have the force and autonomy to break the ordering imposed on them by the conscious mind, and demand new articulation and meaning:

Some seem to protest against the selection which intelligence attempts to subject them to. And then they reappear unexpectedly, as if asking for new meanings, or making fleeting new gibes or pointing everything in a different direction. (*OC* II 49–50)

They are never still, constantly circulating and maintaining *en jeu* the mystery he seeks to elucidate:

Objects, facts, feelings, ideas: they were all elements of the mystery; and at each point in life, mystery arranged everything in the strangest manner. In that strange meeting of the elements of an instant, an object finished up beside an idea (perhaps neither of the two had had any relation before, nor would have later) [...]. Suddenly the mystery would shift unexpectedly; then I thought the soul of the mystery was a movement disguised as different things: facts, feelings, ideas; but suddenly the movement disguised itself as something still and was a strange object of surprising immobility.   (*OC* ii 102)

This is very close to Cortázar's idea of mystery: 'Mystery is not written with a capital letter as so many writers imagine, but always lies *between*, in the interstice. Do you imagine the I knew what would happen after [...]?' (*UR* a 108)

In another story, 'El caballo perdido', the relation between 'mystery' and 'intelligence' is studied more deeply. The dichotomy is expressed in slightly different terms: there is a *dédoublement* of the hero into the subject of the story, obsessed with his memories to the point of being totally alienated from the present, and his double, or 'partner', the representative of his life in the present and in society, of concepts, adulthood and remorse.

The parallels in the following two passages begin to make clear the similarities between Hernández's concept of the double and 'my paredros'. In the first, from Hernández's 'Tierras de la memoria', the body seems to be an embryonic form of the 'partner'. The dichotomy in the second passage, from *62*, is between an essential 'tacit life' and superficial, everyday life:

I was never particularly at home with my body; I did not even know very much about it. I kept up some relationships with it which alternated between clarity and obscurity, but always with interruptions which took the form of long periods of forgetfulness or sudden bouts of concern. At home they had looked after it like a little animal, were fond of it and treated it kindly. And when I undertook a journey, they charged me with looking after it. At first I accompanied it as if it were a very young child and I found it unpleasant to take on the responsibility of its care.   (*OC* iv 93)

What saves us all is a tacit life which has little to do with the everyday or the astronomical, [...] which bears little relation to our photographic identity [...], life like something belonging to someone else but which one has to look after all the same, the child we are charged with while its mother goes out on an errand. (62)

It is 'my paredros' who has the job of looking after this essential, subterranean life, seen as a child. 'My paredros' is described as 'an associate entity, a sort of *compadre* or substitute or baby-sitter of the exceptional' (23). A *compadre* is either member of the pair formed by the father and godfather of a child, i.e. a substitute father. A baby-sitter obviously fulfils the same role.

After the story of 'El caballo perdido' has been told, the subject realizes that 'he himself' has not told it, but his 'partner':

I felt the anguish of the person who discovers that unwittingly he has been working half and half with another and that it has been the other who has taken charge of everything [...]. I mused that it had been he, my partner, who had dealt, over my shoulder, with my own memories and intended to speculate with them: it was he who had written the story. (*OC* II 28–9)

He had left the memory alone, like the mother in the passage in *62*, while he attended to other business: 'He was like one of the family by now, and I could leave him alone, attend to something else and return to him' (*OC* II 28).

This is important because his 'partner' would falsify his memories on telling them, simplify them, suppress some, introduce foreign concepts from the 'city': 'Moreover, my partner would bring a lot of ideas in from the city, take away a lot of objects, change their lives and make them into servants of those ideas: he would repaint them and they would lose their souls and their clothes' (*OC* II 42). Perhaps most important, especially in the context of *62*, is the fact that the 'partner' would introduce the idea of sin and remorse into the memories of an innocent childhood, thus creating two sets of memories, the innocent and the contaminated, and a barrier between the subject and his own past: 'because I was on the other side of memories, those with their backs loaded with remorse' (*OC* II 38–9). This idea of sin is introduced by the almost commercial use made of memories:

In the person I was to become there was already a hint of the money-lender's smile at the value attributed to his memories by the person who takes them in to pawn them. The hands of the moneylender of memories weighed a different quality in them: not the personal past, loaded with intimate, private feelings, but the weight of their intrinsic value.[14] (*OC* II 34)

Nevertheless, the subject needs the 'partner' if he is to write at all, but accepts his help on the latter's terms: 'He helped me to convert my memories (even those which were loaded with remorse) into writing. And that did me a lot of good. I forgive him for his smiles when I refused to set my memories within the co-ordinates of time and space' (*OC* II 44).

This same dichotomy between the (pure) elements of a work of literature, Juan's memories presented chaotically in the spontaneous *coágulo* (clot) in the restaurant Polidor, and analysis, 'telling', is basic to Cortázar's novel. Juan realizes this as soon as he tries to come to terms with his experience:

As soon as I try to analyse, I will put everything into the good old reticular lunch box and falsify it beyond repair;   (11)
as if memory was of any use divested of that other force which in the restaurant Polidor had been able to cancel out the past tense in it;   (12)
that material which was becoming more and more language, an *ars combinatoria* of memories and circumstances, knowing full well that [...]
everything I recounted would be irremediably falsified, ordered, proposed as an after-dinner riddle.   (30)

But Juan too comes to the conclusion that he cannot do without his intelligence and language, that they are an integral part of him, that, parodying Ortega, 'he was that [intuition, visceral knowledge] *and* his thought' (13). It is interesting to compare this last statement with the following: 'There were even times when we felt that my paredros was so to speak existing on the margin of us all, that we were ourselves *and* him, like the cities where we lived were always the cities *and* the city' (28).[15] 'My paredros', on this level of analysis, that is writing, is a double who represents the attitudes involved in 'telling' (intelligence, language, anonymity), as against personal experience, in this case, that of Juan. In other words, 'my paredros' is the author of *62* in the same way as *el que te dije* is the author of *Libro de Manuel*, where Andrés makes the comment, 'In my case it was a personal affair and there was no reason why I should project it onto a sort of clarity for any third party, but *el que te dije* was in a different position' (*M* 212).

It is significant that the theme of the double is made most explicit when Juan begins to tell his story. He himself says, 'I will see Tell, and Juan (for it is possible for me too to see Juan at that moment in the zone)' (20). It is also significant that an increasingly impersonal use of verbs is made when Juan's telling his story is discussed:

He who is thinking that at some point he will have to start telling;

(16, my italics)

supposing that *he who* tells;   (19, my italics)

it will be necessary to start telling;   (15, my italics)

Of the city *there will be word* when its time comes (there is even a poem which *will be* quoted or *will not be* quoted).   (27, my italics)

'My paredros' exists when a member of the group in the 'zone' attributes to him something said or done which he is unwilling to accept as his own: 'The status of paredros seemed to consist above all in the way certain things that we did or said were always said or done by my paredros, not so much to evade responsibilities, but rather as if deep down my paredros were a form of *pudor*' (27).

As we have seen, it is the 'exceptional' which is delegated to 'my paredros', those aspects of the individual which are related to the 'city'. Or perhaps the 'city' is simply a product of the same operation, since 'to attribute any design or any action to my paredros always had a facet turned towards the city' (28). Exactly what is delegated is put in rather ambiguous terms: 'a delegating of what was one's own (*lo propio*) in that momentary dignity of somebody else's (*ajena*), without really losing anything of our own (*lo nuestro*)' (23). It is clear, however, that *lo propio* and *lo nuestro* are not synonymous: *lo propio* is personal, whereas *lo nuestro* is collective. The two are in a relation of antagonism, as can be seen in the even less explicit phrase, 'a force which came from myself against myself' (25). *Lo propio*, the most intimate part of oneself, is destructive, perhaps revolutionary in nature. To entrust it to 'my paredros' is, in a sense, to repress it, in order to defend *lo nuestro*, to defuse the threat. *Lo nuestro* would thus correspond to the anchylosed, conservative ego, 'our precious daily ego' as discussed with reference to *Los premios*. This interpretation of *lo propio* is confirmed to a certain extent by the fact that 'my paredros' is also entrusted with what is most innocent in the group, the 'damp innocence' (63) of Osvaldo the snail.

'My paredros' comes to be seen as used as a *comodín*, i.e. a playing card which loses its face value and can be used in place of any other card according to the necessities of the game: 'Being it [*paredros*] gave him something like the value of the *comodín* in a pack of cards, a ubiquitous and slightly disquieting efficacy which we liked to have at hand and throw on the table when circumstances demanded' (28). Thus, he fulfils a similar role to the money-lender in 'El caballo perdido', and it becomes increasingly clear that 'my paredros' represents 'l'être du langage', what is described in a passage quoted above as '*ars combinatoria* of memories and circumstances'. It is a significant paradox that the *paredros* should always be referred to as '*my* paredros', when he is a collective, impersonal construct. This is equivalent to the paradox of the Neurotics Anonymous believing that 'the individual is *unique*' (*UR* back cover, my italics).

Just as Hernández's 'partner' is seen as a mother ('a mother who warned me against a danger' (*OC* II. 41)), we have seen that 'my paredros' is a father figure (baby-sitter, etc.). Thus, 'my paredros' can be taken as the superego, that which represses, controls, orders and imposes sanctions. In this context, it is significant that it is 'my paredros' who takes over on the island (203), who pays in the café (147). More importantly, he is given the role of confessor – it is to him that Nicole confesses her infidelity, addressing him as 'padre, paredro mío' (171). Calac and Polanco form a group with 'my paredros' in this respect. Polanco, for example, becomes the confessor of Austin (120). Calac claims that he and Polanco have been like fathers to Marrast (152); Marrast himself calls Calac 'padrecito' (154). What is described as a *lapsus* on the part of 'my paredros' when receiving the confession of Nicole, the Italian phrase 'visto: se ne permette la stampa' (171), which would seem to be a sort of *imprimatur*, establishes him in the analogous role of censor.

Without wishing to digress too far, there is another aspect of Calac which links him with 'my paredros', as well as 'my paredros' with writing, and illustrates the vicarious, substitutive nature of this writing. Calac is presented at various points as being the author of the novel, the presence of Cortázar in it:

He was beginning to write a book as an antidote against bad memories;   (221)
The hand gripped the notebook, and the pencil had stopped at the word stopped;   (244)
Is that what I had abandoned my homeland for! Loads of essayists and critics reproach me for it with bitter words.   (151)

Calac's role in the novel and his description of writing correspond to all we have said of 'my paredros':

Yes, when you've been around a bit, you learn to be others too, to get inside their skins;   (204–5)
I don't count in the slightest in all this, let's say that I'm prepared to live vicariously, as if you were a character in one of my books.   (150)

In the examples quoted above, 'my paredros' emerges as superego, repression of personality and individuality, as substitution and language. There remains another aspect of him: his introduction into the story (like Hernández's 'partner') of elements foreign to any of the characters – conventional concepts which are never questioned, tested or felt, but which are taken for granted. This, of course, totally contradicts the original project of *62*. Such elements are introduced when 'my paredros' ceases to be one of the group, and becomes an independent agent:

A lot of things about the city must have come from him, because nobody remembered anyone else having said them, somehow they became part of what we already knew and what we had already lived of the city, we accepted them unquestioningly although it was impossible to say who had brought them first; it did not matter, all that came from my paredros, my paredros answered for all that. (29)

The word *tacit* often links 'my paredros' with such concepts:

My paredros served as a *tacit* testimony of the city; (27, my italics)
that *tacit* complicity which had gathered us round my paredros;
(83, my italics)
the status of paredros alluded, *as was well known*. (23, my italics)

The significant decision, for example, to eliminate any personal aspects from a conversation about Nicole and Marrast is *tacitly* understood: 'Between us it was *tacitly* understood that such problems were not collective and even less dialectical material, besides which they did not even seem to be problems' (132–3, my italics).

In this context, the 'zone', that is, the group of friends listening to Juan, can be taken as the readers of *62*. If much is tacitly understood by them, if they are likely to read conventional concepts into what they hear, then there is no point in telling the story, writing the novel, which would be able to say nothing new, discover nothing. The reader is perhaps warned against the *paredros* in him:

Supposing that he who tells the story were to tell it in his own way: that much were already *tacitly* told for those in the zone [...] one would have to ask oneself whether it makes sense for them to be there waiting for you to start telling it, for somebody at any rate to start telling it. (19–20, my italics)

THE COÁGULO

In 'Cristal con una rosa dentro', Cortázar relates an experience of his own which corresponds to the *coágulo* of Juan and becomes the nucleus of *62*. Various disparate elements, objects, memories and actions suddenly became linked for him in a unity, a *figura* which pointed to a 'different reality' (*UR* b 99). He makes the distinction, an important one in *62*, that experiences of this kind can either be experienced passively, or provoked intentionally. The two categories correspond to the *coágulo* and to the *coup de dés* of Marrast in throwing together the Neurotics Anonymous and a painting from the Courtauld Institute.

A passage from Nabokov's *Pale Fire* quoted in 'La muñeca rota' (*UR* a 107) brings us closer to seeing exactly how language works to discover *lo otro* and to order the 'original' chaos of the text. The two moments of Juan's experience can be clearly seen here too. John Shade, the fictional author of a poem within *Pale Fire*, faints and, while unconscious, believing himself dead, has a vision of a white mountain. He later reads an article of a woman who, having been resuscitated from a coma by a doctor, also claims to have seen a white mountain. He takes this coincidence as a confirmation of eternity, but it turns out that the woman had originally written 'fountain' rather than 'mountain'. 'Life everlasting based on a misprint!',[16] exclaims Shade. He comes to realize that it is impossible to gain any independent certainty or transcendent truth outside time. His experience nevertheless points to a truth which would lie in a pattern or structure within disorder:

> But all at once it dawned upon me that *this*
> Was the real point, the contrapuntal theme;
> Just this; not text, but texture; not the dream
> But topsy-turvical coincidence,
> Not flimsy nonsense, but a web of sense.
> Yes! It sufficed that in life I could find
> Some kind of link-and-bobolink, some kind
> Of correlated pattern in the game.[17]

A verbal coincidence which occurs in the Polidor restaurant produces in Juan a moment of eternity and unity, 'instantaneous plenitude' (14), an 'instant outside time' (12). This instant, however, immediately dissolves away into a network of analogies: 'the pure paradox of fleeing from the net which trapped it within the minute mesh of its own dissolution' (15). But it is this system of analogies which forms the *figuras* which later structure the whole text and constitute the unconscious motivations of the characters' actions. While the analogies hide and disperse this truth and presence, it is through the *figuras* that the characters (and the reader) have the opportunity of recovering what Juan was unable to grasp.

Juan's experience is essentially one of self-apprehension. He senses a vital force which is revealed to him as at once alien, 'this which comes from somewhere else' (13), threatening to the survival of his ego, 'a force which came from myself against myself' (25), and yet profoundly personal: 'profoundly mine' (19), 'what was most mine' (13). The total presence and 'instantaneous plenitude' that he fleetingly experiences can be understood both in its temporal implications ('memory which has escaped from its noose of time to be' (12), 'instant outside time'), and as an ontological presence. It is also a 'knowledge' of the deepest identity of Hélène.

The experience is, then, seen as total contradiction, present and immediately or simultaneously absent, 'something which was experienced as an instantaneous contradiction, which coagulated and fled simultaneously' (10). No sooner has Juan received this knowledge than he is 'expelled' from it: 'It cannot be that once again I should find myself at the centre of this that comes from somewhere else and at the same time be expelled from what is most mine' (13). It is this plenitude and knowledge which, after the 'expulsion',[18] becomes the absence (of Hélène) and the void (of meaning) discussed earlier.

The *coágulo* scene is both within and outside the time of the novel. Juan refers *back* to it at certain points (e.g. 'a succession of links which began who knows when, in the Blutgasse centuries before or one Christmas Eve in the Polidor restaurant' (219)), yet all the main episodes of the novel are presented as having happened *before* it. In so far as it is outside the time of the novel, the *coágulo* is an indication of an *original* presence, an experience previous to the structures of the alienated ego, of the type sought by Oliveira in Paris.

LA DIFFÉRANCE

Repression, postponement and recovery of lo otro: la différance

The expulsion discussed above presents an interesting duality: 'I got lost in analogies and bottles of white wine, I reached the edge and preferred not to know, consented to not knowing, even though I could have' (262). It is both an active refusal or repression ('I preferred not to know') of the knowledge and presence offered, and a passive complicity ('I consented to not knowing'). These two modes correspond to a certain extent, however, to both the psychological and linguistic levels of the phenomenon. If languages conceals and reveals, Juan represses and seeks.

If Juan represses the meaning of the *coágulo*, it is as a strategy of self-preservation, a defence of the 'precious daily ego'. He senses that it threatens the survival of his ego: 'a force which came from myself against myself'. The novel itself, Juan's expanding and recounting the *coágulo*, is, however, an attempt to recover the lost or repressed presence. Thus, what he does is effectively to postpone the assumption of the knowledge in order to avoid its possible cataclysmic consequences for his life. This coincides with the classical Freudian pattern:

Under the influence of the ego's instinct of self-preservation, the pleasure principle is replaced by the *reality principle*. The latter principle does not abandon the intention of ultimately obtaining pleasure, but it nevertheless demands and carries into effect the postponement of satisfaction, the abandonment of a number of possibilities of gaining satisfaction and the temporary toleration of unpleasure as a step on the long indirect road to pleasure.[19]

This postponement is incorporated into the literary and linguistic theory of Jacques Derrida. Language is based on a system of oppositions, differences: 'Dans la langue, il n'y a que des différences *sans termes positifs*.'[20] Thus, by its very nature, it cannot immediately express a unity or non-dual experience as such, 'an instant outside time', but temporalizes it, defers its possession (to the end of a word, sentence, work, etc.). The two important factors of 'differing' and 'deferring' are synthesized in Derrida's neologism *la différance*. This seems to be a similar idea to that expressed in the phrase 'the pure paradox of fleeing from the net which trapped it with the minute mesh of its own dissolution' (15). The hollow doll which passes from scene to scene in the novel, becoming increasingly heavy, is an image of this meaning *en souffrance*.

The *figuras*, in whose functioning we are initiated in the *coágulo*, are the medium of this *différance*, the trajectory of (in, through) the characters towards the recovery of the original presence (fulfilment of the desire). Analogously, they are codes by which the reader can reverse the entropy of the text, discover potential meanings.

The ambiguity of la différance *and the transformation of* lo otro

The recovery we have discussed is far from straightforward. Derrida asks whether *la différance* can in fact recover the presence or whether, with the repetition of sublimatory tactics, the death instinct and entropy will prevail, whether the presence is impossible and, in Cortázar's words, language will simply produce 'a fine, useless rain of dead moths' (27):

Nous touchons ici au point de la plus grande obscurité, à l'énigme même de la différance, à ce qui en divise justement le concept par un étrange partage. Il ne faut pas se hâter de se décider. Comment penser *à la fois* la différance comme détour économique qui, dans l'élément du même, vise toujours à retrouver le plaisir ou la présence différée par calcul (conscient ou inconscient) et d'autre part la différance comme rapport à la présence impossible, comme dépense sans réserve, comme perte irréparable de la présence, usure irréversible de l'énergie, voire comme pulsion de mort et rapport au tout-autre interrompant en apparence toute économie.[21]

The possibility of recovering through the *figuras* what was originally repressed is equivalent for Juan of reaching the rendez-vous in the subterranean 'city', presented as a final, unifying meeting with Hélène. A fundamental structural link is thus made with the pattern of recovery established in *Los premios* and *Rayuela*. The ambiguity of Oliveira's killing la Maga becomes far more important here. Oliveira kills la Maga both in order to purify, 'demonsterize' her, and to destroy the threat she posed to his life. This ambiguity is reflected in the recovery, which is presented as either a fulfilment or a punishment: 'paying or collecting'. What the *coágulo* tells Juan about Hélène, or what he reads into it, is that she is a monster, in that it links her with Erzebeth Báthory, a Hungarian 'vampire'. We have already seen that the only way to destroy a monster (a tabooed natural force) is to accept it, and that it is the refusal to accept this

force that makes it monstrous and decrees that it should be eliminated. Juan not only refuses the link between Hélène and Erzebeth
Báthory ('What were you doing here? You had no right to be among
the cards of that sequence' (31)), but insists on projecting the (*ipso
facto*) monstrous aspects of Hélène onto another character. More
exactly, this projection or transference has the effect of inventing
the monstrous character of Frau Marta.

Juan substitutes Frau Marta and the English girl for Hélène and
Celia:

> The first to yawn would be Polanco, and you too, Hélène, when instead
> of your name I started putting smoke rings or figures of speech. [...]
> right up to the end I will prefer to name Frau Marta [...], I will obsti-
> nately keep substituting a girl from Paris for one from London, one face
> for the other.   (36–7)

This type of substitution, when the story is told, has the effect of
altering the actual course of the plot. 'My paredros' is that part of
the characters or the narrative which carries out the substitution.
There are many instances of less important substitutions: when, for
example, Calac talks of 'my paredros' rather than of Marrast to
Nicole, out of *pudor*. Thus to *tell* a story is to substitute, which might
suggest why Tell, Juan's substitute for Hélène as a lover, is so called.

One very basic aspect of the novel is becoming clear, that is, that
there are two antagonistic forces in the narrative: those which go to
form the *coágulo*, and false, vicarious ones which are introduced
a posteriori:

> that instant outside time and what associations incorporate into it in
> order to attract it, to make it more yours, to bring it more over to this
> side;   (12)
> trying to distinguish between what rightly belonged to that abrupt
> conglomerate and what other associations were able to incorporate
> parasitically into it.   (11)

'Yours' in the first phrase is the opposite of 'what is most mine', and
'bring over to this side' means to defuse a threat, to make it as falsely
innocent as the exterior of the doll.

As in Lacan's analysis of 'The Purloined Letter',[22] the message
always reaches its destination, the *figura* is fulfilled. But the original
vital message of the *coágulo*, what was seen as 'most mine', becomes,
through the *détour* of *différance* and substitution, increasingly alien.
When the doll-novel of M. Ochs is broken open, and meaning
finally extracted, it is seen to contain something terribly repulsive.

Juan's substitution indirectly confirms and ratifies the taboo on the vital force, and Hélène's action is interpreted as, indeed becomes, vampirism. On her arrival at the rendez-vous, she is executed as a vampire.

THE CODES

The coágulo, *genesis of the codes, their archetypal nature*

A brief outline of the stages of the episode is necessary. The first element is Juan's inexplicable purchase of a novel by Butor, *6 810 000 litres d'eau par seconde*, which he has no intention of reading. The second is his sensing the presence of the Countess Erzebeth Báthory on a street corner. The street names are important in spite of Juan's denial that 'there was anything about that corner to remind him of the countess' (17): the word *vampire* is clearly present in *M*onsieur le *P*rince and *VAugIR*ard. Lastly, on entering the restaurant, with the same absolute absence of motivation, he opens the novel and reads a passage containing the name of Chateaubriand at exactly the same moment as another diner orders a *château saignant*. This verbal coincidence reactivates in him a literary knowledge of the Hungarian Countess Erzebeth Báthory: 'the legend, the mediocre chronicle that Juan had read years earlier' (18). The repetition of *château* refers him to the castle of Csejth, the habitual residence of the countess, and *saignant* to *sanglant*, from the title of what was probably the chronicle mentioned, Valentine Penrose's *La comtesse sanglante*.[23] The coincidence is expanded when he orders a bottle of Sylvaner: 'Sylvaner, which contained in its first syllables as in a charade the middle syllables of a word where in its turn throbbed the geographical centre of a dark ancestral terror' (24). The reference is to Transylvania, homeland of the early Báthorys and the traditional territory of vampirism.

The novel opens with a series of questions which suggest a traditional type of causality: 'Why did I go into the restaurant Polidor?[24] Why, now I've started asking questions like that [...]?' (9) Such causality is however soon destroyed: 'Any possible ordering of the elements seemed unthinkable' (27). The elements of the *coágulo* are in a causal relation of mutuality; they 'cause' each other. It is impossible, for example, to decide whether Juan bought the book because he was going to enter the Polidor, or whether he entered the restaurant because he had bought the book.

The group of coincidences is referred to as a 'constellation': 'the constellation would emerge intact' (14); 'the privileged horror of the constellation' (21).[25] The concept of constellation is an important element in the thought of Jung:

> The term simply expresses the fact that the outward situation releases a psychic process in which certain contents gather together and prepare for action. When we say that a person is 'constellated' we mean that he has taken up a position from which he can be expected to react in a quite definite way. But the constellation is an automatic process which happens involuntarily and which no one can stop of his own accord. The constellated contents are definite complexes possessing their own specific energy.[26]

In a later work, 'Synchronicity, an acausal connecting principle',[27] Jung develops the idea of constellation in an unexpected direction, expanding it to cover the field of actual events. Groupings of chance happenings are made meaningful by the activation of unconscious archetypes.[28] He posits a correspondence between the psyche and the world of phenomena similar to Leibnitz's 'pre-established harmony'. One type of synchronistic occurrence is described as 'the coincidence of a certain psychic content with a corresponding objective process which is perceived to take place simultaneously'.[29] It is quite clear that Juan's experience falls within this category. The 'psychic content', his sensing the presence of the countess, is confirmed by the 'corresponding objective process' of the verbal coincidence. Jung notes, as does Juan, the ambiguity of the relationship between the subjective state and the objective process: 'The numinosity of a series of chance happenings grows in relation to the number of its terms. Unconscious – probably archetypal – contents are thereby constellated giving rise to the impression that the series has been "caused" by the contents.'[30]

All this has important consequences for our text. The coincidence of two or more elements in the text 'constellates' an archetypal content in the reader and the character, as is the case with the story of Erzebeth Báthory. At the same time, this constellation gives meaning[31] and order to the randomness of the (original, hypothetical) text. Thus, we have the 'previous opening' (C 18) demanded by Cortázar, and the impression is given that the text has produced its own meaning. This seems to be what Cortázar means when he talks of 'being conscious that the plot (la trama) should produce the text rather than it being the latter which conventionally wove the plot and was subjected to it' (UR a 107).

The Polidor episode is thus a model of how the text itself produces the *figuras*. Whereas in *Rayuela* the *figura* was formed by the repetition or, at least, influence of the acts of partially the same group of people elsewhere and thus on a different level, in *62* the *figuras* are based mainly on independent literary texts and myths which will be referred to here as 'codes'. These texts are given the 'numinosity' of archetypal structures, unconscious patterns which dictate the behaviour of the individual and the functioning of reality. Various sub-codes can be distinguished. They appear in a different way from the main ones, of which they can be seen as versions, and have a slightly different status, but will not be studied separately. The histories or myths of the following have been studied as codes:

(a) Parsifal;
(b) Diana and Actaeon (connected with *La mariée mise à nu par ses célibataires, même*);
(c) St Sebastian;
(d) Erzebeth Báthory (connected with Sheridan le Fanu's character Carmilla);
(e) La Malcontenta;
(f) Heliogabalus.

The emergence of the codes in the text

The emergence or genesis of the other codes is not nearly so magical as that of the Countess, though they do follow the pattern described quite consistently. There are parallels to be drawn between their emergence and the appearance of 'my paredros'. 'My paredros' emerges from a situation, from an act or acts of communication, as the *moi* of the individual or group, or more interestingly, its *moi-autrui* as in the phenomenology of Merleau Ponty: 'From postcards from Tell or news from Calac, from the web of telephone calls that went from destination to destination, there arose a picture of my paredros which was no longer that of any one of us' (28–9). The text of the novel is similarly conceived of as a web (*tejido*), a mobile,[32] a system of signs from the many combinations or constellations of which a set of codes and hence *figuras* emerge, like 'my paredros' from the 'web of telephone calls'.

Any reference to 'my paredros' has the effect of by-passing the process of the actual production of a code; having him introduce a code aims to give the impression that it has emerged spontaneously from a sort of metatext. The code is introduced either directly by 'my paredros', as in the case of the myth of Diana and Actaeon ('Do you know what my paredros called me one day? Actaeon. He's very cultured, you know' (235)), or in an ill-defined letter or a reported conversation. Once constellated by a knowledge of the literary text or myth both in the characters concerned and in the reader,[33] the code creates the *figuras* in the text. Readings of otherwise often meaningless elements are made possible through the codes, which give different meanings and articulations to seemingly banal or unintegrated episodes. The *figuras* are created or indicated by textual means – echoes and analogies within the 'web' of a type similar to the 'château saignant'–'Chateaubriand' word play.

The Countess emerges in the word play mentioned and constellates in Juan the literary archetype of Valentine Penrose's *La comtesse sanglante* (or any other account of Báthory's life), 'the mediocre chronicle that Juan had read years earlier'.

The Heliogabalus code emerges in a conversation in a greengrocer's shop. Roger, the greengrocer, retells the porter's version of the 'crimes' of M. Ochs, and this constellates in Juan the literary archetype: 'The lottery of Heliogabalus suddenly took on an interest in Juan's eyes which it had never had in the days when he used to flick listlessly through the chronicle of Spartianus Aelius' (100).

The code of St Sebastian emerges in a dream of Marrast which does not even correspond to him. (In this sense Marrast is the *paredros* of Juan. He has the 'ironic notion that he was robbing images from Juan, that it was the latter who should see Hélène like that during his bouts of insomnia' (92–3).) He sees Hélène tied to a tree and pierced by arrows, which constellates in him the code of d'Annunzio's libretto for Debussy's *Le martyre de Saint Sébastien*: 'At one time, when I was young, I had known long passages of the poem off by heart, and especially that moment when everything seemed to condense and revolve around the marvellous line, "j'ai trop d'amour sur les lèvres pour chanter", which now came back to me with the image of the torture of Hélène' (92).

Great emphasis is placed in the last three examples on the distance of the literary memory: 'that Juan had read years earlier'; 'which it had never had in those days when'; 'once, when I was young'. This distancing of the texts has the effect of investing them with an archetypal aura, of situating them almost in the unconscious of the characters concerned.

The Parsifal code emerges in a letter written by Polanco and related to Tell: 'Because Polanco suggests that there is a lot of the Parsifal in that English lad' (89). This constellates her knowledge of Wagner's libretto: 'Austin, *"der Reine, der Tor"* ' (89).

The Malcontenta code emerges in Marrast from a state of semi-consciousness, a state where 'we feel truth right here in the middle of our stomach, that same truth which, later on, with our eyes open, we refuse to accept' (73). There does not seem to be any literary version of the legend.[34]

The second set of codes, which are in a sense 'added', vary in means of presentation from those discussed above. They are made less explicit, their texts are more modern. *La mariée mise à nu par ses célibataires, même*, for example, a 'glass' by Duchamp, emerges in a strange passage about Hélène attributable to no particular character in the novel (77). Not being an actual text with any measure of development (though we have the *Green Box*), it affects the novel in only a slight way. It does nevertheless add nuances to the Diana code.

The text of 'Carmilla', a vampire story by Sheridan le Fanu, also seems to be operative in the novel. Apart from one mention of this author (85), no direct reference is made to the text. There are, however, distinct parallels between the two texts, which will be explained later. In this case, however, the actual text is not all-important. The influence of the pretty well-defined genre to which it belongs is more significant.

READINGS OF THE TEXT THROUGH THE CODES

Parsifal

It is to Austin that most features of Wagner's Parsifal are attributed. Parsifal was brought up by his mother in complete ignorance, so that he might avoid the fate of his father, killed in war. He is the 'guileless fool', *der Reine, der Tor*, referred to in the prophecy made to Amfortas:

> By pity 'lightened
> A guileless Fool;
> Wait for him,
> My chosen tool.[35]

Austin too is totally innocent as is seen in the extremely amusing account of his unfortunate experiences with the prostitute Georgette.

He lives with his mother (94), who treats him as if he were a child (173).

Just as Parsifal, dazzled by the passing of knights in splendid armour, abandons his mother, Austin is lured away from his mother's side and from the protection of the Neurotics Anonymous by the 'tartars' and Celia: 'I recognize that you have opened up new horizons for me' (146). He is seduced by Nicole as Parsifal comes close to being seduced by Kundry. When Parsifal is rejected by the knights of the Grail because of his ignorance, he goes off in search of the holy spear originally in the keeping of Amfortas and treacherously had from him by Klingsor. On retrieving it, he uses it to heal the wound of Amfortas.

Juan's desperate search for Hélène in the 'city' can also be read through this code. When Parsifal recovers the magic lance from Klingsor, Kundry curses him and predicts that he will never be able to find his way back to the castle of Amfortas (*Pa* 28–9).

Another character from *Parsifal*, Kundry, provides a number of readings. Having been present at the Crucifixion, she had mocked Christ, and since then, in various incarnations ('She-Lucifer! Rose of Hades! / Herodias wert thou, and what else? / Gundryggia there, Kundry here' (*Pa* 29)), had been forced to search for Christ through the ages to 'stand before Him in deepest woe'. But whenever she comes near him, she laughs again and all is lost:

> Through endless ages for thee I've waited,
> The Saviour – ah, so late!
> At whom I scoffed in hate.
> Oh! –
> Couldst thou know the curse,
> Which through me, waking, sleeping,
> Through death and lifetime,
> Joy or weeping,
> While ever steeled to bear fresh woes,
> Endless through my being flows! –
> I saw Him – Him –
> And – mocked Him! [...]
> I caught then His glance, –
> I seek Him now from world to world,
> Once more to stand before Him:
> In deepest woe –
> Sometimes His eye doth seem near,
> His glance resting on me.
> Returns then th'accursed laughter on me, –
> A sinner sinks in my embraces!   (*Pa* 45)

She is under the control of the evil Klingsor, now in possession of the holy lance, and is often summoned from her sleep to carry out his orders. Hence her desire to sleep peacefully: 'Oh, unending sleep, / Only release, / When – when shall I win thee?' (*Pa* 32) After these missions, or, from the point of view of the Knights of the Grail, absences, she is found stiff and only half alive, and resuscitated by Gurnemanz. When not required by Klingsor, she tries to make amends by acting as servant to the knights and travelling to distant places in search of a potion to soothe the wound of Amfortas inflicted by the holy lance. Klingsor forces her to seduce her victims, as she did with Amfortas, and it is only by being rejected in her seduction that the curse can be broken.

When Parsifal arrives at Klingsor's castle to recover the lance, Kundry is ordered to seduce him. She kisses him, and on this kiss Parsifal feels, mingled with passion, a sharp pain in his side. This pain is the pain of Amfortas's wound and, by extension, the wound in Christ's side. Parsifal is thus revealed as the Christ-figure for which Kundry has been searching; Kundry's attempted seduction of Parsifal as an involuntary repetition of the Crucifixion; her laughing at him, her possible saviour, as a repetition of her mocking Christ.

There are various signs in *62* which point to the fact that Hélène can be read as Kundry. Just as Kundry has lived in several incarnations, Hélène too has been the Countess, and Frau Marta. (The repetition of archetypal structures clearly evokes the idea of reincarnation.) Kundry is summoned from her sleep to the side of Klingsor in the same way as Hélène is forced to walk through the streets and hotels of the 'city'. Kundry's search for Christ is Hélène's endless search for the person or place where she will be able to rid herself of the packet, symbol of her guilt, that she is obliged to carry. There is a significant suggestion that Hélène has already been in this place in the past: 'a lift which ended in something that Hélène no longer remembered' (145). Hélène, like Kundry, longs for true, peaceful sleep: 'perhaps before that, in order to get some real sleep afterwards, she would succeed in reaching the room where they were waiting for her' (144); 'perhaps I would have been saved without realizing it [. . .] and then it would be possible to sleep as you are sleeping' (176). The 'accursed laughter' of Kundry is the involuntary laughter of Hélène after her night with Juan: 'I heard her laugh a dry laugh [. . .]. The shaft of light pierced the final moments of

Hélène's laughter and Juan saw on her face [...] an expression of primordial evil, an unwitting refusal of her own desire' (258).[36] Just as Kundry makes up for her misdeeds by tending the wounds of Amfortas, Hélène is by profession a kind of nurse: an anaesthetist.

Given this identification of Hélène, three important episodes of the novel can now be read according to the *Parsifal* code: the death of the young man referred to as *el muchacho muerto*, Hélène's rape of Celia, her subsequent conversation with Juan and the night they spend together. These episodes are linked together in a *figura* by the repetition in them of certain elements and by other analogies existing between them, some perceived by the characters, others of which they are presumably unaware.

The identity, for example, between Juan and the 'dead lad' who dies under the anaesthetic administered to him by Hélène is established by Hélène herself: 'Something in the cut of his hair [...] had reminded her of Juan' (103); 'I didn't kill you for pleasure', she explains to Juan (238). Another element, 'pulling up the sheet', establishes a common identity between even more characters: Celia puts to bed the doll that Tell (Juan) had sent Hélène, and then expects to be treated in the same way: 'the little girl who puts her doll to bed [...] and then [...] expects the same gestures to be repeated with her, [...] to have the sheets pulled up to her neck' (166). The same element is repeated in the case of the 'dead lad': 'someone would have pulled a white cloth up to the dead lad's chin' (166). Finally, Hélène imagines Juan saying to Tell: 'You ought to give the doll to Hélène', and 'pulling the sheet up to her neck before going to sleep' (167). Thus, the common identity of Juan, the doll, the 'dead lad', and Celia is firmly established, 'and so Tell's doll was Celia who was the dead lad' (166–7).

A second important element is opening or wounding. Hélène 'wounds' the lad by giving him an injection in the arm. He would also be opened up in the post-mortem, hence his identification with the doll: 'They would already have opened him up as one opens up a doll to see what it has inside' (168). Celia's body is described as 'opening' when she is raped by Hélène: 'the naked skin opened up with lashes of foam' (183). It is only shortly after this scene that the doll falls and breaks open.

The following reading of these three episodes according to the *Parsifal* code is thus possible. The death of the young lad is the crucifixion of Christ. This is borne out by several factors: the 'initial' aura given to his death at several points in the text, for example 'at the end (but that end had perhaps been the beginning) the image of a dead lad in a hospital' (81). His last words before dying, 'hasta luego', promising an imminent, unfulfilled return, also take on new significance. The guilt felt by Hélène, which will be discussed in greater detail later, is that of Kundry at having mocked Christ at the Crucifixion.

Kundry's encounter with Parsifal is staggered over the following two episodes, perhaps to express the dislocation of time, destiny and consciousness in this episode, perhaps to attain a greater density of meaning in the scene with Celia, which is the cross-roads of several codes. Celia is an emissary of Juan, the presence of Juan, in that she 'is' the doll which was indirectly sent by Juan: 'Now I know that you are the real doll, not that blind little machine sleeping [...], and he who sent you is here, he has come with you, carrying the doll under his arm' (175). Juan, in turn, is the 'dead lad', and thus Christ–Parsifal.

Celia, then, represents the possibility of salvation for Hélène. Her presence in Hélène's bed ceases for a moment to be a 'scandal' (the death of the lad–Christ was 'the absurd, a scandal' (103)): 'Somehow there was no scandal and [...] she was so to speak reconciled, accepting without protest the disorder of Celia being in her house and her night' (170). We will see that the 'disorder' that Hélène has always rejected is that which Juan represses in the Polidor scene. Celia's vitality and innocent naturalness is the possibility of making reparation for her sin, and gaining salvation by restoring life to the 'dead lad':

If I could take away a little of all that life you have without hurting you, without pentothal, if I were allowed to use the perpetual tomorrow which envelops you and take it to that basement where there are people crying uncomprehendingly [...] and he opened his eyes and felt the warmth of return, of forgiveness entering his veins [...], perhaps I would have been saved without realizing it [...] and wake up closer to you, and to Juan, and to the world, to the beginnings of reconciliation and forget-fulness. (176)

Her rape of Celia, Kundry's attempted seduction of her saviour Parsifal, becomes an unwitting destruction of her possible salvation. Her idea of a closer, more physical union with Celia is introduced in such an unobtrusive, yet totally unexpected fashion (charac-teristic of Cortázar's style) as to give it the force of destiny, or a curse: 'a hope and now this new element, Celia, this new element which is perhaps another way of understanding or of finally destroying oneself' (178). The breaking of the doll, the revelation of its (presumably) putrid contents (the putrefaction of sin) is a confirmation of the inevitability of the failure of her attempt.

The relation between the arrival of Celia and a previous (original) sin is exactly that which exists between the arrival of Juan and the earlier rape of Celia, which renders his arrival futile. Hélène still harbours the hope that Juan can save her: 'She said yes, she would stay with him, she asked him to throw the doll into the rubbish bin, to free her of the last remnants of the smell of death in her house' (259). Various elements, however, point to the fact that her night with him is simply a repetition of her night with Celia: her impression that Juan has already been in her flat ('Are you sure you haven't been here before?' (224)); her involuntary laugh similar to that of Kundry; the doll, still lying in the cupboard as if on an operating table.

The nature of the experiences described in these three scenes breaks, as did the initial *coágulo*, with any conventional conception of time. Thus, we have strange sequences like the following, when Celia sees the contents of the doll: 'She screamed without understanding, her scream was an understanding previous to herself, a final horror preceding blind flight' (186). She understands and is responsible for an act which took place centuries before her birth: the Crucifixion. Though this act puts an end ('final horror') to an age of 'innocence', it was the beginning ('preceding') of our own, a headlong rush ('blind flight') to hide and forget. Hélène too realizes that the timeless repetition of archetypal structures makes nonsense out of concepts of time: 'At the extremes, thought Hélène, [...] in ultimate situations, the before and the after touch and are one' (144). Celia's weeping is likewise timeless, being a repetition or continuation of an 'original' grief: 'Before and after it was [...] the same remains of an interminable weeping which had begun in the midst of darkness, so many centuries before, in such a different world that it was exactly that same world where now [...]' (185). The tragedy lies, of course, in the irreversibility of the temporal succession within the repeated archetypal pattern: 'Why him first and afterwards you, why him before and you after. To believe that one can reorder the factors, abolish that death from here, from this futile hope of insomnia, what stupid deceit' (176-7).

As we have already seen, the *Parsifal* code 'emerges' in Tell. It is also Tell who sends the doll, the 'carrier' of the codes, to Hélène, confirming and activating the latter's role as Kundry. Tell would seem to be, at this point, the *paredros* of Hélène. On closer examination, Tell turns out to be a less well-defined Kundry, almost an 'echo' of Hélène–Kundry. (There are many seemingly meaningless echoes of this type, which perhaps have the function of 'jouer le hasard', i.e. giving the impression of chaos from which order emerges.) Looking back at Tell's emphatic rejection of the attributes of Kundry ('but on the other hand, I'll be damned if I'm like Kundry' (89)), a familiar pattern of wounding occurs. She is present when Juan cuts himself while shaving, immediately after she has announced her visit to the 'city'. Her having been there means a change in their relationship, in that she no longer cures his wound, but in a sense causes it: 'That distances you, makes you an active agent, you are on the side of the wound, not the bandage' (61).

A few days later, while drinking Campari (Cam*pa*ri – *Par*sifal?), Tell remembers another accident to someone dear to her, the death in a road accident of her negro lover. The stretcher on which he is carried (87) links him to the 'dead lad' (234). The description of his death suggests that it was a sort of crucifixion: 'his red car twisted round a tree trunk' (87). Hélène, martyred as St Sebastian, is 'tied to a tree' (92). His name, Leroy, also suggests Christ. It is from the coincidence of this memory-postcard from the dead ('the past on its back with its eyes open, all those dead folk who sometimes send postcards' (87)) and the postcards from London with news of Austin ('It's almost insolent the way they all talk about Austin in those postcards they send of the Tower of London' (89)) that the idea of Parsifal eventually emerges.

Immediately after this 'emergence', there is a very interesting lapsus on the part of Tell: 'don't you think I'm in absolutely brilliant form, that I'm the worthy whore of an interpreter from [...]?' (89). This later surprises her: 'Why did I call myself a whore before this inconsequential fantasizing in front of the mirror [...]?' (89). Her calling herself a 'whore' indicates her assumption of the role of Kundry. It is thus not surprising that the next step is to imagine herself seducing Austin–Parsifal: 'almost on the point of imagining Austin in bed' (89). Rejecting this aspect of Kundry, she defines herself in Kundry's second role: 'I don't fit the definition of the term at all, in fact I'm the great consoler, she who washes my little numbskull's love wounds' (89–90); 'I wash him of words' (86). Kundry was both the seducer of Amfortas and tended his wounds. She also washes the feet of Parsifal. When Tell goes to look after Nicole, she both bathes her (212), and is referred to as the 'trained Nordic nurse' (249).

Actaeon and Diana

We have seen that several characters take on the same role from an archetypal text: Hélène, Nicole and Tell can be read as Kundry. Similarly, one episode can often be read according to several codes. After the introduction of the Actaeon code by 'my paredros', the relationship between Juan and Hélène can be read, not only by the *Parsifal* code, but by the former too. The myth recounts that Actaeon, while out hunting, comes across Diana bathing with companions and pauses to gaze at her. Angry that a mortal should have seen her naked, she sprinkles him with water and changes him into a stag, whereupon he is torn to pieces by his own hounds.

Hélène sees Juan's love for her as an intrusion into her private life which has the effect of leaving her naked: 'The passage of your image through any of someone else's memories strips me naked' (140). She describes him as 'my denouncer, he who through loving me and being loved strips me and leaves me bare and makes me see myself as I am' (141). There are two scenes which can be read as Actaeon's seeing Diana naked. The first is a minute account of Juan putting sugar into Hélène's coffee, when Celia observes 'a refusal, an infinite rejection of Juan's gesture' (142). It is as if Juan, after glancing at her, 'bitterly submitted to an injustice' (143). The second instance is when Juan sees her cry in her flat, and senses that having witnessed this intimate scene constitutes a threat to him: 'I would have liked to spare her it, return her to her courteous distance so that some day she would forgive me for having witnessed that defeat' (236). (This weeping is also the conclusion of the *Parsifal* code: Kundry finally weeping when baptized by Parsifal.)

It becomes obvious that, even before this second occasion, Juan has already been punished for the offence: 'I am not Diana [explains Hélène] but I feel that somewhere in me there are dogs waiting and I would not have liked them to tear you to pieces' (238). The idea of the consummation of the punishment is introduced by a strange non-sequence of tense between 'there are' and 'I would not have liked'. The teeth of the dogs were the needle she used to anaesthetize the 'dead lad': 'now they use intravenous injections, symbolically, of course' (238). The resultant paradoxical treatment of time is exactly the same as in the episodes affected by the *Parsifal* code. In the latter it corresponds to the nature of the story, as well as to the idea expressed here – the dislocation of time between the 'city' and the 'zone', between unconscious intentionality and consciousness: 'One kills somebody long before receiving him at home and giving him whisky and crying over his death while he offers us his handkerchief' (238).

The code also orders the otherwise inexplicable occurrences of dogs in the text. In Juan's poem on the 'city', there is a feeling of dread together with the anxious search for the meeting place. The dread is described as a 'dog': 'something which is not yet fear but which has its shape and its dog' (32). The rendez-vous with Hélène is a meeting of separation, or as Cortázar would call it a *desencuentro*, and this separation is the 'dog': 'you were lost and shouting in my city, so near and unfindable, for ever lost in my city, and that was the Dog, it was the rendez-vous, without appeal it was the rendez-vous, separated for ever in my city' (35). What separates them is the attitude involved in Hélène–Diana's killing the 'dead lad'–Juan–Actaeon. When Tell relates to Juan how she saw a dog in the 'city' (65), this is an anticipation of his fate. When Austin is bitten by a dog in Bath (230), (apart from the Bath–Báthory echo) he is probably contaminated by the meaning of the word which, as we shall see, is repression and taboo. Hélène too sees dogs (169), and people looking for dogs (166) in the 'city'.

La mariée mise à nu par ses célibataires, même

The mention of Hélène as 'la mariée' does little but confirm the Actaeon code. The similarity between Duchamp's glass and the classical myth is clearly brought out by Paz in *Apariencia desnuda*. In the glass, however, the myth is given a more critical dimension: 'la mariée' is composed of what seem to be agricultural instruments; her relations with her uniformed admirers are expressed in mechanical terms; she is exited by the 'love gas' from her own containers. Significantly, Hélène's life is also seen as a machine: 'your soul is a cold machine' (112); 'the rigorous machine of my life' (141). In this version of the myth, there is not even the human contact of violence.

Le martyre de Saint Sébastien

One receives the impression from certain formal similarities between the codes that one produces the other. It is a basic oxymoronic structure that links the Actaeon myth with *La mariée*, as Paz suggests: 'I have already pointed out the similarity between the myth of Actaeon and the two works by Duchamp: the gazer is gazed at, the hunter is hunted, the virgin strips in the gaze of him who gazes at her.'[37] The same relationship is present between these two codes and a third, d'Annunzio's *Le martyre de Saint Sébastien*, the story of the 'archer struck by arrows' (77). The oxymoron is, in fact the most salient feature of that work:

Je suis le but qui est frappé / et je suis le trait qui le frappe.[38]
Est-il vrai qu'au solstice / tu as blessé le ciel? / – Le ciel / m'a blessé.[39]
Je meurs de ne pas mourir.[40]

The role of St Sebastian is difficult to attribute to any one particular character in the novel. Marrast, for example, believes that in his dream St Sebastian was Hélène, but later realizes that this was the result of unconscious censorship, and that he had really dreamed about Juan, whom he would presumably like to see crucified. The name of Hélène's murderer, however, Austin (in Spanish, Agustín), might point to the latter's identity with the 'César Auguste' of the work, Diocletian, responsible for St Sebastian's death. The problem is of little importance as the series of oxymora expresses a major theme of the work: the contradiction between traditional psychology and the pattern of behaviour imposed by the codes, between personal freedom and predestination.

Though less obvious, there are important, unindicated coincidences between archetypal characters mentioned in *62* and others, from different codes, which are not mentioned. These coincidences serve to increase the 'numinosity' of the attributions. One of the most significant is the similarity between Kundry and a character from *Le martyre de Saint Sébastien*, 'la Reine malade des fièvres', who was also present at Calvary, and since then has lived on in various incarnations, as Magdalâwit and Mariamme. She was entrusted then with the Holy Shroud and with it cleaned the blood from Sebastian's cut hand, another 'repetition' of the wound of Christ. She herself is 'une plaie divine'.[41] Her wound was a cavity burned into her breast by an angel as a resting-place for the shroud. Could there be an echo of this in Hélène's murder by Austin: 'Hélène did not live to know where that fire that was entering her and opening out right in her breast came from and who had caused it' (266)?

Erzebeth Báthory

The initial *coágulo* links Hélène with the Countess Erzebeth Báthory. The *coágulo* scene, however, is presented, as we have seen, as both previous to the main body of the novel and later. This has two consequences here. Firstly, Hélène is only *potentially* the Countess, and secondly, although the reader has been introduced to the code, it has not necessarily emerged in the 'zone', that is, in the minds of the characters.

The Vienna 'emergence' is far less spontaneous and convincing than those previously discussed. It is prepared by an almost gratuitous introduction of the archetypal text by Juan in conversations with Tell. On arriving in Vienna, he tells her the story of the Countess simply because she had lived there, and Tell becomes obsessed with it: 'I was a little worried by that mental vampirism which the countess had exercized on Tell because of me the first nights in Vienna when I had talked to her at length about the countess' (80). He had introduced her to the story of the dolls of M. Ochs on a train journey to Calais and, due to a strange synchronistic occurrence ('right at the end of the story of Monsieur Ochs' (109), a woman had entered the compartment with a box from which she had taken a doll), had decided to give one of the dolls to Tell.

After such an elaborate preparation, it is not surprising that a pattern seems to emerge from a series of rather forced coincidences. Wandering through the streets of old Vienna, Juan comes across the *Basilisken Haus*. The sculpture of a basilisk[42] he sees there immediately creates in his mind a constellation of figures. The Vienna basilisk reminds him of the basilisk brooch worn by Hélène and the silver basilisk ring of M. Ochs. There is a fourth element in the constellation which Cortázar gives the impression Juan is trying to play down (it is mentioned twelve pages after the main grouping): 'Had the arms of the countess perhaps contained some fabulous animal, perhaps a salamander?' (108–9). Her arms did in fact contain, as the cultured Juan would know, the dragon of the ancient Báthorys. This fourth element has the effect of linking Hélène to the Countess. Juan also attempts to break the link between Hélène and M. Ochs by arguing that it is not so much Hélène's basilisk that reminds him of M. Ochs, as the atmosphere of the Blutgasse (Blood Alley), the residence for a time of the Countess, whose fame as a torturess reminded him of the mutilated dolls of M. Ochs. The forced nature of the argument is reflected in the prose:

The Blutgasse was ever present, and so having remembered Monsieur Ochs was not perhaps so much a consequence of the basilisk house which led me to him through Hélène's brooch, as perhaps of the dolls, in that the dolls were one of the signs of the countess, who had lived in the Blutgasse, since all Monsieur Ochs's dolls had ended up tortured and torn after the affair in the rue du Cherche-Midi.   (96)

Now that the presence of the Countess in the novel has been established, it will be useful to give a brief account of her activities. She lived in Hungary from 1560 to 1614. Suspected of being a lesbian, she showed incredible cruelty and perversity towards her servants during the absences of her soldier husband. An extremely attractive and vain woman, she was particularly preoccupied with the whiteness of her skin. On noting one day that the blood on her own skin of a girl she had punished especially cruelly left it white and smooth, she began to experiment in this direction, hoping to slow up or halt the ageing process. Aided by her servants, who scoured the countryside for victims, she slaughtered hundreds of girls, and is claimed to have bathed in their blood. Her eventual punishment was to be walled up in a room of her castle, and left to die.

Two points must be made in relation to Cortázar's treatment of the Countess. Though by her activity she wished to ward off death, she was not a vampire in the traditional, literary sense. Though often associated with Gilles de Rais, and known to be under the influence of the witch Darvulia, her activity was not consciously sacrilegious like that of her French counterpart. Thus, Cortázar's attribution to the code of religious connotations is significant in relation to the meaning which he himself wishes to attach to it, and forms a common denominator with other codes:

Or perhaps the blasphemous, the continuous transgression which the countess's life must have been [...]. One could not help thinking that the countess must have particularly enjoyed blood on a night like that, amidst the bells and midnight masses.   (17–18)

The basilisk with which she is associated also has sacrilegious connotations. It is seen to wear a crown of thorns (108), and not just
the normal crown or crest from which the animal takes its name.

Only after the presence of the Countess has been established in
this way does Frau Marta, an innocent if slightly sordid figure,
come to be seen by Tell and Juan as the heiress to her inclinations.
This constitutes a different pattern from that followed with other
codes, where the emergence of a code and its attribution to a
character, the forming of a *figura*, is simultaneous.

The signs which point to a common identity between Frau Marta
and the Countess are extremely subjective, and the idea is first
considered simply as a hypothesis: 'I eventually accepted that the
evocation of the countess was at least a valid working hypothesis'
(80). Juan and Tell were bored in Vienna. Their linking Frau Marta
with the Countess and more generally with vampirism is presented
as a game to fight off this boredom: 'The atmosphere of the hotel
must have had something to do with it, or the tedium which would
overtake us and which we fought off in that way' (78). The episode
is described by Tell as an 'invention' to pad out the vacuity of their
lives: 'For want of a future worth its name, which means a future
with Hélène, one has to invent one and see what happens' (87).
Sinister aspects of Frau Marta are snatched upon in order to confirm
the hypothesis: her hands, for example, 'were rather like owls, like
blackish hooks' (79), a description worthy of Valle-Inclán. Literary
references of a type not found elsewhere in *62* also point to the
'apocryphal' nature of the episode. Sheridan le Fanu (85), John
le Carré (127), Raffles (162), and Nick Carter (162) are mentioned,
while Tell is 'absorbed in a spy thriller' (94). Use of thriller techniques such as the suspense created by leaving thirty pages (129–160)
between parts of the episode also point in the same direction.

Carmilla

The points discussed above (that Frau Marta is presented as a
vampire in the literary tradition; the lack of spontaneity of the
constellation; the very literary nature of the episode; Tell's talk of
invention, etc.) suggest that Juan and Tell introduce a new, different
force into the novel, which then acts as a secondary, 'false' archetypal
code for 'later' episodes, transforming and replacing that of the
Countess.

The name of Sheridan le Fanu is mentioned. It would seem that the code that Juan and Tell introduce is the text of the latter's vampire story 'Carmilla'. Thus, if it is true that Frau Marta is made a vampire to clear Hélène of any connexion with the Countess (i.e. the dangerous, revolutionary force repressed by Juan), then the transference is totally counterproductive, as Hélène's 'later' action is dictated by this second, even more sinister code.

'Carmilla' is a more or less straightforward vampire story. A young girl, Carmilla, is accepted as the guest of a noble Styrian family and befriends the daughter of the house, Laura. At the same time, young peasant girls in the vicinity start dying mysterious deaths. The relationship between the two girls becomes increasingly lesbian and morbid. Laura begins to suffer from a strange wasting disease and 'dreams' at night that Carmilla is at the foot of her bed in a blood stained night-dress, or in the form of a cat. She also experiences a pleasant sensation focused below her throat. A wound is discovered at that spot, and Carmilla is revealed to be the vampire Mircalla, and definitively killed in the traditional fashion.

Several elements in the Hélène–Celia episode seem to confirm the hypothesis. Just as Austin discovers a mole on Celia's body, Carmilla–Mircalla has a similar mole on her neck – the mark left when she was 'visited' by a suicide-vampire and changed into a vampire herself. The sensation felt by Laura, when visited by Carmilla, is repeatedly described as that felt while bathing:

Certain vague and pleasant sensations visited me in my sleep. The prevailing one was of that pleasant, peculiar cold thrill which we feel in bathing, when we move against the current of a river.[43]

When Celia awakes to a realization of what Hélène is doing to her, she remembers that she has been dreaming about bathing in a Yugoslavian swimming pool:

It must be a beach or perhaps the irregular edge of a large swimming pool [...]. Celia half opened her eyes in the dark and realized that she had been dreaming; as always, like everybody, she felt the injustice of waking already far away, without even being able to remember who had been with her a second before, someone who must have just come out of the water because there was still a sort of feeling of dampness around, an idea of bronzed skin and summer.   (181)

It is later suggested that the 'dream' had been provoked by Hélène's caresses: 'Hélène's hair lashed her mouth with the sea smell of her dream' (182).

One patent result of Juan and Tell's contrivance is that the episode of Frau Marta and the English girl is too easily and literally read, whereas the reading of other parts of the novel according to the codes is symbolical. The transference, nevertheless, produces the text: Frau Marta is eventually discovered making her way through the hotel towards the room of the English girl, whom she has captivated by her knowledge of Viennese monuments. The old lady enters the room, followed by Juan, and with the co-operation of the English girl, undresses her. Though her intentions were presumably to bite her throat, she does not finish the act. Two teeth marks, however, are clearly visible: 'the fact that Frau Marta's lips had not yet pressed against the English girl's throat, and that the mark of consummation should scarcely be distinguishable as hardly more than two minute purple spots easily mistaken for two moles' (179). These marks take on the significance of inherited stigmata. Although nothing has actually happened to the girl, it is already too late when Juan arrives: 'So they had got there too late, they already knew so without having to say anything to each other, and it would have been almost ridiculous to shout, to put on the light and wake up all the hotel for something already consummated, which could not get worse even if it were repeated an infinite number of times' (174).

This dislocation of time is surely analogous to the impossibility of Kundry being saved by Parsifal (though she eventually is) since the curse of her seductions will force her to repeat her original mocking of Christ; to Hélène's futilely receiving Juan, whom she has already killed. There remains the question of the responsibility for the chain of vampirism. Though it is in a sense independent, it seems to lie to a certain extent with Juan and Tell, in that it was they who provoked the Frau Marta episode. There is a semi-conscious realization in the characters themselves of their complicity: as Tell muses, '*Tiens*, now I remember that last night I asked Juan whether we might not unwittingly be the accomplices of Frau Marta' (88). Juan, after making an effort to understand why, for example, Frau Marta had left her door open and why she was seemingly unaware of their presence, again becomes indifferent, and 'everything merged back into a passive acceptance which was not far from complicity' (179).

It is according to the Frau Marta–Carmilla episode, which becomes a secondary code, rather than according to the actual history of the Countess, that Hélène's rape of Celia must be read. The doll is the first link between the two episodes in that, just as Tell had received it before the happenings in the hotel, Hélène receives it from Tell shortly before Celia comes to her flat. The phrase 'at the foot of the bed', mysteriously repeated throughout the novel, serves to establish the identification of Celia with the English girl, whose pyjamas, removed by Frau Marta, 'fell at the foot of the bed in the exact shape of a lap-dog curled up at the feet of its mistress' (180). Likewise, Celia's dressing-gown 'had finished up at the foot [of the bed] in a ball' (185). Celia's warning that 'there will always be one of my stockings on the floor at the foot of the bed' (117) points in the same direction. Another pointer is Hélène's impression that Juan was present in her bedroom when she was with Celia (as he had been present in the original scene in the Vienna hotel):

Poor Juan so far away and so miserable, all that could have been different if he had been at the foot of the bed in the dark, looking once more for the answer which now arrived too late, for nobody;   (170)
He who has sent you is here, has come with you, carrying the doll under his arm.   (175)

Hélène is rather unexpectedly linked with the English girl by an insistence on their both having their eyes open in the dark. This is characteristic of the 'undead', as can be seen in Bram Stoker's description of Count Dracula in his coffin: 'He was either dead or asleep, I could not say which – for his eyes were open and stony, but without the glassiness of death.'[44] A strange aspect of this link is that Hélène here seems to be the original model for the English girl, rather than the other way round. Attention is focused on Hélène's eyes at various points: in bed with Celia, she has 'her eyes always [still?] open in the darkness' (170); in the midst of their reconciliation, Juan 'saw her eyes wide open, with dilated pupils, an expression of primordial evil' (258). Even after her death, her eyes remain obstinately open: 'Face upwards, Hélène's eyes were open' (266). It is with these data in mind that it is 'inevitable' (163) that the girl should have her eyes open when visited by Frau Marta (though they are presented 'afterwards', and indication of the non-linearity of the narrative, the necessity of more than one reading). The fact that the girl should be awake leaves Juan on the point of understanding the situation, as if he had some knowledge of what was to happen, or had happened, between Hélène and Celia:

'Suddenly and darkly he thought he understood why [...] the English girl was awake' (178–9).

The temporal and causal relationships between the two episodes thus become totally paradoxical in a way characteristic of the whole novel. After witnessing the Frau Marta scene, Tell sends the doll to Hélène (unconsciously but significantly realizing that it really belongs to the latter (190)), whereupon the rape takes place; Hélène senses the presence of Juan in her room, which suggests that he had already been present at a similar scene. Yet Juan's impression of *déjà-vu* on seeing the English girl's eyes suggests the opposite temporal sequence – that the Celia–Hélène scene is previous. Juan too senses the paradox: 'just like that night in the Polidor restaurant crossing like a shot through something which was not exactly memory, suddenly there, in absolute violation of time, everything on the point of being explained with no possible explanation' (179).

The most overt link between the two episodes pointing towards Hélène's 'vampirism' is the insistence on her touching Celia's neck and throat, the two words being repeated eight times. This motif is repeated elsewhere in the novel with slightly bizarre results if taken as anything more than an echo: Juan's throat is painful after his night with Hélène (263), which would suggest that he has become her victim; Austin is brought into the group when he seeks 'Nicole's neck with a first lukewarm kiss' (173).

Hélène's death can be read as that of a vampire. One traditional way of destroying a vampire is to pierce its heart with a pointed stake[45] and Hélène receives the fatal blow 'right in her chest'. In this, it is the death of Carmilla, not that of Erzebeth Báthory. Vampirism is one of the most important themes in the novel. It is chosen by Cortázar due to the obvious 'monstrosity' of the vampire, and because the self-perpetuation of a chain of vampires is a very eloquent image of the timeless repetition of unconscious archetypes.

La Malcontenta

This code seems to concern almost exclusively Nicole and Marrast. It is linked to the Countess code in that, just as the Countess was punished for her crimes by being walled up in her castle, the 'Malcontenta', a lady of the Foscari family, was exiled to a Palladian villa of her own in the Moranzano area near the lagoon of Venice, to expiate the sins of too loose a life. The code emerges when Marrast, in a state of semi-wakefulness, gives Nicole the name 'la Malcontenta'. This reminds him of the legend they had heard in Venice and how, on the road between Venice and Mantua, Nicole had suddenly become sad and fully conscious of the fact that she no longer loved Marrast, but Juan.

Bracketing off for the moment her own motivations and the 'chance' happenings which make her act possible, Nicole's seduction of Austin must be read as fulfilling her role as Malcontenta. The guilt which henceforth surrounds her and her subsequent punishment when she is carried off by Frau Marta along the canal of the 'city' (perhaps the Brenta canal, which leads to the Villa dei Foscari or Malcontenta) is thus logical within the code. Not only Marrast, but also Juan (his *paredros* at this point, as is seen in Marrast's vision of Hélène's punishment) play the role of strict male justice present in the legend. When Marrast writes to Juan (though nominally to Tell (192), a typical substitution) about Nicole's infidelity, he does not have the address and decides to make a paper boat with the letter and post it on the Thames. This boat becomes the one Juan launches on the Saint Martin canal: 'He smoked without taking the cigarette out of his mouth while his hands were automatically constructing a little boat with the blue paper from the packet: afterwards, approaching the edge, he threw the boat into the water' (263). *Automatically* suggests the involuntary nature of his act. Juan's boat in turn becomes the barge on which, the 'following' night, he sees Nicole prisoner on the canal of the 'city' (267).

Heliogabalus

Various different aspects of Heliogabalus are emphasized by different commentators on his life, and most of them seem to be present in *62*. The code is therefore extremely rich, indeed, most of the characters and the actual writing of the novel seem to be affected by it. Heliogabalus's greatest claim to fame is the fact that he is said to have been the originator of lotteries.[46] These lotteries have impressed for two reasons. One is the disparity between the prizes: 'Ellus Lampridius, in *The Life of Antoninus Heliogabalus*, relates that the emperor wrote the destinies designated to his guests on shells, so that one received ten pounds of gold and another ten flies, ten dormice, ten bears.'[47] The other, the enjoyment the emperor took in witnessing the bloody fights over the prizes in the people's lottery:

Chacun se dispute ces dons; lui cependant rit des coups que l'on se porte. C'est ainsi que, dans ses largesses au peuple, au lieu de distribuer de la monnaie, il expose au pillage des bœufs gras, des chameaux, des ânes, des cerfs. La mêlée que ce pillage occasionne, est pour lui un spectacle d'autant plus divertissant, qu'il y a plus de monde de blessé; car l'esprit de cruauté semble présider à toutes ses folies.[48]

One must be careful not to attribute the moral tone of nineteenth-century commentaries like the one above (though seemingly echoed by Juan (100)) to Cortázar, who would, one suspects, share Artaud's enthusiasm for the emperor. Artaud insists on his anarchism, the chaotic mixing of opposites in him, especially the male and female principles, as in his religion, that of the god Baal:

Mais ce qui beaucoup plus que l'Androgyne apparaît dans cette image tournante, dans cette nature fascinante et double qui descend de Vénus incarnée, et dans sa prodigieuse inconséquence sexuelle, image elle-même de la plus rigoureuse logique d'esprit, c'est l'idée de l'ANARCHIE.[49]

His homosexuality or androgynous nature leads him to a fascination with castration which he imposes on others as if, according to Artaud, he himself were the victim:

[...] au milieu des castrations qu'il impose, mais qu'il impose chaque fois comme autant de castrations personnelles, et comme si c'était lui-même, Elagabalus, qui était chatré. Des sacs de sexes sont jetés du haut des tours avec la plus cruelle abondance le jour des fêtes du dieu Pythien.[50]

Herr Urs: Cambio de piel

In the context of the creation of M. Ochs, there is a curious coincidence, worthy perhaps of commentary. Written at the same time as 62, Carlos Fuentes's Cambio de piel has a character, Herr Urs, who is similar to M. Ochs in many ways. The coincidence begins with the names: 'Ur' in German means 'aurochs', Bos primigenius. 'Ochs' means 'ox'. Like M. Ochs, Herr Urs made, or rather repaired, dolls. The dolls he received were subtly transformed, their innocence destroyed. Each male doll would be given some female attributes and vice versa: 'One hussar displayed, under his little jacket with gilt buttons, a little lace bra'.[51] Herr Urs is a sort of terrorist, his work a recreation of 'the original catastrophe which we will never recover as unity'.[52] His attitude is contagious but will destroy those who cannot face their freedom: 'The rebel infects the world with freedom [...]. The unknown freedom which makes us ill because we have believed that health lies in subjection.'[53]

When I asked Fuentes about this, he replied that the two authors had been amazed and amused on exchanging the relevant chapters and summed up their reaction in the following way: 'Let's let the critics tie themselves in knots.' A further indication of the affinity between the two authors appeared with the Mexican's *Terra Nostra*, where various ambiguous archetypal figures, recurring throughout history, are associated with the advent of the millennium.

THE DOLLS, GUILT

Perhaps the most outstanding characteristic of the dolls of M. Ochs (like those of Herr Urs, and like Heliogabalus) is their sexual ambiguity. The first of the hollow female dolls he circulated, opened by *Eve*line *Rip*aillet (*Eve* because in it the young girl discovers sin; *Rip* – Jack the Ripper, a favourite figure of Cortázar)[54] contained what was presumably a penis: 'An innocent little girl [...] turns up holding in her hand, like that... [...] Roger took his realism to the extent of lifting up a certain vegetable and proposing it to the world with a gesture which Juan thought sublime' (98). M. Ochs was an anarchist (precursor of the *pre-Joda* in *Libro de Manuel*), who aimed to create public scandal and at the same time generate a mistrust in what is presented to society as most 'natural'.

The most important aspect of M. Ochs–Heliogabalus's activity is his experimentation with, and demiurgical control of, chance. It is impossible for the individual to know what is inside the doll he has bought, since the prizes vary as much as those of Heliogabalus: 'a used toothbrush or a glove for the left hand or a thousand-franc note' (99). In this context, the aleatory–anarchistic gestures of Tell and Marrast and the *coup de dés* of the author himself all take M. Ochs as an archetype.

The codes in the novel are fulfilled through causal chains established by chance, rather than by (indeed usually against) the conscious intentions of the characters. The presence of M. Ochs is felt at key moments in these chains, for instance when Nicole seduces Austin: 'the first kiss on the mouth in a doorway decorated with plaques concerning the import of guaranteed Swiss toys' (173). This would confirm M. Ochs's 'lottery' as the distributor of the codes. This chance distribution is epitomized by the trajectory of the doll which identifies Hélène with the Countess–Carmilla.

The doll is originally given to Juan by M. Ochs himself. After telling Tell about M. Ochs on the train and the chance entry of the woman with another doll, Juan decides to give it to Tell. He has it sent from Paris to Vienna by 'my paredros'. Tell 'capriciously' sends the doll to Hélène; Celia 'accidentally' breaks the doll and its contents are revealed.

What the doll contains when it arrives at its destination, though not made explicit, represents guilt and sin: ' "It wasn't a suspicion," said Hélène, "there was no possible word for it. A sort of blot or vomit, if you like" ' (231). The lack of verb or attribution in this last sentence is very characteristic. The guilt is given no *locus* in Juan, Hélène, or the doll. The guilt felt by Nicole and Marrast is very similar; 'It wasn't even a question of forgiving him because it was not his fault, it wasn't anybody's fault, the worst sort of fault lodged there like an intruder who eventually got himself accepted' (70).

This brings us to one of the most important paradoxes in the novel, that is, that the guilt is involuntary, and seemingly independent from the person who feels it ('as if the fault [*culpa*, guilt] had travelled of its own accord in that doll' (232)), yet at the same time the contents of the doll vary, and this particular doll concerned them, and no one else: 'It's as if at the bottom of it neither you nor I had anything to do with it. But it's not like that and we know it. It has happened to us, not to anybody else' (232). Their guilt becomes a destiny which is fulfilled through a network of chance occurrences: 'Thus, underneath and in spite of all the chance and the improbabilities and the ignorance, the path was abominably straight and went from him to Hélène' (226). They are, nevertheless, totally responsible for this destiny created by chance: 'all his responsibility in that which had happened through the double chance of a whim and a blow against the floor' (226–7).

In order to expand and dialecticize this contradiction, the following sections examine the relation between the *figuras*, the 'patterns which are fulfilled from outside', and the guilt connected with them; the symbolic, labyrinthine 'city'; the real situation and behaviour of the characters in the 'zone'.

THE FIGURAS

The pattern of transgression of taboo and subsequent punishment is the common factor of all the codes and the *figuras* they create in *62*. The 'offences' can be divided into two groups, those connected with sexual taboo and those involving a specifically Christian concept of sin and related to the Crucifixion. In relation to the second group, it is significant that the novel opens on Christmas Eve and that various elements in Juan's supper at the Polidor give it connotations of the Mass.

In the first group, la Malcontenta breaks the taboo on sexual freedom in the woman; the Countess at least that on sexual heterodoxy; Heliogabalus breaks the taboo on homosexuality and indeed most social conventions. Actaeon comes up against the most radical taboo of all, perhaps at the base of all the others, where all human and sexual contact is outlawed, even the vision of the naked body. Here, the isolation of the individual is decreed absolute.

The second group is formed by *Saint Sébastien* and *Parsifal*. Kundry's offence is to have mocked Christ on the cross. St Sebastian's offence is simply a belief in the outlawed religion of Christianity. His crucifixion is a repetition of that of Christ. The wound of Amfortas, the pain of Parsifal when kissed by Kundry, and the cut on Sebastian's hand are repetitions of the wound of Christ.

The punishments are as follows: la Malcontenta is imprisoned in her own house; the Countess is likewise walled up in her own castle; Heliogabalus is slaughtered (M. Ochs imprisoned); Actaeon is torn to pieces by his own hounds and, likewise, St Sebastian is pierced by his own arrows; Kundry is condemned to search throughout the ages for a Christ-figure in order to undo her original offence.

The protagonists of the *figuras*, most obviously the Countess Erzebeth Báthory and Heliogabalus, are clearly the monsters of previous works. In *Rayuela* we saw the return of the monster as a redemptive force after its original death as promised in *Los reyes*. The force behind the monster, the 'other side' of man, his lost presence and unity, returns in *62* in a literary form much as expressed by Fuentes[55] in the following passage from a chapter which can be summed up by the exhortation 'Pity the monsters!':[56]

Can't you see that nature ordered them to do that and that sanctimonious old Orestes, a real boy scout in buskins, when he wrung the Furies' necks, was only giving them the advantage of negation: allowing them to reappear with their blood poisoned but with the pretence of order, without the real spontaneity of their place in the world, disguised as order to sow disorder? But there you are: the heroes of Antiquity invented literature because they obliged the natural forces to hide and reappear in disguise.[57]

It is up to the characters (their good faith, rebellion, consciousness of language, etc.) to separate this 'natural force' from the monstrous aspects added to it by 'literature' and with which it is only tenuously linked in the *coágulo*, and thus avoid its condemnation and destruction (punishment) inherent in the code. Guilt in the lives of the characters is thus of fundamental importance. For them to rid themselves of guilt on assuming the rebellious force of the monster is equivalent to breaking the repetition of its repression, the fulfilment of the code. Their attempts to do so are most clearly seen in the symbolism of the 'city'.

THE CITY

Literary antecedents

The influence of Butor's *La modification* is suggested by the novel that Juan buys in the first pages of *62* and later abandons in a doorway. There is a similar episode in *La modification*, where the character buys a book without knowing the author, which he never reads, but which becomes the book he will write in order to come to terms with his experience. The novel is an account of a journey which the character makes from Paris to Rome in order to offer his Roman lover a post in Paris, thus breaking with his own family and past. As the journey goes on, he gradually abandons the idea when he considers that the charm of his lover Cécile lies simply in the fact that she represents for him the idea of ancient Rome, and will disappear when she is in Paris. His nostalgia for Rome is a nostalgia for a centred world, 'une croyance secrète à un retour à la *pax romana*, à une organisation impériale du monde autour d'une ville capitale'.[58]

The distance which opens up between the character and Cécile is the reflection of a larger gap between modern civilization and the Golden Age of Rome:

Mais maintenant qu'elle s'est déclarée il ne m'est plus possible d'espérer qu'elle se cicatrise ou que je l'oublie, car elle donne sur une caverne qui est sa raison, présente à l'intérieur de moi depuis longtemps, et que je ne puis prétendre boucher, parce qu'elle est en communication avec une immense fissure historique (*Mo* 274).

It will be the function of the novel to bridge the gap between the two civilizations where the character has failed personally: 'Ce serait pour moi le moyen de combler le vide qui s'est creusé, n'ayant plus d'autre liberté, emporté dans ce train jusqu'à la gare, de toute façon lié, obligé de suivre ces rails' (*Mo* 272). Though he personally is not free, his novel will be an image of a freedom possible in the future, and, in a sense, will establish that freedom: 'Donc préparer, permettre, par exemple au moyen d'un livre, à cette liberté future hors de notre portée, lui permettre, dans une mesure si infime soit-elle, de se constituer, de s'établir' (*Mo* 274). The novel will abolish the absence of Cécile in the same way as *62* that of Hélène, 'combler le vide de ces jours à Rome sans Cécile' (*Mo* 273). (There are two Céciles: the Cécile of the *cité éternelle* and the woman–Cécile in Paris, as there are two Hélènes: the Hélène of the 'city', the 'deep' Hélène, and the Hélène of the 'zone', of the Juan who 'still hoped to have tea with Hélène' (77).)

Though the preceding notes may throw some light onto the nature of the 'city' in *62*, there are even greater similarities between *62* and the novel planned in *La modification*, that is, the idea in Butor's work of an almost physical interpenetration of Rome and Paris. By turning a corner in the area of the Panthéon in Paris, one might arrive in the streets near the Roman Pantheon. Only certain privileged people would be able to find the access to the other city: 'On pourrait imaginer ces deux villes superposées l'une à l'autre, l'une souterraine par rapport à l'autre, avec des trappes de communication que certains seulement connaîtraient sans qu'aucun sans doute parvînt à les connaître toutes' (*Mo* 277). But just as the 'city' in *62* is usually referred to as 'my city', conserving a certain measure of individuality, and varies according to the person who visits it, it is also possible that the Parisian and Cécile would miss each other there:

Cette femme romaine de temps à temps passerait à Paris; ayant longue-ment voyagé pour la retrouver il s'apercevrait qu'involontairement sans doute elle est parvenue au lieu même qu'il vient de quitter, recevant une lettre d'un ami la décrivant par exemple,
    de telle sorte que tous les épisodes de leur amour seraient conditionnés non seulement par les lois de ces relations entre Rome et Paris, lois qui

pourraient être légèrement différentes pour chacun d'eux, mais aussi par le degré de connaissance qu'ils en auraient (*Mo* 280).

The relation between the 'city' and the 'real' cities in *62*, Paris, London, and Vienna, is very similar:

One or other of us had had the experience of passing from the city to a bed in Barcelona, unless it was the other way around;   (22)
Any image of the places we frequented could be a delegation of the city, or the city could delegate anything of its own [...] onto the places we frequented and lived in at the time.   (23)

Juan, for example, entering the 'city' from Vienna, sees Hélène who has entered from Paris. She does not, however, see him, since her task in the city is different from his.

It is likely that there is some relation between the mysterious packet that Hélène is forced to carry through the 'city' and hand over at a place not revealed to her, the contents of which are only partially discovered by the reader at the end of the novel, and the box carried by the soldier in Robbe-Grillet's *Dans le labyrinthe*. The character has forgotten the name of the street where he had agreed to meet the person to whom he was to give the box, which is finally revealed to contain only the uninteresting possessions of a dead soldier.

Some of the physical aspects of the 'city' seem to be related to the paintings of Giorgio de Chirico: the arches, towers, chimneys and vague red light. The anguished atmosphere is reminiscent of Kafka, and of some of the stories of Martínez Estrada, such as 'Sábado de Gloria', and 'La cosecha'. As a sort of Hades, it has much in common with the nether regions of Buenos Aires described in the 'Informe sobre ciegos' in Sabato's *Sobre héroes y tumbas*, and by Marechal in *Adán Buenosayres* as 'Cacodelphia'.

The 'city' and the rendez-vous

The 'city' is a symbolic account of the deep aspirations of the characters, the progress of which is monitored in much the same way as that of the passengers in *Los premios* by Persio. The labyrinthine streets of the 'city' have much in common with the corridors of the *Malcolm*, and to visit it is the descent to Hades discussed in relation to other novels and stories. Though the more obvious symbolism

of the descent is found in an intermediate level between the 'zone'
and the 'city', where Eurydice is the 'dead lad' Hélène wishes to
bring back to life by descending to the morgue, a parallel recovery
is, nevertheless, present in the 'city'. To reach the rendez-vous
there (the stern of *Los premios* and the 'centre' or 'unity' of *Rayuela*)
is to recover the force and possibility of Hélène, her true nature,
present and lost in the *coágulo*.

The passivity of the characters' actions in the 'city', 'where there
was always something passive about walking: it was so inevitable
and decided, so fatal' (102), indicates the dictation of their lives by
the codes and their negative connotations, but also the impersonal
search for a state which would transcend such connotations, as
described in chapter 62 of *Rayuela*: 'inhabiting, foreign forces,
advancing in search of their citizen's rights; a search which is
superior to us as individuals' (*R* 417).

Indeed, one invariable activity in the 'city' is an anguished and
often frustrated search: 'It was as if Nicole was looking for (and
could not find and it was heart-breaking) those necklaces with big
blue stones which were sold in the streets of Tehran' (59). The
necklaces do not hide the real object of the search – the rendez-vous.
Juan searches relentlessly for Hélène, and is always prevented from
reaching her by the inert masses of passengers on the trams; Hélène
for the rendez-vous where she would hand over the packet containing the doll.

Perhaps even more important is the constant search for cleanness.
It is clear from our discussion of the contents of the doll and the
references to a 'blot' or 'vomit' that the feeling of dirtiness in the
city is an indication of guilt. Juan makes this presence very clear
in his poem: 'to arrive where it is necessary and putridness, rottenness is the secret key in my city' (33). The desire to find a shower
or toilet symbolizes the desire to rid oneself of this guilt. It occurs in
all the main characters:

[Marrast:] to look as so often before for a bathroom;   (82)
[Nicole:] You were always tired and sort of dirty in the city, and that
was perhaps why so often you wasted an endless amount of time in the
corridors of the hotel which led to the bathrooms where it was then
impossible to have a bath because the doors were broken;   (244)
[Juan:] You have to go out of the lift and look for a shower or a toilet
because you have to, for no reason, because the rendez-vous is a shower
(*ducha*) or a toilet, and it is not the rendez-vous, to look for happiness
(*dicha*) in your underpants [...].   (34)

The near-equivalence of *dicha* and *ducha*, 'happiness' and 'shower', is significant, and perhaps an additional indication that cleanness is a prerequisite to reaching the rendez-vous, or rather to the rendez-vous signifying the culmination to a process of self-realization. 'After the shower I shall go to the rendez-vous', says Juan (34). Similarly, for Hélène, to reach the rendez-vous is to hand over the doll and its contents, after which, she would be free (to love Juan). She must 'go on and carry the packet to the place of the rendez-vous, and perhaps only then, from that moment on [...]' (257).

The rendez-vous would offer Juan the possibility of a final possession of the real Hélène, union with her: 'that last illusion, that the rendez-vous would be with him' (257). Hélène hopes the rendez-vous will be the rebirth of the 'dead lad', i.e. the Juan who had offered her the knowledge she had been unable to face and had repressed. It would also suppose the destruction of her guilt. On arriving at her rendez-vous, she imagines that 'the dead lad was calling her [...] so that Juan would wake up naked in bed to receive the packet and destroy for ever the rottenness which it doubtlessly contained' (265–6). In a sense, this union is a union with the lost part of themselves – the *coágulo* was a revelation of the truth of both Juan and Hélène in the same way as Medrano's dream of Bettina in *Los premios* was really about himself.

Finally, the rendez-vous would free them from subjection to the codes, the repetition of repression and destruction of vitality, 'as if reaching Hélène and freeing her from the weight of the packet could have closed, left behind one of those patterns which were fulfilled from outside, as if finally to meet in the city could have washed them of one of those faults (*culpas*) which travelled of their own accord' (233). Juan's phrase about journeying in the 'city' 'towards a destination which I know but which I will forget on my return' (32) is perhaps an additional indication that the rendez-vous presents the possibility of recovering a presence lost at some point.

Their hopes, however, are far from being realized, and the two real events in the 'city' confirm the pattern of punishment in the codes. Hélène is given the death of a vampire by Austin on arriving at the rendez-vous, and thus effectively transformed into a monster. Austin is significantly referred to at one point as St George the dragon-killer: 'little St George [...] who disembowels your basilisks' (261). Nicole, imagining Juan offering her a cigarette by the canal, is approached with a similar offer by Frau Marta and carried off by the latter on a barge, presumably to become a vampire too. The meeting becomes 'a rendez-vous with fingers, with pieces of flesh in a cupboard' (32). The trams in the 'city' are a possible meeting-place for Juan and Hélène, and also an image of destiny: 'Destiny is always waiting in trams' (189). They too are turned into monsters and destroyed: ' "That's why there are less and less of them", said Tell brilliantly, "men have realized and are killing them, they are the last dragons, the last gorgons" ' (189).

Such transformation or 'monsterization', introduced by *différance*, substitution, and bad faith, determines the whole development of the novel. Two amusing possible examples of this process can be seen in the transformation of the most innocent characters into their opposite. The change is indicated only anagrammatically: *Feuille Morte* is linked with *Frau Marta*, and O*sBaldo* the snail, whose 'damp innocence' is an important image within the novel, with the *basilisco*. (The vampire of le Fanu's 'Carmilla', Mircalla, is similarly linked to her more innocent identities Carmilla and Marcilla.)

THE ZONE: REBELLION

The code articulates a taboo, which is, as we have seen, a negative indication of a vital force. In order to liberate this force, the logic of the code must be reversed by some form of transgression: 'In the light of archetypal figures, any prohibition is an obvious piece of advice: open the door, open it right away' (*UR* b 50).

The clearest example of this inversion can be seen in *Prosa del observatorio*, where faith is expressed that Actaeon will return to possess Diana finally:

Actaeon will survive and return to the chase until the day he finds Diana and possesses her under the foliage, [...] Diana enemy history with its dogs of tradition and commandments (*PO* 66).

The same inversion is present in *Rayuela*:

People got hold of the wrong end of the kaleidoscope, so you had to turn it back to front [...] throw yourself onto the floor like Emmanuèle and then to start looking at things from the mountain of dung, looking at the world through the eye in your arse (*R* 253).

Marrast's building his statue upside down is an expression of the same rebellion. There is a similar revindication of the repressed, faecal aspects of man:

The statue would radically invert the traditional elements, [...] it would raise against the heavens the heaviest and most boring part of itself, the everyday matter of existence, projecting its base of faeces and tears towards the *azur* in a genuinely heroic transmutation. (54)

The general attitude in the 'zone', the 'obstinate and cheerful trampling of decalogues', Hélène's 'rape' of Celia, Nicole's 'seduction' of Austin, are part of the same rebellion.

We have seen, however, that the characters are unsuccessful in breaking the force of taboo, that their acts of rebellion turn them into monsters. It is in the 'zone', in the ambiguous attitudes of the characters and the meaning of their actions that this transformation can be approached.

The antithetical pair conformism–rebellion are continually permutated in the 'zone'. Marrast's sending the letter to the Neurotics Anonymous, for example, as an image of provocation, is revolutionary, yet taken in the context of his relationship with Nicole it is simply a means of evading their false situation, and results in her 'betraying' him with Austin and becoming guilty (a whore) in his eyes.

In any chain of transformations there is one basic potential element which is repeated in three forms: an initial intuition or revelation (in Juan, as to the nature of Hélène); a 'literary' version (the episode of Frau Marta and the English girl); and the actual fulfilment of the code (Hélène's rape of Celia). It must be realized that there is no one unique relation between them. Causally, each one presupposes the others and they are as resistant to ordering as the elements of the *coágulo*. Thus, no one element is chemically 'pure', free from the effects of the writing, and can be extracted from its context for analysis.

A measure of their textuality may be seen in the fact that there are three equally important, parallel forces working on them: their being told, the attitudes (conscious or otherwise) of the characters in them, and perhaps also the influence of the reader. Moreover, each element is included in three different types of causality: superficial verisimilitude, the causality of the codes discussed, and the psychological–existential. It might also be added that not even the traditional Sartrean definition of character can be relied upon: 'My paredros is right when he says that Sartre is mad and that we are more the sum of other people's acts than that of our own' (246).

Thus, the basic pattern in this area of the novel is parallel to that

I described in terms of *différance*, equivalent to the terms used by Cortázar and his characters of *aplazamiento* (postponement), *plazo* (the time for which something is postponed), 'truce'. Schematically, the pattern is as follows: repression (of the original intuition); sublimation (*différance*, *aplazamiento*); the return of the repressed, often transformed. The effect of the sublimation depends to a great extent on the measure of good or bad faith displayed by those involved, but not only in the individual directly involved, but also in those around him. Foreign influences enter from the network of relationships, like 'my paredros' from the 'web of telephone calls'. The various possible origins of any transformation must thus be followed through the network of the text as it is presented to us.

THE ZONE: THREE GROUPS OF CHARACTERS

Hélène, the 'dead lad', Celia

Though one runs the risk of creating false perspectives by extracting any episode from the various causal chains to which it belongs and by starting one's analysis at any particular point in the 'zone', as its elements are in a sense simultaneous, I have nevertheless begun by taking the episode of the death of the 'dead lad' as a revelation to Hélène of the full force of 'the absurd, the scandal' (103).

The terms *scandal* and *absurd*, used to describe the death of the young man, link his death with that of Rocamadour, in the context of which both are used (*R* 183, 197). The 'dead lad' thus belongs to the line of children in the novels (Jorge, Rocamadour and Manuel) constantly threatened by illness and death. It would seem to be Hélène's orderly, anti-vital life ('to me that life of hers was like death' (158)) that is responsible for the death, in the same way as Oliveira feels responsible for that of Rocamadour: 'A more modest proposition: he has killed us because we are guilty of his death. Guilty, that is to say the accomplices of a state of affairs...' (*R* 185). The 'dead lad' is, as we have seen, also Juan, whom Hélène kills (as Actaeon) for discovering the 'dangerous' force in her and for denouncing the inauthenticity of her life ('my denouncer, he who [...] makes me see myself as I am' (141)), in the same way as la Maga denounces Oliveira, and is 'absolutely perfect in the way she denounces the false perfection of others' (*R* 369), and as Oliveira denounces Traveler: 'I don't hate you either, brother, but I denounce you' (*R* 394). In this sense, the young man's death is also Hélène's repression of her own deeper identity.

As soon as the young man has died under the anaesthetic administered to him by Hélène, the repression of the 'scandal' begins. This repression is usually referred to in *62* as a *coartada*, or *escamoteo*. (The term *coartada* ('alibi') links this activity to the concept of 'my paredros'.) One of the main forms of the *coartada* is the *aplazamiento* (postponement) discussed earlier as *différance*. It revolves around the last words of the young man, 'hasta luego'.

These words refer to various distinct things. The first is the claim that the young man (Juan) makes on Hélène's future, a claim which the latter has always rejected: 'She has only surrendered her body when she was certain she was not loved, and only because of that, in order to separate the present clearly from the future, so that afterwards nobody would come knocking at her door in the name of feelings' (141). In another sense, it is an indication of the *plazos*, the postponement that will follow the death, i.e., promises to return to the memory of the scandal which will never be kept (*la différance* as 'pulsion de mort'): 'a postponement *sine die* for her on this side' (118). Hélène, despite her efforts, will forget the death: 'I too will say "hasta luego" like you, and we will both have lied' (104). The dead man's friends and parents will act in a similar fashion: 'until they too said [...] "Hasta luego", and went down for a glass of cognac' (168).

The *plazo* sometimes has the meaning of a cleaning, making the scandal innocent (like the doll, as Juan does to Hélène) for later presentation: 'the time (*plazo*) necessary for preparing the corpse decently' (117); 'The body [...] would be a horrible blue and red and black map, hurriedly covered by a nurse, [...] the beginning of the sleight of hand (*escamoteo*)' (168). The 'hasta luego' is nevertheless an invitation to a rendez-vous, and creates the possibility of the meeting in the 'city', that is, the recovery of the young man and what dies with him. It is the bad faith involved in the *plazo* as an attempt to forget that makes this recovery problematic.

The effect of the young man's death on both Hélène and his friends is to wound them and leave them naked:

café and office friends [...] naked and open;   (168)
[Hélène] applying distances and compresses, the first absorbent pads, [...] the bandages which would protect the skin from rubbing too roughly against things.   (102)

This is exactly the same effect that Juan's eyes have on Hélène (Diana):

How can I tell anyone if you yourself cannot know that the passage of your image through any of someone else's memories strips me naked and wounds me [...], that in my own way I love you and that this affection condemns you because it turns you into my denouncer, he who through loving me and being loved, strips me and lays me bare and makes me see myself as I am.   (140–1)

These characteristics also correspond, of course, to the 'dead lad': 'naked and open like the dead man' (168). We thus have the beginning of a strange circular or repetitive logic. Juan wounds Hélène with his gaze; Hélène, by rejecting this gaze, wounds Juan (Actaeon); his death in the form of the 'dead lad' wounds Hélène...

The young man is Hélène's most intimate life, and the wound inflicted on her by Juan is self-knowledge: 'he throws me into myself' (140); 'he makes me see myself as I am' (141). And thus to forget (repress) the memory of the 'dead lad' is to forget what she has done to her own life. This becomes clear in her use of personal pronouns: the 'I will forget you' (104) addressed to the young man becomes 'you will forget yourself in time' (112) when she addresses herself. The same is the case with the dead lad's friends: 'until they too said, said to themselves, said to him: "Hasta luego" ' (168). There is no contradiction here, for it is in the most intimate and personal lives of Hélène and Juan that the possibility of the union lies. Celia reinforces the idea by calling Hélène's life a 'death' and a 'scandal'. The young man's real death is also, significantly, described as a 'scandal'.

'My paredros' would have called her, she muses, a 'deferred suicide' (103). This suggests various related ideas:

(a) *Deferring* suggests *aplazamiento* and thus, by postponing the first message of Juan (repressing it), she is committing suicide.

(b) Her attempt to forget the 'dead lad' is simply a renewal of the *plazo*.

(c) The suicide is not definitive (like the death of a victim of vampirism), and hence the hope she conceives on the arrival of the doll and Celia, 'the true message of Juan' (177).

(d) *Suicide* might be as ambiguous as other elements of the novel and contain the idea of the killing of the alienated 'precious daily ego', and thus become a positive term.

Let us examine the ways in which Hélène represses the 'revelation' and her 'true self', the *coartadas* (excuses) she employs 'so as never to speak of herself, so as never to be Hélène when she was with us' (160). It is 'intelligence' (superego) which invents the bandages with which she protects her 'wound': 'a consecutive system of shock-absorbers and insulators which her intelligence would set up' (102). A very significant comment is made about these barriers set up by intelligence: 'A life based on cotton wool and insulators seemed to me the worst kind of spitting (*escupitajo*) in the face of what had just happened' (103). This *spit* obviously corresponds to the rotten contents of the doll, described as 'guilt' and 'blot', while it is a 'really thick spit' (245) that forms the barrier that Osvaldo the snail has to cross in his race across the train seat, a symbol of the characters' attempt to reach the rendez-vous. (This spit is in turn described as a 'blackish blot' (251), which connects it with the 'black blot' of *Libro de Manuel*.) It thus becomes clear that it is repression that introduces the idea of sin into whatever is repressed. Repression as we have discussed it (*différance*) is a factor also inherent in writing, so the two levels are parallel and both refer us back to the figure of 'my paredros'.

The company of others, the 'zone', providing potential contact and union, can paradoxically be a means of escape and repression. Hélène uses Celia at first simply in order to forget: 'I ought to have gone straight home, had a shower and drunk whisky until I forgot [myself], but you see, I came to dunk my croissant too and it's not all that bad, we'll keep each other company until we feel better' (120). The same idea is expressed in *Rayuela*: 'So, paradoxically, the height of solitude led to the height of gregariousness' (*R* 120).

Hélène's most important arms are order and habit. It is habit which makes 'hasta luego' a negative term: 'the friendly gesture which in turn contained a promise and which habit turned into two empty words' (101). The absolute orderliness of her flat is repeatedly described as a defence: 'The only function of the green and the third shelf was a geometrical defence of your solitude' (138). Otherness, Juan's look, the 'dead lad', threaten to destroy this sterile order, constitute an 'irruption into the obstinate order of her alphabet' (141). Thus, disorder means scandal and death to her. This is implied in the relief she feels at being able to accept the presence of Celia in her flat, the hope she conceives: 'Somehow there was no scandal and [. . .] she was so to speak reconciled, accepting without

protest the disorder of Celia being in her house and her night' (170).
It is by considering disorder and vitality a scandal that she converts
it into death. Hélène herself seems to realize this when she warns
Celia, 'Flee from Catharists' (176).

Another repressive strategy of Hélène is time: 'You will eventually
forget yourself with method, with a before and an after' (112). (For
Hélène as well as for Juan the possible state revealed to them would
be 'another present' (112).) Another is language, which serves just
as often to separate as it does to unite or to reveal *lo otro*, becoming
itself a barrier: 'the screen phrases' (158).

Yet there is a way out of this circularity for Hélène. At a certain
point the concept of forgetting takes on two opposite meanings: 'No
game will make you forget: your soul is a cold machine, a lucid
register. You will never forget anything in a whirlwind which razes
the large and the small to throw you into another present' (112).
The ambiguity of this passage is remarkable, and only by keeping
in mind all the modulations of the sense of *forgetting* can it be understood. Here the 'cold machine' compels her to remember, is a 'lucid
register'; elsewhere in the episode, 'the rigorous machine of her life',
her 'system of shock-absorbers', etc., aim to make her forget. Thus,
to remember and forget in sublimation are equivalent, which is, in
fact, a decent definition of the negative aspect of *différance*. 'No game
will make you forget' suggests forgetting as something positive, as if
forgetting the death implied the possibility of coming to terms with
Juan and otherness. The cataclysmic, chaotic forgetting of the
'whirlwind' (described in a similar way to the positive message of
Juan's *coágulo*: 'an instant outside time', 'razes', 'tears') becomes
equivalent to Hélène's initial attempt to remember the scandal of
the death of the young man, come to terms with it ('she would
have liked to be able to keep for ever every proof of the absurd and
the scandal, refuse life its cotton wool' (103)). A new opposition is
thus formed: *remembering–forgetting (whirlwind) | forgetting–remembering
(cold machine)*, which corresponds to the two sides of *différance* stressed
earlier.

It is the madness of the whirlwind that Hélène invokes in her
'absurd will for madness' (112). Only authentic madness and disorder can abolish (make her forget) the scandal of the death and
recover (make her remember) the initial promise of Juan in the
'hasta luego' of the 'dead lad', and by-pass – *déjouer* – the traps of a
more lucid *différance*. The idea is a continuation of the irrationalist

element of the earlier novels, like Oliveira's 'only by living absurdly could one hope to break this infinite absurdity'.

All the absurdist action of the novel is of this nature. The absurd situation against which the action is directed is not only psychological, ontological and linguistic, but is also given a wider political context:

In Burundi there was an uprising, my dear; the rebels captured all the members of parliament and the senators, some ninety in all, and shot them en masse. Almost at the same time the king of Burundi, who has an unpronounceable name followed by an impeccably roman III, was having talks with de Gaulle, great ceremony in a hall with mirrors, salaams and probably technical aid and all that. So it's impossible not to understand that Marrast and Tell who are sensitive to things like that, and even Juan who is less sensitive because to a certain extent he makes a living out of them, should decide that the only possible course of action is to make life impossible for the director of a museum or that they must immediately send a doll to their solitary friend in the rue de la Clef?

(143–4)

When absurdist action is not combined with good faith, it becomes 'idiotic games, life' (30), a ratification of the absurd. Hélène realizes that the authentic 'madness' she is looking for is not so easily achieved:

No, none of them is mad, none of us is. Only this afternoon I was thinking that not everybody can go mad, you have to deserve things like that. It's not like death, you see; it's not total absurdity like death or paralysis or blindness. There are some of us who pretend to be mad out of sheer nostalgia, as a provocation. (141)

Though the passage is rather ambiguous, it seems that a distinction is made between 'madness' and the total absurdity of death. Thus, 'madness' would demand a measure of reflexion, which is, of course, in Cortázar, the source of inauthenticity. Marrast and Tell, for example, pretend to be mad, try to be mad, but do not achieve it, just as Oliveira at the beginning af *Rayuela* does not (which results in the death of Rocamadour). This stems from the ambiguity of their anticonformist stance. Oliveira confesses to being 'buried in prejudices which I scorn and respect at the same time' (*R* 116), and the 'zone' is similarly ambiguous. Marrast claims that he and the others radically refuse to be serious and are totally unconventional:

None of us was really serious [...] and what had gathered us together in the city, in the zone, in life, was precisely a cheerful and obstinate trampling of decalogues. Each in his own way, the past had taught us the profound futility of being serious, of appealing to seriousness at moments of crisis. (83)

Elsewhere, however, we learn that they were 'profoundly serious when it came to my paredros or the city' (28).

Hélène's 'madness' finally finds an expression in her 'seduction' of Celia. By recreating the intensity of the original force discovered by Juan and repressed by them both, she hopes to recover the force and consequently bring the 'dead lad' back to life, 'reorder the factors, abolish that death from here' (176).

This transgression, expressed in the rape, belongs to the long line of such episodes in Cortázar's novels: the rape of Felipe by Bob; that of Francine by Andrés in *Libro de Manuel*; Oliveira's kissing Talita. The rape always takes place before the descent to Hades to recover the dead (Eurydice). Hélène talks of taking Celia down to the morgue, 'to that basement where there are people crying uncomprehendingly' (176). In the corresponding episode of *Libro de Manuel*, Andrés similarly talks of taking Francine down to the 'basement': 'I can no longer search with reason, I need to go down those steps of cognac with you and see whether there is an answer in the basement, whether you can help me to get out of the black blot' (*M* 292).

For some reason, however, her rebellion, though seemingly total, is unsuccessful. Celia breaks the doll and its contents restore the death and sin Hélène had tried to abolish. The anarchy of Erzebeth Báthory is changed into the evil of Frau Marta–Carmilla. Hélène finds not the 'dead lad'–Juan in the 'city', but Austin, who kills her. Why is this? Keeping in mind the precept 'we are much more the sum of other people's acts than that of our own' (246), it is to the actions and attitudes of other characters and to other causal chains that one has to look for an answer.

In spite of all, the rebellion does constitute a partial victory, perhaps a 'move closer to the final mutation' (*R* 417–18). Whereas Hélène had always hidden her face (Diana), in the same way as the 'horrible blue and red and black *map*' (168, my italics) of the 'dead lad's' body is hidden by the nurse, she now defiantly displays it to Austin: 'What can we do, Juan, apart from lighting another cigarette and letting the outraged baby have a good look at us, giving him a straight full-on view of the *map* of one's face so he can learn it by heart' (247, my italics). Juan too talks of 'something which had torn her from that thorough negation of life, which forced her to weep while looking me straight in the face' (236).

It is obviously Juan who is responsible for the transformation in the meaning of her act, since it was he who sent the doll. But Celia is also responsible. Oliveira realizes that gestures like that of Hélène can only be meaningful if there is a response from *lo otro*, from the other side of the 'original unity' which Cortázar's characters constantly strive to restore: 'True otherness [...] could not be achieved just from one side, the outstretched hand had to be answered by another hand from the outside, from the other (*lo otro*)' (*R* 121). Oliveira's overtures to Berthe Trépat are frustrated by the lack of such a response. In *Libro de Manuel*, it depends on the response of Francine whether the act of sodomy becomes a rape or not: 'Something new was emerging in her tears, the discovery that it was not unbearable, that he was not raping her' (*M* 313). Celia, however, totally rejects Hélène's action and this makes an important contribution to the effect of Juan's sending the doll (or perhaps is the result of it, a typical ambiguity in *62*).

Juan and Tell: the doll

Juan's initial *coágulo* experience can be taken as part of the action of the novel for the purpose of this analysis of the 'zone', though it does not belong there in any strict chronological sense. The *coágulo* is a revelation to Juan of the common identity of Hélène and the Countess, of Hélène's free, rebellious nature. This is just as much a revelation about himself, since the whole possibility of his union with Hélène is implicated therein. This union, in immediate terms, would destroy his everyday identity, his 'precious ego'. It is described as a 'unity [...] which destroys me and tears me from myself' (11). His fear of this destruction is parallel to his horror at the activity of Erzebeth Báthory and Heliogabalus.

The rest of the novel for Juan in the 'zone' is an attempt to come to terms with this revelation, but mainly by repression and sublimation, *différance*. He makes the experience itself harmless by telling it, makes Hélène harmless by excluding her from the *coágulo*, refusing to understand her inclusion in it:

What were you doing here? You had no right to be among the cards of
that sequence [...]; Why did you insist on joining [...]?   (31)
the refusal to admit what was thrown into my face tonight;   (38)
I could have known the truth, accept that you were ...   (262)

He thus insists that Hélène has no life outside the 'zone', that there is a possibility of union on the superficial level of the ego. He is described as 'he who still hopes to have tea with Hélène, receive Hélène's telephone call' (77). It is this negation of the most essential Hélène, its repression and transference that creates her 'absence'. This attitude on the part of Juan is just as important as her own self-repression. Hélène's 'absence' for Juan is thus equivalent to the 'death' of the young man for Hélène.

Though only by insinuation, and in a light, humorous fashion, the revolutionary nature of Hélène, as seen in the *coágulo*, is given political dimensions. The realization of Hélène's potential depends on Juan, who is a representative of the establishment, a translator at international conferences. He is unwilling to 'free' Hélène, or incapable of doing so, since this would destroy his personal order, as Celia suspects: 'A man would have swept away [Hélène's rigid order] with one flick of his hand, almost without realizing, between two kisses and a cigarette burning the carpet, Juan. No, Juan of all people no, because in his own way he was also too fond of carpets' (138). But, no less importantly, it might also destroy the political order through which he earns a living. He is 'less sensitive' than the others to political contradictions and absurdity 'because to a certain extent he makes a living out of them' (144). Without the *coartada* of Tell to mask the absence from his life of what Hélène could represent, Juan would no longer be able to maintain this order: 'If he didn't have me waiting for him [says Tell], let it be said in all modesty, he would most probably drink a whole bottle of slivovitz and then the following day his simultaneous or consecutive translations would mark a new era in international relations' (86).

Let us examine the *coartadas* (excuses, alibis) of Juan. The sense of vacuity in his life (the absence of Hélène) is vicariously filled or masked by his relations with Tell: 'Wasn't two or three weeks in a no man's land [. . .] just the right void to fit Tell's slim waist?' (60). Tell anchors him firmly 'on this side' giving him 'a sort of functional happiness, of reasonable everyday humanity' (67). As in case of Hélène, the revelation he receives is described as a wound, 'a concretion [. . .] which denies its own importance after wounding mortally' (13), and Tell, before becoming involved in the 'city', is, like routine for Hélène, the bandage he uses to dress this wound: 'You are something different, a sort of refuge or first-aid kit with bandages [...] and suddenly you are so close, you have walked in the city at the same time as me, and even though it may seem absurd, that distances you, makes you an active agent, puts you on the side of the wound, not the dressing' (61).

The essential theme of *aplazamiento* is also present. Tell helps Juan put off facing the real issues in his life, 'she knew how to [...] give me that postponement of Paris with everything that Paris was to me at that time (with everything that Paris was not to me at that time), that neutral interregnum [...]' (60). Paris is something negative (i.e. the absence of Hélène) and at the same time positive in that 'absence' is only the negative of what had been, in the *coágulo*, 'plenitude', and could presumably become 'presence' again. We later see that the 'neutral interregnum' mentioned, like the 'truce' (256) formed when Juan eventually sleeps with Hélène without establishing any deeper contact with her, has the function of exorcizing the imminence or impossibility of 'that other postponed meeting' (256), the rendez-vous in the 'city'.

The equivalent of Hélène's 'madness' in this sequence is the invention of the Frau Marta episode by Tell and Juan. Tell gives the operation the sense of providing Juan with an alternative future without Hélène: 'For want of a future worth its name, which means a future with Hélène, one has to invent one and see what happens' (87). Juan, however, apparently believes that it will give him the possibility of a future with Hélène, because, by transferring what he finds unacceptable about Hélène to Frau Marta, Hélène will become conventionally acceptable. He 'would accept or invent anything as long as he did not have to accept that other future without Hélène' (88). There is a characteristic ambiguity in their invention in that here 'invention' can be equivalent to its normal opposite 'acceptance'. Their 'madness' is thus a sort of conformism. Tell remarks significantly that 'it's as if there were much that had already been invented in our inventions' (88). Their invention is the ratification of something tacitly understood, conventional, which reminds us of the role of 'my paredros'. In no way is Tell's madness like that demanded by Hélène. Rather than being a 'whirlwind' it creates 'minute waistcoat tempests' (59).

The substitution is a major element in the *aplazamiento* process. Hélène's physical presence is substituted by Tell, the more essential Hélène by Frau Marta: 'right to the end I will prefer to name Frau Marta' (37). As I have suggested, this has the effect of making innocent, of 'absolving', both Hélène and Juan. The theme of absolution is repeated throughout the novel. It is this absolution that creates the crime. Tell seems to give Juan a dispensation: 'as if I had a dispensation, without betraying a sworn faith, I who had sworn no faith' (60) (the dispensation creates the faith); Austin pardons Celia in the same way: 'a sort of forgiveness that neither she had any reason to ask for, nor he to give, a certificate for that life of happy fools' (246); Hélène's forgetting of the 'dead lad' is similar: she is 'absolved by forgetfulness, returned to competence and efficiency' (102–3). Such absolutions are reminiscent of the *paredros*'s role of confessor and surely correspond to the creation of the doll. The doll's exterior is made unnaturally innocent ('the innocent crotch' (109)) at the expense of its 'natural', vital nature, its contents, being transformed into something sinful.

The second part of Tell's 'madness' illustrates the negative side of *la différance*. She comes to realize that her own possession of the doll was simply a *détour*, and breaks the substitution by sending it: 'I would feel him enter the simulacrum, make me another, take me as another, knowing only too well that I knew and despising himself. "Why should he give me Monsieur Ochs's doll?", I thought before falling asleep. "Tomorrow I shall send it to Hélène, it's only right that she should have it" ' (190). But this act has negative results. One reason is temporal: had she sent it before the Frau Marta episode, it might not have had the same contents. The spite she feels against Hélène (according to Marrast, 'bitterness (*rencor*), void of voids' (84)) also seems to be of importance. Whatever her superficial motives, the doll sent is Hélène's potential act of liberation, made guilty *a priori* by Juan and Tell in the Vienna *détour*.

Nicole, Marrast

The relation between Nicole and Marrast is far less complex than the relation between Juan, Tell, Hélène and Celia, though it follows the same general pattern: realization of personal truth, the repression and *aplazamiento* of this truth, and the return of what was repressed in a 'contaminated' form.

The realization, provoked by a visit to the Palladian villa la Malcontenta, is that Nicole no longer loves Marrast, but Juan. Their relationship which, up to that time, had been 'a battle of threatened freedoms' (71), becomes sterile, empty, petrified. Yet both of them reject the knowledge that they have changed:

'But you are not like that, Mar.'
'Existence precedes essence, my dear.'
'No, you are not like that. You weren't born to be like that.'   (75)
Why should I have to maintain my pre-established image, the one you had invented? I am the way I am, before you thought I was one thing and now I am the *malcontenta*.   (108)

The stratagems or *coartadas* they employ in their attempt to ignore the fact that their relationship is over are similar to the ones discussed above: postponement, routine, hope, substitution. Their passive hope that the situation will resolve itself has much in common with postponement: 'first the hopeful denial, the it's not possible, the let's carry on for a bit' (84). It is seen as a 'void', and as a 'whore dressed in green' (148). Postponement is also present in its more literal form. They continually put off going to the art gallery, and their purely sexual relationship is a way of putting off the real dilemma:

That postponement which would repeat so many others since the afternoon on the Mantua road [. . .] opened up a zone of rituals and games, old ceremonies which led to the love of selfish bodies, stubborn deniers of the other solitude which would be waiting for them at the foot of the bed. It was the precarious truce, the no-man's-land where they would fall entwined [. . .], hastening into a false, recurrent eternity.   (75)

Substitution is present in various forms. Calac, for example, chides Nicole for her hope that simple affection for Marrast can act as a substitute for real love: 'When I talk about loving him, I'm not talking about being fond of him or being good to him and those amiable substitutions which are the flower of our civilization' (149). Habit replaces thought and feeling: 'Everything had the familiar air of a pre-established ceremony, a well-ordered substitution' (53).

The result of this *escamoteo* is a feeling of 'emptiness', equivalent to the 'absence' of Hélène and formed in a similar way. Nicole dare not look at herself in the mirror because she would see 'a black hole, a funnel which swallows down the present with a disgusting gurgle' (71). Marrast sees emptiness everywhere: 'doubt, a void (*hueco*), hope, an even bigger void, bitterness, void of voids, manifestations of the big hole' (84).

Marrast's sending the letter to the Neurotics Anonymous, an Ochsian provocation of chance, has much in common with Tell's

sending the doll to Hélène: 'But you let the eagles loose and afterwards it's good to watch where the hell they finish up [...]. Look,
it's not the first time I have freed an eagle [...] because the idea of
unleashing something, anything, seems to me obscurely necessary' (124). This action, however, again like that of Tell, is described
as *vicariously* filling the void: 'the vicarious attempts to fill up the
void, for example the sprig of *Hermodactylus tuberosis* and the Neurotics Anonymous' (84). Thus, it is hardly different from the empty
conversation Nicole and Marrast make, described as 'stuffing' (69).
The same word is used to refer to the contents of the dolls: 'the object
hidden in the stuffing of the dolls' (97).

Nicole's seduction of Austin constitutes an honest and coherent
action, a return to the consciousness of her freedom. Yet by seducing
him she becomes guilty and conforms to the repressive aspects of two
codes, becoming Kundry and la Malcontenta. Returning once more
to the phrase 'we are much more the sum of other people's acts than
that of our own', we see that it is the vicarious nature of Marrast's
action, his bad faith and conventionality, which activates the archetypes and fulfils the *figura*. It is he who provides Nicole with the
instrument of her liberation, Austin, in the same way as Juan is
presented as having sent Celia to Hélène. Marrast comes to be aware
of his own conventionality: 'I discover that I am as conventional
as anybody else, as much of a husband without being married' (196).
He realizes that the guilt is in him, and that the code is in his own
mind, but he is incapable of ridding himself of it: 'But it is not she
who is dirty and I know it and I can't help it, the blot is in me, I
who am unable to remove from my blood all this which allows itself
to be thought so clearly, and it's useless for me to say silly little
girl [...], I feel her dirty in my blood, a whore in my blood' (196).

And the familiar pattern of the formation of the doll is repeated –
Marrast prefers to save his 'precious ego', his *hombría*, the innocent
exterior of the doll, and pronounce Nicole a whore: 'all of them
whores and I a man Tell with his outrage saving his sex [...] a
man safe with his whore inside' (198). After such a statement and
the parallel admission of complicity by Juan, Nicole can be punished
by Frau Marta and become a vampire in her turn, initiate another
chain of victims, another *figura*.

4

Libro de Manuel

INTRODUCTION

Socialism and literature: the debate

After the complex, subtle, and ultimately minority novels *Rayuela* and *62*, we are faced with a very different sort of literature in *Libro de Manuel*, published in 1973. The literary level is patently lower. The repetition of structure and character types from earlier works is mechanical; the language is often stereotyped Cortázarese bordering dangerously at times on rhetoric. It is nevertheless a brave and honest book, and is an important experiment within the political fiction which characterizes the seventies (1970, Vargas Llosa's *Conversación en la catedral*; 1974, Carpentier's *El recurso del método*; 1975, Roa Bastos's *Yo el supremo* and García Márquez's *El otoño del patriarca*; 1978, Fuentes's *La cabeza de la hidra*). Perhaps more radically if not necessarily more successfully than the authors mentioned here, Cortázar in this novel faces up to the tension between a politically committed message, and serious literary experimentation which often tends towards a relativization of any message. *Libro de Manuel* was written quickly and was designed to reach a wide reading public. It is thus unfair to judge it exclusively according to the same purely literary criteria as his other novels, or in isolation from its context.

The 'double text' of earlier works provides the structure with which he approaches the problem. A new discourse is articulated through another, more conventional one, which it uses but subverts and attempts to renew. In *Rayuela*, the alienated discourse corresponds to the conventional world of Traveler which Oliveira wants to join but must first infiltrate and modify. In *Libro de Manuel*, dogmatic Marxism and literary realism are taken as a partially alienated main discourse and vehicle, through which and against which a secondary, irrational, erotic and taboo discourse is established to liberalize and widen the first.

161

To understand the emphasis of *Libro de Manuel* it must be placed in the context of the debate on socialism and literature in which Cortázar was involved before its publication and which reached a crisis point with the imprisonment of the Cuban poet Herberto Padilla in 1971.

Since 1961, after a visit to Cuba, Cortázar has unequivocally proclaimed his adhesion to the cause of socialism in Latin America.[1] In *Viaje alrededor de una mesa* (1970), an account of a round table on commitment in literature, in which Vargas Llosa also participated, he forcefully criticized the attitude of many revolutionaries who, in the name of the socialist 'new man' of the future, proscribe from literature those aspects of man not directly accessible to rational analysis:

[Neo-social realism implies] a perspective where many subjects which are delicate and equivocal but which are just as genuine a part of human personality as political faith and economic necessities (I am referring among many others to eroticism, play, imagination beyond any subject matter which can be checked out against reason or 'reality') are proscribed or mutilated in the name of a certain notion of the *hombre nuevo* which, in my opinion, would have no reason for coming into being if he were condemned to read what he is offered by those who obey similar concepts of revolutionary freedom (*VM* 28–9).

In a reply to this and other similar declarations, Miguel Alascio Cortázar, in *Viaje alrededor de una silla*, accuses Cortázar of various heresies: the irrationalism he practises leads to confusion, a state propitious to the rise of fascism;[2] his distance from social reality leads Cortázar to view any revolutionary change as spontaneous, a position which leads to *repentismo*, anathema to the classical Marxist;[3] Cortázar's claim, after Plato, that art is one of the highest forms of eroticism (*VM* 51) is countered by an assertion that Plato was essentially a reactionary whose eroticism was but an apology for the elegant vices of the aristocracy,[4] and that Cortázar's eroticism simply uses the ideal of widening the horizons of literature for the *hombre nuevo* as a pretext for writing little more than commercial pornography.[5] The Colombian Oscar Collazos, in 'La encrucijada del lenguaje', repeats many of these arguments, and suggests that the formal difficulty of texts by Cortázar and Fuentes springs from an inferiority complex *vis-à-vis* the Europeans and an attempt to prove themselves superior to the *barbarie* of Latin America: 'We can and must be capable of being superior to *our* barbarism. We too are capable of reaching the "heights" that they have achieved' (*LR* 31). Perhaps the most important accusation of Alascio Cortázar and Collazos is that Cortázar condones a dichotomy between the politics and literature of a writer, leading him to ignore reality: 'Cortázar's basic approach, reading between the lines, is simple: to authorize, to "legalize", to present this dichotomy, the split of the literary being and the political being, not only as possible, but as valid too. But also to establish a deep scorn for the reality he suspends' (*LR* 15).

Cortázar's answer to all this is that 'reality' is far more than the 'socio-historical and political context'; that any literature worth its name 'approaches man from all angles' (*LR* 65); that what is needed is writing which is revolutionary in itself rather than writing dictated by revolutionary theory ('the revolutionaries of literature rather than the literary men of the revolution' (*LR* 76)) if revolutionary language is to be cleansed of the 'rotten corpses of an obsolete social order' (*VM* 33). Repeatedly, however, he demands a great personal sense of responsibility in the writer if these ideas are not simply to embody escapism (e.g. *LR* 57). The general affirmation from the time of *Rayuela* is still basically valid: 'Historical results like Marxism or whatever you like may be achieved, but the Yonder is not exactly history' (*R* 509).

What Fuentes has called the 'tragicomic'[6] case of Padilla consti-tutes an important crisis in Cortázar's theoretical position. Padilla was arrested in 1971 by the Cuban authorities for anti-revolutionary attitudes: pessimism, escapism, individualism, etc. His *autocrítica* brought a strong reaction from left-wing writers in Latin America and Europe. Cortázar signed the letter of protest. Castro's reply was devastating. He would have nothing to do with 'pseudo-revolution-aries', 'bourgeois liberals' writing from the 'bourgeois salons' of Europe, unaware that the real problems of Cuba were not the temporary imprisonment of a poet, but underdevelopment, edu-cation, the real threat of invasion, the blockade. 'But as for Cuba', he concluded, 'they will never be able to utilize Cuba again, never!, not even by defending it. When they are about to defend us we will say to them: "Don't defend us, friend, please don't defend us. We are better off without your help" ' (*CP* 119–20). Cortázar was strongly affected. He did not sign the second letter of protest, but published his 'Policrítica a la hora de los chacales' (*CP* 126–30). While defending the writer's right to criticism and creative freedom,

he denounced facile liberalism, and reaffirmed his adherence to the
Cuban revolution:

You are right, Fidel: only in combat do we have the right to be dis-
                                                              [contented,
criticism, the search for better formulae, can only come from inside,
yes, but inside is sometimes so outside,
and just because today I abandon for ever violet scented liberalism, the
                                            [signatories of virtuous texts
be – cause – Cu – ba – is – not – that – which – their – wri – ting –
                                            [desk – sche – mas – de – mand,
I know I am not an exception, I am like them, what have I done for
                                                       [Cuba beyond love,
what have I given for Cuba beyond a desire, a hope.
But now I abandon their ideal world, their schemes,
just now when
I am shown the door of what I love, I am banned from defending it,
right now I exercise my right to choose, to stand once more and more
                                                               [than ever
by your Revolution, my Cuba, in my own way (*CP* 128).

Such statements cannot be ignored when considering the genesis
of *Libro de Manuel*, nor the fact that the royalties were given to
organizations defending political prisoners in Argentina. The central
mystery of the novel is a set of instructions given to the main character by a cigar-smoking Cuban which can only be known once they
have been carried out. The open eyes of the corpse at the end of the
novel reminded Cortázar, after the novel had been published, of
those of Che Guevara.

The 'dispensable chapters' of *Rayuela*, where the readers and the
characters too in many cases are exposed to the cultural context of
the author, are replaced in *Libro de Manuel* by newspaper cuttings on
current Latin American political issues (plus information on political
violence in France and torture in Vietnam). Cortázar himself,
as he says in the prologue to the novel, was rather disappointed
by this experiment – he transcribed all the important news items
of certain days in the hope that this somewhat aleatory way of introducing political reality into the lives of his characters would
radically affect their personal trajectories (7–8).

Cortázar's somewhat contradictory attitude to his own creation
cannot however be ignored. In the prologue to the novel, he announces the 'convergence' of his two roles of political essayist and

novelist: 'If for years I have written texts concerned with Latin American problems, and at the same time novels and stories where those problems were absent or only came in incidentally, here and now the waters have merged' (7). In an interview given after the publication of *Libro de Manuel*, however, he admits that, due to the nature of his literary texts, his political commitment would have to find its expression in separate activity: 'I do not believe that we should falsify our goals as writers for the sake of so-called political commitment. The problem is how to insert that political commitment, if one cannot do so in the book because the book is, as you say, "hermetic", then in other lines of behaviour.'[7]

A more interesting contradiction concerns the level at which the writing of the novel is pitched. In 'Corrección de pruebas en Alta Provenza', written while proof-reading the novel, Cortázar claims that the urgency of the information contained in the novel forced him to write 'horizontally', that is, to follow a traditional, linear narrative mode, thus excluding formal innovations which take time for the reader to assimilate, a time-lag which was not important for *Rayuela*:

But right from the start I realized that, paradoxically, if this was a book of our *here and now*, i.e. of the immediate, it did not make sense to distance it through experimentation and technique: the deepest contact would be blocked by the very methods applied to establish it (*C* 19–20).

But Cortázar later firmly rejects the possibility of lowering his standards or abdicating his literary personality in order to make his work more accessible: 'You hinted at the possibility of lowering one's tone to make literature more accessible. I am totally opposed to this option [...] because I believe that every writer has his own destiny.'[8] When taken in isolation, such statements are simply contradictory. In the novel, however, Cortázar's by now familiar use of two discourses, two 'authors', explores such contradictions thoroughly and dialectically.

Irrationalism and revolution in Libro de Manuel

Cortázar is well aware of the kind of argument which links irrationalism with totalitarianism, Nietzsche with Hitler, Unamuno with Franco. His views on the subject were well defined as far back as 1949, as can be seen in his reply to Guillermo de Torre, where he makes the point that only combined with the strictest rationalism can irrationalism become a collective danger. His views are summarized here by García Canclini:

Reason is an ally of our aims, and it is up to us whether it is creative or destructive. Cortázar explained this intelligently in a reply to Guillermo de Torre, who held existentialist irrationalism responsible for the crimes of the Nazis. The desire for such crimes, which was an irrational impulse, would never have become a bloody reality if it had not been programmed by rigorous reason. The irrational is never a collective danger *per se*; only when organized by reason can it engender inquisitions, torture techniques and death chambers.[9]

The same idea is present throughout the work in often surprising forms. In 'Simulacros', from the 'Ocupaciones raras' section of *Historias de cronopios y de famas*, a family builds a scaffold in its front garden, but does so with the sole purpose of having dinner there and perhaps scandalizing the neighbours. The even less likely superman-like figure Fantomas repeats the point in comic-strip language: 'The world won't be destroyed by books, Steiner, but by men. Men exactly like you!' (*F* 34).

One of the most important points made in *Libro de Manuel* is that the revolution must aim to transform the whole of man, not just those aspects of him defined by Marxism. As Lonstein says, 'I'm referring to man himself, what he is and not what the others see of him from the *Capital* outwards' (226). Breton proposes a synthesis of Marx and Rimbaud (' "Transformer le monde", a dit Marx; "changer la vie", a dit Rimbaud: ces deux mots d'ordre pour nous n'en font qu'un')[10] which is taken up by Ludmilla in *Libro de Manuel*: 'I wonder if there was all that much difference between Lenin and Rimbaud' (90). A similar comment is made in *Prosa del observatorio*: 'Thomas Mann said that things would be better if Marx had read Hölderlin; but on the other hand, madam, I agree with Lukács that it would also have been necessary for Hölderlin to read Marx' (*PO* 71–2). Cortázar believes with the surrealists that there is little point in breaking the dualism capital/labour if at the same time parallel dualisms such as dream/waking life, imagination/reality, unconscious/conscious, illicit and licit sex, all variations on the same 'terrible interdit'[11] are not abolished.

Benedetti, whom Collazos quotes in order to criticize Cortázar, makes a similar point, defending the free imagination of the writer within the revolution and pointing to the convergence of imagination and revolution in the 'événements de mai '68':

A revolution must encompass everything: from ideology to love [...]. A writer, an artist, must use his imaginative capacity to defend, within the revolution, his right to imagine more and better.

It is perhaps in that word, *imagination*, where culture and revolution can really meet. 'L'imagination prend le pouvoir', read an inscription on the steps of the Faculty of Social Sciences in Paris during the recent *May revolution*.[12]

It is thus not surprising that the 'May revolution' had a strong surrealist element. Its slogan, according to Cohn-Bendit, was 'sous le pavé, la plage'.[13] What its enemies denied was 'personal liberty, the innocence of desire, the forgotten joys of creativity, play, irony, and happiness'.[14] Cortázar's own interest in these aspects of the Paris events is well documented in his 'Noticias del mes de mayo' (*Ultimo round*).

Such faith in gratuitous humour and 'pataphysical' irrationalism explains the occasionally delirious methods Cortázar has his revolutionaries use. In order to finance the kidnapping of the leader of an anti-revolutionary group presumably connected with the CIA, they smuggle counterfeit dollars into Europe in a container carrying a turquoise penguin and two armadillos, which are later to be seen walking by the Seine. In what is denominated the *pre-Joda*, they seriously shake the absolute faith of the Parisians in the infallibility of their government institutions by inserting old cigarette stubs in apparently untouched packets, violate their everyday order by effusively thanking the bus-driver for a pleasant drive,[15] standing up to eat in elegant restaurants,[16] and other similar Dadaist provocations.

'Madness', according to one character, is a way of disconcerting political enemies, as it was used by Morelli in order to *descentrar, desencasillar* the reader. But it is also a means of self-defence, a way of avoiding falling into the strategies used by the enemy and perhaps reproducing his ideology in a future socialist state: 'Binary revolutions [...] are condemned before they triumph because they accept the rules of the game. While they believe they are smashing everything, they become so deformed you wouldn't believe it. How much necessary madness, my friend, intelligent and aggressive madness to finally dislodge the ants' (200). (The 'ants', enemy agents, have connotations similar to those of the ants of previous works, minus the positive aspects.) The *pre-Joda* is thus, in general, a continuation of the provocative activity of Marrast. The madness referred to above is a development of the final madness of Hélène, itself inherited from Oliveira.

The most surprising symbol of the necessity of 'superfluous' beauty in the revolution is the mushroom for which Lonstein insistently demands such attention: 'the superfluity of certain beauties, certain toadstools in the night, all that which can make any project for a future meaningful' (183).

LONSTEIN: A NON-DUALISTIC LANGUAGE

Lonstein, in many ways the Morelli of *Libro de Manuel*, decries in the other characters the dichotomies which Cortázar tries to reconcile in the novel, the dualism between love and politics, chance and will, etc.: 'In all of you there is a binary functioning which would have sent even Pavlov to sleep watching you behave in the *Joda* or in sex' (335). He develops an ideolect, an almost private language, composed of what he calls 'fortrans', neologisms combining two normally exclusive lexical items, which are interspersed with innumerable gallicisms. The 'fortrans' point towards a new mental structure, 'a new struculture' (structure, culture) (338), which would transcend the 'binary functioning' of the others.[17]

It is highly ironical but characteristic and significant that the term 'fortran', chosen by Lonstein to express his new 'struculture', should be taken from computer technology. Throughout the novel, computers are an image of an alienated discourse: Lonstein's poem 'Fragmentos para una oda a los dioses del siglo' is described as 'cards to feed an IBM' (83); Francine, the representative of the intellectual Paris bourgeoisie in the novel, is seen as 'a little IBM machine' (137). Lonstein's attempt to 'artifucklate [*articulear*: *articular*, *culear*] the wholworld' (338) within but against an alienated language and discourse is an image of the task of the novel as a whole. It demands that the sign of this discourse should be changed from negative to positive, turned upside-down in the way Oliveira transforms the meaning of *piedad*. Like Marrast with his statue, like Jai Singh with the cold fatality of the stars in *Prosa del observatorio*, Lonstein is an 'inverter': 'but man there, the inverter, he who turns destiny upside-down, the acrobat of reality: against petrified ancestral mathematics' (*PO* 42). If the enterprise were at all successful, the 'lorpro' ('logical organization of any programme') of the deterministic world of computers (of the social novel, of fanatics) would become 'ilorpro' ('the illogical organization of any programme') (200).

Miguel Alascio Cortázar's accusing Cortázar of being a pornographer is perhaps not irrelevant to the latter's attempt in *Libro de Manuel* to treat the erotic, and especially tabooed sexuality (masturbation, sodomy), with great honesty, with 'that delirious degree of verbal nudity' that he found to be a necessary purification before any revolutionary change, 'an indispensable condition for Verrières on Friday night' (219). *El que te dije* aspires to a style which would not change key on approaching such subjects: 'The problem is closer to us: to search for something like not noticing it when we move from one area to another, and we're not capable of that yet. Paradoxically, we look on prohibited themes as special' (232). There are indications that Cortázar found such a resolution highly embarrassing at times:

I drop my biro and pick it up again, these hairy cheeks of mine blush because I find it hard to talk about fingers up arses [. . .], but I pick up my biro, take the fluff off it and start writing again and feel disgusted, I've got to go and have a shower, I feel like a slug or like when you slip on a pile of shit. (233)

Lonstein, more than any other character, is aware of the censorship inherent in language and tries especially hard to talk openly about taboo subjects, those which fundamentally contradict the laws and logic of his society, such as his relationship with the corpses he washes in the morgue. It is mainly through the 'fortrans' that he attempts to solve this problem, which Andrés defines as 'naming the things that it was impossible to describe' (213). Bataille, who fought a parallel battle at the limit of language and thought, comments succinctly that 'les mots disent difficilement ce qu'ils ont pour fin de nier'.[18] One of his characters, l'Abbé C., uses a language which may well have inspired the 'fortran' in this context. He believes that the only way to express the *indicible* is in the form of an enigma: 'Il serait donc apparemment, dans la nature de cet objet de ne povoir être donné comme le sont les autres: il ne pourrait être proposé à l'intérêt que sous forme d'énigme. . .'[19] The same character can only express himself to his loved one by defecating under her window and writing highly enigmatic letters to her. Both these elements are combined with a series of gallicisms in the following passage of Lonstein:

I can't keep conjugating my boulow at Marthe's bistrow, as my coupans say, and that condemns me to silence besides which as I am a bachelor and a chastonanist I am left with no other outlet but solliloquy apart from the toiletbook where from time to time I defeposit (*defepongo*) one or two turdscripts (*sorescriptos*).   (40)

Defepongo (*defecar, deponer*) is very similar to Bataille's 'soulépadé-pone'[20] (*souiller, padir, déposer*), which is even more disguised than Lonstein's neologism, as 'sous le petit pont'.

VERTICAL OR HORIZONTAL WRITING: THE TWO AUTHORS

Cortázar claims that in order to explore 'vertically', deeply, the experience recounted in the novel, he found himself obliged to write 'horizontally', linearly: 'And thus, through one of those curious workings of the world of communication, I realized that only by writing "horizontally" could I transmit vertical movements of meaning, a questioning of frontiers, without too much loss' (C 19–20).

A difficult issue is at stake in this paradoxical assertion, which is at the nerve centre of the formal tensions of the novel. Eco provides a clear introduction to the problem in his *Opera aperta*. A language is a system of predetermined probabilities.[21] Intelligibility and information (i.e. a new message) are in opposition. Any information represents an element of disorder in the established code: 'the message introduces a crisis into the code';[22] 'the more clearly the message communicates, the less it informs'.[23] A large amount of information, a very new message, runs the risk of creating chaos, incomprehension. The only way of transmitting this message is thus a dialectic between a conventional code and the message which threatens it: 'Between the offer of a plurality of formal worlds and the offer of undifferentiated chaos, void of any possibility of aesthetic enjoyment, the distance is short: only a pendular dialectic can save the composer of an open work.'[24]

Andrés, the Oliveira–Juan of *Libro de Manuel*, and also its 'final' author, faces this problem on listening to Stockhausen's *Prozession*. He finds that he is alternately able and unable to concentrate, that he can concentrate only on the passages where the piano is used among the electronic sounds. *Prozession* had represented for him the music of the *hombre nuevo*, yet, in the midst of this new experience, 'even so the old man is still alive and remembers' (26). It becomes clear to him that although intelligibility demands the presence of the old code (of expression, of behaviour), this code is likely to project into the future the alienated structures to be transcended:

And now it is even simpler to understand how history, temporal and cultural conditioning is inevitably fulfilled, because every passage where the piano is predominant sounds to me like a recognition which concentrates my attention, wakes me up more acutely to something which is still attached to me by that instrument which serves as a bridge between the past and the future. (26)

Andrés believes that the novel will only be valid if understood: 'A bridge is a man crossing a bridge, mate' (27). The problem is thus posed of communication through a medium which implies an alien view of the world. He asks how one can 'find the way to say intelligibly, when perhaps your technique and your deepest reality are demanding the burning of the piano and its replacement by some other electronic filter' (27). His choice between the two alternatives available to him is unequivocal. He decides to trust in the comprehension of future generations, 'to build the bridge anyway and leave it there; from that suckling infant in the arms of its mother, a woman will walk away some day and will cross the bridge on her own [. . .]. And then the piano will not be necessary' (28). When Patricio complains that no one will ever understand the scrapbook finally compiled by Andrés, the latter answers, 'Manuel will understand, [. . .] Manuel will understand some day' (385).

The 'horizontality' referred to by Cortázar finds its main expression in the 'plot'. This plot is almost a commonplace: a group of revolutionaries in Paris kidnap an important official in order to secure the release of political prisoners in Latin America. The characters converge on Verrières to carry out these plans, and such a simple narrative structure and well-defined action allow and oblige Cortázar to combine the difficult symbolism of the rendez-vous (as discussed in 62) with the 'real' problems he has newly decided to approach. The plot imposes a certain discipline on material which otherwise might take on a circularity that would exclude a wider reading public.

Within this framework, there are two clearly discernible types of causality, corresponding to the two authors Andrés and *el que te dije*, which I will follow in the next two sections. The first is what might be called the mystically horizontal trajectory of Andrés from a state of uncommittedness to a participation in the events at Verrières, and reflected in his 'later' writing or rewriting of the novel. The second is the linear causality that *el que te dije* tries to impose on the lives of the characters by deterministic logic, classification and

selection of the elements of the narrative. This imposition is parallel
to the censorship imposed by 'my paredros' in *62*. His motivations
are strictly and limitedly 'revolutionary' and his (unfinished) discourse forms the alienating and official code against which Cortázar's
own causality (the writing of Andrés?) expresses itself, thus forming
the *dialettica pendolare* referred to by Eco.

ANDRÉS

The dream

The position of Andrés at the beginning of the novel is much the
same as that of Oliveira in Paris. His life is plagued with dualism
and he is symbolically torn between two women: Ludmilla, like la
Maga, a totally natural and 'true' figure who 'seems to have a sort
of right to violate all chronology' (15), and Francine, like Pola,[25]
middle-class, cultured and significantly the part owner of a bookshop:
'The man astride the roof trying to encompass the Ludmilla world
and the Francine world [...] and of course the continual buffeting
from the binary, the irreconcilable double view from the ridge of
the roof' (167). His attempt to break with what he considers the
bourgeois institution of the couple is only partially honest in that he
takes a lover in a totally 'bourgeois' fashion, wishing to maintain the
status quo with Ludmilla. He himself realizes the difficulty of
knowing whether his choices are made freely or dictated by unconscious taboos: 'When I choose what I believe to be a liberating line
of conduct, a widening of my world, I am perhaps obeying pressures,
coercions, taboos, or prejudices which spring precisely from the side
which I am wanting to leave behind' (168). As in the case of Oliveira,
Andrés's lucidity and intellectuality, his incapacity to choose
between the piano and the electronic filters, leads him into a state of
total inactivity.

In the dream, Andrés enters a cinema to see a mystery film,
which indicates that he is a spectator in life. In the cinema, there are
two screens, an indication of the duality of his life. A waiter
approaches and menacingly informs him that a Cuban is demanding
to see him. When he comes out from the interview with the Cuban
(Castro), he realizes that the scene has been cut in the dream, that he
has been given a message to deliver, a mission, but he does not know
what it is. He is now, however, both an actor in the film and a

spectator, but before he finds out the conclusion of the film (his mission), he is woken by the postman.

The almost obligatory nature of the reference to the writing of Coleridge's *Kubla Khan* (103) must not make one underestimate the importance of the unconscious in the dictation of the message. The idea is also reminiscent of other works: *El sueño de los héroes* by Bioy Casares, where the hero has to re-enact a dream in order to find out its conclusion; García Márquez's 'Ojos de perro azul', where the hero, on waking every day, forgets the password by which he will recognize the 'real' lover he meets in his dreams; in a different way Borges's '*Inferno* 1, 32' from *El hacedor*.

The cut in the dream is referred to as the 'black blot' (*mancha negra*) and has extremely wide and paradoxical implications. It is censorship in that it separates Andrés from a knowledge of his destiny, and, as such, is connected with many other alienating manifestations of taboo in the novel, and thus demands destruction. It is the bulwarks cutting off access to the stern in *Los premios* and the string barrier between Oliveira and the other side of his reality, Traveler, which creates the 'black mass' in *Rayuela*. Yet at the same time, on returning to the film, there is absolutely no dualism in Andrés for the first time: 'But all this about it being double is what I say now I'm awake, there was no doubleness in the dream, I perfectly recollect that while I was returning to my seat I felt all this which I am now segmenting in order to explain it, however partially, as one single block' (103).

Paradoxically, only by doing what he has to do will he be able to know what it is: 'Rather as if only thanks to that action which I had to carry out could I find out what the Cuban had said to me, a completely absurd inversion of causality, as you can see' (103). A very similar reversal of causality was important in Oliveira's behaviour in the second part of *Rayuela*: 'I have the impression that as soon as I've got nice straight nails I'll know what I need them for'; 'First the nails and afterwards the purpose of the nails' (*R* 278). The connotations of such a reversal are complex and work on different levels. In *Rayuela*, we sensed a faith in the spontaneity prescribed by Zen, and in an impersonal causality or force which would direct Oliveira's action.

The problem becomes clearer when Andrés, after tortured attempts to penetrate intellectually the 'black blot', comes to the conclusion that 'I can no longer search with reason' (292). This is,

of course, the position reached by Oliveira, largely through the
example of la Maga. Intelligence is seen as accomplice of the
barrier of the 'black blot', as in *Los premios*. The theorizing of Andrés
leads him into a vicious circle of dualism and inactivity. The possibility of looking beyond revolutionary action to a hypothetical and
very different future is considered in very similar terms in Callado's
Bar Don Juan: 'We cannot think consecutively. We cannot manage
to produce integrated analytical thought. Our barrier of guts and
blood is too dense. We think with our whole body, inside the problem.'[26] Thus the 'black blot' denotes both the impossibility of
thinking beyond revolutionary action towards the state such action
might produce and also the necessity of renouncing a type of thought
alien to the revolution.

There is also a much simpler moral side to the issue. The sort of
intellectual activity symbolized by *Prozession* is a luxury which
Andrés has to win the moral right to indulge in. To renounce
intellectual thought in favour of pure and purifying action and
violence will transform this thought in the same way as Oliveira
abandons *la piedad* (conventional human sentiments) in order to
return to it in a freer, less alienated form:

Mais viendra le moment où il comprendra que pour écouter *Prozession*,
il faut d'abord gagner le droit à l'écouter, et pour cela, remplir certains
devoirs, accomplir certaines tâches, jouer certains jeux. Un jour, alors,
oui, on peut s'asseoir dans un fauteuil et écouter *Prozession*, sans que ce
soit, une fois de plus, l'égoïsme, le solipsime, la solitude, l'échec.[27]

Andrés does go to Verrières and thus, symbolically, joins the
revolution. The question of what sort of causality it is which leads
him straight to this destination remains. His poem 'Maneras de
viajar' and the fact that he travels to Verrières by underground and
by train are reminiscent of the city in *62*, and suggest the passivity of
an unconscious destiny. Such a destiny is reflected in a mystical faith
on the part of Andrés himself: on reaching a fork in the road to
Verrières, he blindly but with obvious symbolism takes the left-hand
turning, exclaiming in the words of St John of the Cross ('aunque es
de noche'),[28] 'Let us turn left, even though it may be night, my
beloved Juan de la Cruz' (352). *El que te dije*, again quoting St John,
rejects such mysticism *a priori*: 'A la caza darle alcance, etcétera. No'
(13). Curiously, this same phrase, 'even though it may be night', is
used by João in the novel by Callado quoted above.[29] In addition to

the meaning of barrier, the 'black blot' takes on the second meaning of a 'dark night of the soul'.

A parallel could be drawn between the Cuban's message, discovered and perhaps fulfilled in the journey of Andrés, and Cortázar's concept of narrative as discussed with reference to *62*, where the *intention significative* with the mediation of *la parole* was seen to discover, by saying it, what was to be said.

One must not forget that this reversal of traditional logic also contains a clear statement on revolutionary strategy – that revolutionary praxis and theory cannot be separated. Hence Cortázar's and Andrés's mistrust of preceptive politicians as typified by Lucien Verneuil. His quotations in 'Noticias del mes de mayo' of Sartre's denunciation of the reactionary role of the Communist Party in 'mai '68', and his comments on the Cuban revolution, are relevant here: 'What is admirable about the case of Castro is that theory was born from experience instead of preceding it' (*UR* a 50). Debray in his controversial *Revolution in the Revolution?* expands this point: revolutionary theory and morality were forged not in the city by party workers, but in the *sierra*. This work would seem to be known to Cortázar. His article 'Literatura en la revolución y revolución en la literatura' is an obvious parallel to Debray's title. One should avoid confusing Cortázar's enthusiasm for the more surrealist aspects of 'mai '68' with a belief in spontaneous revolution. The lack of explicit revolutionary theorizing in *Libro de Manuel* is explained by *el que te dije* (252).

The arrival at Verrières: return to the childhood garden

Borges tells us that in 'La muerte y la brújula', a story based like *Libro de Manuel* on the ambiguity between personal motivation and destiny, he was able, through 'that voluntary dream called artistic creation',[30] to describe what he had tried unsuccessfully to describe for many years: the atmosphere of the outskirts of Buenos Aires. This he does effortlessly, for he had – consciously – tried to describe not the Androgué of his youth but the estate of Triste-le-Roy near Paris.[31] Similarly, Andrés, on arriving at Verrières, is reminded of his childhood in the Buenos Aires suburb of Bánfield:

> My grandmother taught me in a garden in Bánfield,
> a sleepy suburb of Buenos Aires,
> – *Snail, snail,*

bring out your horns into the sun.
That must be why in this suburban night
there are snails.   (353)

For Andrés to reach Verrières is thus to return to his childhood, to
his origins. The stern in *Los premios* and the blind impulse of the eels
through their life cycle to their origins in the Sargasso Sea in *Prosa
del observatorio* have similar connotations. The journey of the eels in
this last work is as distorted by the classification and separation of
the scientists as the journey of Andrés would have been by analysis
and consciousness. We will later see the importance of a provincial
garden in the trajectory of Oscar towards revolutionary commitment. With the importance of the origins in mind, it may well be
relevant to the failure of *el que te dije* as author of *Libro de Manuel*
that, on beginning to write, he turns his back on his childhood
garden, on the table his grandmother has set and on the light around
which the insects are flying (24), an image of the original *intention
significative*. The origins will take on greater significance in our
discussion of taboo.

Synthesis or schizophrenia?

The journey of Andrés to Verrières, in spite of its mystical directness,
is as ambiguous as that of Julien Sorel to the Verrières of *Le rouge et
le noir*. It is haunted by a duality which points either to a vital
synthesis of the personal and political, or to the schizophrenia
attributed to Cortázar by Collazos.

Andrés has personal, individual reasons for going to Verrières:
Ludmilla is there with Marcos, the leader of the revolutionaries,
whose lover she has become on leaving Andrés. It is suggested that
by arriving late he brings the enemy agents, the 'ants', after him
(358). One interpretation would be that it is his individualism that
has introduced the 'ants', with all their connotations, into the
revolutionary action. This interpretation corresponds, however, to
only one reading of his relationship with Ludmilla, that is, that he is
motivated exclusively by jealousy in going to Verrières. It may be
licit to recall from *Rayuela* that Traveler's interpretation of Oliveira's
actions in Buenos Aires, strongly coloured by jealousy, is an instance
of bad faith aimed at distorting the causality which culminates in the
synthesis Talita–la Maga.

But the 'ants', according to Lonstein (368), had already been hiding at Verrières four hours before the arrival of Andrés, and a very different reading becomes equally possible. Andrés's male-centred triangle had been an indication of his insincerity: 'Might not a lot of us be trying to smash the bourgeois moulds on the basis of equally bourgeois nostalgias?' (168) On going to Verrières, however, he accepts a triangle centred round Ludmilla, a far more difficult exercise for a male 'Argentinian'. This inversion of a triangle formed by one man and two women into one formed by one woman and two men constitutes an important structural link with *Rayuela*: the triangle Ludmilla–Andrés–Francine becomes Andrés–Ludmilla–Marcos in the same way as the triangle la Maga–Oliveira–Pola becomes Oliveira–Talita–Traveler.

Though the inversion of the triangle is important, the symbolic role of Ludmilla must be considered the prime factor in the deep causality of the journey of Andrés. Ludmilla is another Maga and, though the monstrous attributes of the latter are considerably sub-limated in her, the spontaneity, naturalness and 'trueness' remain, as does the force of the monster. Ludmilla joins the revolution, and for Andrés to recover her or at least to rejoin her *is* to join the revolution, to accept its essence, the most valid forces behind it. The parallel with la Maga is absolute: Ludmilla is frustrated by Andrés, who gives her no children (92–3), is made egoistic and superficial, as reflected in her profession of actress (la Maga sings Hugo Wolf and Rocamadour is abandoned to a *nourrice*); she leaves Andrés for Marcos, whose wounds she cures (214) (la Maga looks after the sick Pola); on disappearing to join the revolution, she is purified by her new role as is suggested in the symbolic shower scene (238) (la Maga is cleansed of her 'monstrosity' by her death or disappearance); Andrés rejoins her and at the same time accepts and is integrated into the revolution (Oliveira recovers la Maga through Talita and is thus reconciled with reality, breaking the dualism which plagued his relations with it).

The synthesis achieved in *Rayuela*, symbolized and effected by the syncretism of Talita and la Maga, becomes in *Libro de Manuel* the synthesis of the individual and the universal and collective. This, for Cortázar, is the highest aim of socialism:

Not only can society as conceived by socialism not annul this concept of the individual, but aspires to develop him to such a point that all the negativity, all his demoniacal aspects which are exploited by capitalist society, will be transformed by a level of personality where the individual and collective dimensions will cease to confront and frustrate each other (*LR* 64–5).

Andrés, on approaching the house, cannot reconcile being an Argentinian (i.e., as in *Rayuela*, a historical individual) and being where he is, involved in revolutionary action: 'what a strange thing to be an Argentinian in this garden and at this time' (355). The paradox is expressed in the macaronically successful 'and the poor *taita* fell, the *taita* who read Heidegger' (355). The nightingale which appears just before the 'black blot' is dispelled is perhaps a symbol of the resolution of this tension. The most universal of birds is brought together with the *teros* and *bichofeos* of Andrés's youth: 'with something singing up there, perhaps the legendary nightingale, I have never heard a nightingale, being brought up on *teros* and *bichofeos* in Bánfield' (355).[32]

We will examine the effect and implications of separating the individual from the political or collective in *el que te dije*'s treatment of Oscar.

The message

The synthesis we have mentioned is further explained by the message which is revealed to Andrés as he approaches the house, and in turn helps to explain this enigmatic message. The message is 'Wake up!' (356) Our hypothesis about all the process is strengthened by Cortázar's essay 'Espeleología a domicilio', where he stresses how, in a dream, the subject and his action are not separated by the conscious mind: 'in that pure living experience where the dreamer and his dream are not distanced by categories of understanding, where every man is his dream, his dreaming of the dream and the subject of the dream' (*UR* b 50). He mentions the myth of Bluebeard's injunction to his wife not to open the door of the room where he kept the bodies of his previous, murdered wives. This door, for Cortázar, is 'underneath your eyelids' (UR b 50),[33] is the door which separates the conscious from the unconscious. He proposes a violation of this prohibition: 'In the light of archetypal figures every prohibition is a clear piece of advice: open the door, open it right away' (*UR* b 50). The way to open the door is 'to wake up in one's dream':

One has only to open it [. . .] and the method is the following: You must learn to wake up within your dream, impose your will on that oneiric reality of which up till now you have only passively been author, actor and spectator. He who succeeds in waking up to freedom within his dream will have opened the door and gained access to a plane of being which will at last be a *novum organum* (*UR* b 50–1).

'Wake up' is thus an order to free the liberatory strength of man's other side, his oneiric world. This is none other than the surrealist programme which has always been more or less implicit in Cortázar's work. Breton talks of 'cette volonté désespérée d'aujourd'hui [. . .] d'opérer à chaque instant la synthèse du rationnel et du réel',[34] and describes the surrealist enterprise in the following way: 'Au point de vue intellectuel il s'agissait, il s'agit encore d'éprouver par tous les moyens et de faire reconnaître à tout prix le caractère factice des vieilles antinomies destinées hypocritement à prévenir toute agitation insolite de la part de l'homme.'[35]

The message does not refer exclusively to the life of the individual, but also to the parallel barriers in social reality, as is suggested in a poem by Cortázar which was inspired by the graffiti and posters of 'mai '68'. One slogan demands 'be realists, ask for the impossible', to which Cortázar replies: 'We are realists, compañero, we are going / hand in hand from dream to wakefulness' (*UR* a 51).

The door of the *Ultimo round* passage is the 'black blot' of *Libro de Manuel*. The incitement to disobedience refers to prohibitions, taboos and censorship on various levels: social, in writing (the censorship of memory by *el que te dije*), and the 'door of horn and the door of ivory' (150) of sexual taboo. The rebellion and turning upside-down of *62*, closely connected with the theme of monsters, thus reappears. The monsters of *Libro de Manuel* are seen, if with less mystery, with greater clarity than elsewhere. We can now understand that the Cuban's message can only be carried out if, *at the same time* as Andrés abandons conscious thought, such prohibitions are violated in order that the repressive order they represent should not return, vampire-like, after the 'dark night' of Andrés.

EL QUE TE DIJE

Chronicler of the Joda

El que te dije is the first author of *Libro de Manuel*. His writing is, to a certain extent, a caricature of the demands from certain Marxist quarters that Cortázar should write something close to social realism, and contains a large element of an almost positivist causality. This tendency in *el que te dije*, however, though never complete or fully realized, produces the rudiments of an alienated and exclusive discourse, the code which, according to Eco and as we have seen in previous novels, is a necessary base against which a new message and causality (symbolized by the journey of Andrés) can be dialectically developed.

El que te dije is, nevertheless, a complex character and is presented with some sympathy. His personal position is very liberal. His very name suggests that he is the 'my paredros' of *Libro de Manuel*, that the other characters have delegated to him, through *pudor*, their own acts. *El que te dije* seems to mean 'the person I told you about', an ellipsis of 'it wasn't me who did it, but. . .'. He has at his disposal all the information on the revolutionary enterprise, registered in a chaotic pile of index cards and scraps of paper. The information is seen, as in *62* by 'my paredros', as insects flying around a light: the empty *intention significative*. Cortázar has always demanded a 'previous opening' on beginning a novel, that the elements of the novel should generate the causality which would link them:

One thing was clear [. . .]: the incapacity I still have to build a novel until the novel itself decides the process, and sometimes it finds it hard. I know that it is impossible but I also know its deep causes, the refusal of literature conceived as a humanistic, architectonic project, the need for a previous opening, that freedom demanded by everything I am about to do and, to that end, there can be no clear idea, no formal plan (*C* 18).

Demands, however, of immediate intelligibility and clarity are made on *el que te dije* as chronicler of the *Joda*. This is the defining difference between his position and that of Andrés: 'In my case [Andrés] it was something personal and I had no need to project it onto a sort of clarity for a third party, but *el que te dije* was in a different position' (212). The personal aspects of the narration can but be neglected or distorted by *el que te dije* due to his very nature as a collective double.

Great stress is laid on the 'neutrality' of *el que te dije*'s position and narrative: 'then *el que te dije* goes to his neutral corner, which is anywhere, not necessarily in a corner' (175); 'this neutrality had led him from the start to stand sort of sideways on, always a risky operation in narrative matters' (11). Yet Andrés, getting his own back for *el que te dije*'s attacks on him, is anxious to explain that this neutrality is not at all honest: '*El que te dije* was like that, as far as he could, he dealt the cards in his own way' (48). More importantly, the ideological character of seemingly neutral concepts such as

memory is carefully brought out. At first, *el que te dije* explains away
the exclusion of names and passages from his narrative as a simple
whim, asking 'why memory should not have its whims' (47). Later,
however, after conversation with Lonstein, he realizes how memory
functions as a defence of 'everyday life', that is of the 'precious daily
ego': 'Forgetfulness and memory are endocrine glands just like the
hypophysis or the thyroid glands, libido regulators which decree
vast twilight zones and brilliantly illuminated crests so that everyday
life will not bloody its nose too often' (230).

We have already noted the inseparability of personal and political
motivations in Andrés. Lonstein, in his turn, stresses the importance
of irrational elements (which the 'technocrats of the revolution'
would consider irrelevant) in the workings of reality and consciousness: 'They are the technocrats of the revolution and think that joy,
toadstools and my landlady are not part of the dialectics of history'
(144). He consequently mixes together all the heterogeneous
information he receives in 'one big meta-*Joda* salad' (108). Even
Marcos, the leader of the revolutionaries, insists that one's personal
and political lives cannot be separated, whereas this is exactly what
el que te dije does: 'Why that obsessive habit of chopping things up as
if they were salami? A slice of *Joda*, another of personal history, you
remind me of *el que te dije* with his problems of organization, the poor
chap does not understand and he would like to understand, he's a
sort of Linnaeus or Ameghino of the *Joda*' (239).

El que te dije is not opposed to the conclusion of others such as
Oscar who come to see the revolution as a wide, all-embracing
movement: 'how everything tended to be the same thing, to be the
Joda right here or far away, in Verrières or la Plata, Gladis or
Silvia' (305). If he could manage not to change key when writing
about erotic experiences, then 'he would begin to feel that everything
is *Joda* and that there are no personal episodes between one moment
and another of the *Joda*' (232).

But *el que te dije* works deductively, starting with the theory.
Moreover, the *pudor* inherent in his constitution prevents him from
writing in the way described. Consequently, at certain points, he
excludes the personal analogies which are so important in the work:
'this café in the rue de Buci had nothing to do with the bar in the
calle Maipú' (48). Similarly, he refuses to accept any relation
between the memories of the garden of his childhood and the
present: 'All this is of little relevance today, after so many years of

good or bad life' (23). Hence, when he receives the trajectory of Oscar, the details of the organizational and political aspects of his involvement in the *Joda* together with seemingly frivolous newspaper cuttings which had fascinated Oscar, *el que te dije* rigorously classifies and separates it: 'one big meta-*Joda* salad which *el que te dije* had to reclassify, putting the astrological cutting from *Horoscope* and the one sent by Oscar on one side, and the problem of old Collins and the counterfeit dollars on the other side' (108).

The inadequacy of his position is finally illustrated when, confronted with the chaotic fight with the 'ants', he is overtaken by events and can only revert to a parody of the *Iliad* before apparently dying: 'This cannot happen like this and here and tonight and in this country and with these people; it's all over, mate (se acabó, che)' (363). His words curiously echo the last moments of Oliveira: 'paf se acabó'.

El que te dije *and Oscar*

There is in Oscar a progressive understanding of his own situation and of the forces which dictate his revolutionary action. The barriers in him which obstruct this understanding (memory, separation) are paralleled by *el que te dije*'s manipulation of the facts of his life. There is an analogy between the alienated discourse which *el que te dije* attempts to impose on his material and the effect of Oscar's superego on his own consciousness. The reader is thus cleverly placed in the same position as Oscar.

El que te dije tries to explain the trajectory of Oscar in one of his many diagrams, the only virtue of which is that it explains absolutely nothing, rather like the taxonomy of Ceferino Piriz. The issue centres mainly around a newspaper article about the escape from a boarding-school in La Plata of a number of young girls, which Oscar sends before him from Argentina with a nostalgic account of his life in doña Raquela's *pensión*, of the scent of the jasmines and his amorous adventures in the light of the full moon. The press-cutting, where no mention is made of the full moon, rather of 'the shortage of light' (109), is surreptitiously introduced as 'the cutting on the full moon' (108). It immediately finds an echo in Monique, who says that 'it was perhaps the full moon as Oscar says' (110) (the reader has not yet heard Oscar's version), and recounts a parallel rebellion in a Strasbourg establishment.

As Oscar flies over the Atlantic to join the 'revolution', and tries hard to concentrate on how he is going to get the counterfeit dollars into France, he becomes increasingly obsessed by the notion of the full moon in the escape of the girls. The infiltration of the full moon into his consciousness is expressed typographically by smaller print over the main text. He has the impression that something is wrong or missing in his understanding. Whereas he himself imagines the girls scaling a wall in the light of the full moon and sexually excited by its influence, the article talks of 'a surprise black-out' (109) and claims prosaically that 'the cause of the trouble was the advertising of carnival dances by neighbouring night-clubs which craze the boarders' (110). A parallel may be drawn between the 'surprise black-out' referred to by the article and the 'black blot' of Andrés, also referred to as a 'total black-out' (267). The suggestion is that there is also some form of censorship at work in the article. To explain the reaction of the girls by the effect on them of the advertisements for dances is equivalent to limiting the motives of a revolutionary to the theory of dialectical materialism.

The full moon which impelled the young girls over the wall is the same full moon Oscar remembers from doña Raquela's boarding house. He recalls how 'in doña Raquela's patio the full moon was an imperious call, an impulse which sent out of orbit one's skin, one's [. . .]' (127). This image of a vital, irrational impulse is not alien to Oscar's decision to join the *Joda*. Indeed, it is suggested that such seemingly irrelevant images can dictate the whole course of a life: 'There is a sort of surreptitious recurrence of the joke or word play or gratuitous act which creeps up onto what is not a joke, onto the plinth of life, and from up there gives out oblique orders, modifies movements, corrodes customs' (125).

The separation of this motivation from his 'real' life ('the flight across the wasteland, nothing to do with this room at the other side of the world' (185)), imposed by his superego and the manipulation of *el que te dije*, leaves the revolutionary present and future he is entering empty and meaningless: 'Opening his eyes [. . .] tipped Oscar into something with no real hand-holds, the perfect, miniskirted and deodorized silhouette of Gladis [. . .], all that absolutely hollow' (128).

Gladis at this point is significantly described as being 'deodorized'. There are two very different types of 'washing' in the novel. This first instance corresponds to the sterilizing influence of the morality of Francine, which is 'as automatic as deodorant on one's armpits'

(266), and to the censorship of *el que te dije*. Consequently, when Oscar finally understands his own position, his memory is like 'an odour before the shower' (164). The other type, essentially in good faith, is, for example, the shower of Ludmilla on leaving Andrés, Lonstein's and Andrés's washing baby Manuel (341), Lonstein's job of washing corpses, symbolically washing away taboo, 'the ancient, rotten corpse of time and taboos and incomplete self-definitions' (233). There is also in *Libro de Manuel* the paradoxical washing and purification by a self-immersion in filth, corresponding to Oliveira's night with Emmanuèle, the self-burial of Heraclitus in the dung-heap to cure himself of dropsy. Lonstein's dissertation on mastur-bation leaves him 'with his face all new and awake and as if washed' (227). Andrés's visit to the strip-club with Francine and his feeling that he ought to let a drunkard vomit on him respond to the same intention.

In his hotel room, in the state of semi-wakefulness when the 'scissors of wakefulness' (142) are relaxed, Oscar allows all the heterogeneous thoughts in his mind to mix together freely: 'It was better to go to sleep and let it all merge since there was no way of separating so many things from one's memory or from the present' (195). Listening on the wireless to Puccini's *Turandot*, he is reminded of his childhood, when he had loved this music, and at the same time of the *pensión* of doña Raquela. (A link would seem to be established between the *pensión* and his childhood.) He remembers that Puccini had died before finishing the work, that it had been completed by someone else, and muses that so many things are given a false appearance of completeness – newspaper articles, the prehistoric animals reconstructed by Ameghino from one bone. (Marcos, as we noted earlier, refers to *el que te dije* as the Linnaeus or Ameghino of the *Joda*.) His own personal version of the girls' escape is then probably right; the hole that the journalist claimed the girls had opened in the barbed wire themselves was already there: 'who knows whether the hole might not have been there already' (164). The 'previous opening' demanded by Cortázar had been there all the time, ignored by *el que te dije* in the lamp in his childhood garden. The barriers within the novel are not absolute, but created in part by the narrative itself. One is reminded of the classification of the eel's life cycle in *Prosa del observatorio*, where Cortázar asks, 'But what is the point of that "why", when all that is asked of the answer is to block off a hole?' (*PO* 41–2)

We can thus see how memories from the past, enclosing an image of the potentiality of the future, can break through the barrier of censorship. The role of analogy in the discovery of the unconscious or repressed motivating force, and in the actual functioning of this force, is essential: 'But it was not a metaphor, it came back in a different way, as if obeying an obscure likeness' (164). Its importance is also stressed in *Prosa del observatorio*: 'Tout se répond, thought Jai Singh and Baudelaire with a century between them' (*PO* 20). Here as elsewhere, the analogy often works through word play, as when Oscar is reminded of the full moon (*luna llena*) on eating a croissant (*medialuna*): 'It may only be the croissant but it is also the full moon, the implacable machine of word play opening up doors and revealing entrances in the dark' (222).

Whereas *el que te dije* understands progressively less of what is happening until his final break-down, Oscar comes to a privileged understanding of the wide, often individual and irrational motives behind his commitment. He realizes that there is absolutely no difference between the girls' scaling the school wall and his girl-friend Gladis, who loses her job as an air-hostess in order to help him, that 'everything tended to be the same thing, to be *Joda* right here and far away' (305). Lonstein initially asks, 'what sort of an idea do you expect Oscar himself to have about what he's doing' (105). Oscar is now in a similar position and able to assert that Lucien Verneuil, apparently the most theoretically motivated member of the group, is 'obeying obscure allegiances to what he thought was pure and practical and dialectic logic' (306).

CONCLUSION

Politics, sexual liberation and monsters

The importance of eroticism in liberation has been a fundamental theme in Cortázar's work since *Los reyes*. The issue in *Libro de Manuel* is centred round the fear of the recurrence of repressive structures in society after the revolution. The strong link between political and sexual revolution is implicitly expressed in the novel, and incorporated into the structures of its text: Andrés can only go beyond the 'black blot' to Verrières after breaking down the parallel 'black blot' of the taboo on sodomy. Sexual liberation in the novel is thus not just a luxury of the revolution, but a necessary condition to its lasting success. Though Cortázar gives few explicitly political arguments, Lonstein significantly links the mental disturbances created by taboo in the individual with the collective illnesses of society: 'the daytime harmony which so many people called morality and which then some odd day, individually, became neurosis and the analyst's couch, and which also on some odd day, collectively, became racism and/or fascism' (218). References, however, are made to Stephen Markus (170) and to Wilhelm Reich (233) who, in *The Sexual Revolution*, was probably the first to note and study the survival in post-revolutionary Russia of reactionary sexual ideas in spite of the destruction of their economic base. Pointing out the cultural backwardness of the old Russia, he stresses the need in the future for a theory of sexual revolution.[36]

The ideas of Marcuse, however, provide the most useful theoretical background to our discussion of the theme. In *Eros and Civilization*, the latter makes a fundamental development in the study of the survivals to which Reich refers. After Freud, he stresses the correspondence between the phylogenetic and the ontogenetic, the repetition in the development of the individual of the stages of the evolution of civilization. The guilt a child feels when, in the Oedipal stage, he symbolically kills his father in order to possess his mother and rejects parental authority to seek gratification in society causes the parental values he has rejected to be reproduced in his superego, a process described as the 'return of the repressed'. Similarly, when the young men revolted against the patriarchal primal horde, where one leader held all the women yet protected the men, the dominant structures of the previous society were repeated, again through guilt, in the collective superego or superstructure. The repetition of this process from generation to generation has the effect of progressively strengthening the repressive laws of the superego.

For Freud, repression, which is used as a blanket term, is inherent in the very nature of civilization, and the process described above becomes a vicious circle. Marcuse, with his distinction between repression and 'surplus-repression', provides an insight which can break this vicious circle, if only in theory. Eros is the tendency towards complete oneness with the world, but the erogenous zones of the body (originally the whole body) have been gradually reduced to the genitals in order to leave the rest of the body free, as a tool, for the tasks of society. Marcuse argues that the scarcity which justified this repression is no longer the rule, that a high level of repression is no longer a historical necessity, but corresponds to the laws of capitalist production which demands that more and more be produced in order to maintain the money surplus. It is this no longer necessary repression that he terms 'surplus-repression'. To present such repression as 'natural' is also to naturalize the historical state which created it. This implies that the destruction of capitalist modes of production opens up the possibility of the reactivation of 'earlier' forms of sexuality, other than the exclusively genital.

In *The Other Victorians*, from which Cortázar quotes extensively, Stephen Markus brings out the ideological connotations of various taboos – the taboo on masturbation, for example, corresponds to the mechanistic view of the world where the body was seen as a machine capable of producing only a limited amount of semen.

The fear of return of the repressed, the perpetuation of alienating structures, conveyed in the repetition of the *figuras*, has been a central theme in all the novels. We have seen that the *figuras* point to a prohibition, but indirectly indicate the liberating nature of the tabooed force, the 'monster', which can be released if the alienating and dualistic prohibition is violated, if Actaeon returns to possess Diana.

The monsters of Cortázar's previous novels are presented in *Libro de Manuel* without the mediation of literary or mythical figures, and simply embody tabooed sexual activity. Masturbation in *Libro de Manuel* is equivalent to the Minotaur in *Los reyes*. Lonstein describes the taboo on masturbation as one of 'the deep ogres, the real masters of the daytime harmony' (218). As in the case of the Minotaur, the only way to kill this ogre (to destroy its monstrosity) is to accept it. This acceptance would have the effect of turning the ogre into a prince (like the Minotaur, son of the queen Pasiphae):

To tear Onan from the inner mass was to kill at least one of the ogres and even more, to metamorphose him by bringing him into contact with the daytime and the open, to de-ogre him, to exchange his sad clandestine coat for feathers and bells [. . .], the ogre which after all was a prince like so many ogres, just that you had to help him to stop being an ogre at last. (218)

Cortázar comments in the context of *Libro de Manuel* that since *Los reyes* he has taken upon himself the task of 'watching over slandered dragons' (*C* 23), the natural forces that 'the establishment defines as monsters and exterminates as soon as it can' (*C* 15). (The 'ants' significantly try to 'slander' the members of the *Joda* by killing their hostage and making it look as if the leader of the group, Marcos, had been responsible. This distortion of events is parallel to that effected by the authorities at the end of *Los premios*.)

There is the same suggestion in *Libro de Manuel* as elsewhere that the monsters preserve the memory of the origins and that only the experience of these origins can revitalize the future. For Andrés, to go to Verrières is to return to his childhood, and in the light of this return, the insistence on the pansexuality of children becomes significant. Children have been an image of the origins throughout the novels, and this novel is explicitly written for baby Manuel. The tender description of the rudimentary masturbation of Manuel is an image of the innocence lost to the guilty world-view of the adults looking on. It is a 'smack in the face (but it was also a caress) given by lost innocence to those who looked at reality in an adult fashion from the other bank, with their idiotic guilt, their stained yellow flowers from the corpses of Hindus' (90).

From the Hotel Terrass to Verrières

Libro de Manuel ends in a characteristically ambiguous and under-stated fashion. Perhaps it ends in a confused fashion, but then 'when there is talk of confusion, what one usually finds is confused people' (12). Without exhausting all the possible readings of the last two episodes (the 'rape' of Francine and Andrés's arrival at Verrières), I have suggested a reading involving the deep structure of recovery followed in earlier works. Though Cortázar may not consciously be proposing such a reading, only this deep structure seems able to account for the concatenation and logic of these episodes.

In the pages before the rape of Francine, the social and sexual are linked in that the 'naturalness' of the taboo on sodomy is presented as parallel to the 'naturalness' of social deprivation in the Paris slums. The taboo on sodomy is referred to as 'the truth, of course, a truth which grows in the earth of genealogical lies' (310). Francine comments on their visit to the slum areas: 'There is no need to come like a cheap doubting Thomas to check on all this inevitable filth' (278). Andrés is quick to pick up the word *inevitable*: 'You said it, my girl, everything was going all right in your speech but at the end you said that little word which is equally inevitable in your *Weltan-schauung*, for your world and mine all that is always inevitable, but we are wrong' (278). In a sense, both naturalnesses are broken down when Francine admits that the sodomy has not been a rape, that 'it was not unbearable, that he was not raping her' (313): 'No, you haven't degraded me' (327).

But the experience is, at the time, presented as a partial failure in that on the following morning both feel guilty: 'Apart from the bed, we were Adam and Eve at the hour of their expulsion, something full of shadows and past, covering our faces so as not to see the daylight on the gravestones down there' (326). The reference to Eve suggests that guilt in *Libro de Manuel* retains from *62* Christian connotations. We are also reminded that it is Jehovah who strikes down Onan for masturbation (225). This failure (when the episode is taken in isolation) is confirmed when Andrés crosses the bridge back to the city, to normality. His attempt at liberation has been a 'false bridge' (290), simply a 'holiday' as against the 'work day' (329) which he rejoins in the city, restoring the old dualism. The dualism of his act, as at the same time a liberation and simple escapism, is inherent in the nature of the hotel as an institution. Its owner 'guarantees a whole lot of Judaeo-Christian values' (287), while offering the therapy of irresponsibility: 'A hotel room is a mini-therapy, unfamiliar furniture, irresponsibility [...] nobody will come and say you're a lout' (286).

But just as in *62* the rape of Celia by Hélène depends for its final value and consequences on the activity and judgements of others, the outcome of this episode is only decided by Andrés's later action. The name of the hotel, suggesting a terrace or balcony, indicates that Andrés is still a spectator, not yet an actor. Only when the two categories of spectator and actor have been brought together will the 'black blot' finally dissolve. It is the close relation in *Libro de Manuel*, as in *62*, between guilt and death which creates the deep link between the two episodes.

Andrés chooses to carry out his transgression of taboo, to rape Francine, in a room of the Hotel Terrass overlooking a graveyard, which he describes as the 'stupid perpetuation of original misery' (292), apparently a reference to original sin.[37] The graveyard signifies the death of the other half of the individual, that which lies out of bounds beyond the 'black blot'. Taboo, the rules and prohibitions of society, in the form of the penalties, fines and traffic lights of the bridge across which Andrés returns to Paris, are ironically seen as protecting the pedestrian from 'death on four wheels' (325). When Andrés 'pataphysically' shows Francine the cemetery, the 'black blot' partially and momentarily disappears: 'The black blot disappeared for one fleeting second, [. . .] something in me had seen across to the other side, there was a sort of final balance to the stock-taking' (293).

The cemetery forms a parallel with the morgue of Lonstein, where the corpses, despised and rejected by society, correspond to 'the ancient corpse rotten with time and taboos and incomplete self-definitions' (233). Lonstein's washing the corpses (of guilt) and caring for them (in a way which flows over into necrophilia) is presented as bringing them back to life, or at least dealing a considerable blow to death (a euphemistic rendering): 'una buena manera de darle por el culo a la pelada' (39). Both transgressions of sexual taboo in the novel are described as descents to Hades. Lonstein's discussion of masturbation is 'a grotesque saga, a descent like that of Gilgamesh or Orpheus to the hell of the libido' (218). Andrés says to Francine, 'I need to go down those steps of cognac with you and see whether there is an answer in the basement, whether you can help me to get out of the black blot' (292).

The rape of Francine is thus clearly a repetition of Oliveira's kissing Talita in the morgue of the lunatic asylum, of Hélène's raping Celia and symbolically taking her blood to the hospital morgue. The descent is always effected, as we know, to bring someone back to life. Though no one is actually dead at this point in the novel, the two characters who could be symbolically recovered are Manuel and Ludmilla. Anxiety is expressed at various points about the safety of Manuel, which links him with Jorge in *Los premios*. There are more indications, however, that Ludmilla is the person symbolically dead to Andrés. Andrés has lost Ludmilla in the same way as Oliveira loses la Maga before symbolically recovering her. Evidence from *62* points in the same direction. To go beyond the 'black blot' is equivalent to the destruction of the contents of Hélène's doll. This destruction opens up the possibility of rendez-vous between Juan and Hélène, and one may assume that the disappearance of the 'black blot' in Verrières has a similar effect for Andrés as regards Ludmilla. That Ludmilla should have received him coolly is in a sense irrelevant, since what Andrés recovers is what Ludmilla represents, that is, the 'essential' Ludmilla: naturalness, spontaneity, revolution.

If at any point *Libro de Manuel* does reach the difficult 'convergence' between Cortázar's twin preoccupations, it is in these final inconclusive moments of the novel. Just as Oliveira reconciles having recovered the force of the dead Maga with going to the pictures with Gekrepken, Andrés, on joining Ludmilla, incorporates the values and force the latter has inherited from la Maga into his real, though tardy, rather superfluous, and perhaps disastrous act of adhesion to the revolution: 'Tell me where there is a gun because I may be drunk but in my time I passed all the tests at the Federal Shooting Gallery, so' (361).[38]

Conclusion

In *Le plaisir du texte*, Roland Barthes talks of an 'alternative excessive' in the field of modern literature, a progressive polarization of writers into two mutually exclusive camps – an elitist sophistication on the one hand and, elsewhere, the pursuit of pure revolution, utopia: 'une pratique mandarinale (issue d'une exténuation de la culture bourgeoise) ou bien [...] une idée utopique (celle d'une culture à venir, surgie d'une révolution radicale, inouïe, imprévisible)'.[1]

Cortázar increasingly takes this dilemma as the very backbone of his work in a way which sets this work in a central position within Latin American consciousness and culture.[2] His prose alternates between a self-deprecatory awareness that he is inextricably caught in the culture of the past, and images of a lost paradise projected towards a future utopia. La Maga, for example, his most 'natural' character, is first seen 'coming out of a bookshop no less'. The encounter is described in a sentence containing three literary quotes, from Darío's *Prosas profanas*, Echevarría's *La cautiva*, and Góngora's *Soledades*: 'It was a small bookshop in the rue du Cherche-Midi, era un aire suave de pausados giros, era la tarde y la hora, era del año la estación florida [...]. My god, what infinite stupidity' (*R* 486). Yet later in the same work we have the hope that 'the labyrinth would unwind like a broken clock spring blowing the time of employees into a thousand pieces' (*R* 253). The two sides of this see-saw are the two discourses of the 'double text' traced through the novels in the preceding chapters. Within its dialectic, each position clearly brings to the surface the partiality and ideological dangers, as well as the real possibilities and values of the other. The humanism and subtlety of bourgeois culture are utilized to the full, while its dead weight on another nascent consciousness is exorcized.

If Cortázar goes some way towards transcending the schizophrenia denounced by Barthes, he is indebted to a set of traits which have become almost a defining characteristic of a certain Latin American literary tradition, the most important of which are a deeply embedded eclecticism, and a very literal interpenetration of utopia and possibility, of fantasy and reality, which would simply be considered literary naivety in a European. Indeed, from a strictly European point of view, the conjunction of traditionally irreconcilable philosophical and literary categories noted by Leo Pollmann in *Los premios* (formalism and magic; Sartrean nihilism and metaphysical meaning; discontinuity of episodes and the continuum of the journey, etc.)[3] might suggest confusion, regression to old-fashioned techniques, and lack of intellectual rigour. When comparing the courses of the French *nouveau roman* and the Latin American *nueva novela*, Pollmann comes up with some decisive differences. Whereas the *nouveau roman* and its theory go hand in hand, and the European rigorously excludes doubtful or ideological categories from his work, the Latin American has an 'aversion to any formal or rational principle and against any sort of abstraction';[4] his attitude towards different methods of approaching reality is synthetic, a general 'not only, but also'.[5] While in Europe 'wanting to represent what things *are* in isolation from their meaning' is 'a "natural" phenomenon deriving from economic well-being', such a theory of knowledge in Latin America, given social conditions, would be a 'really perverse luxury'.[6] In Latin America, he adds, aesthetics are inseparable from nationalism, society, ideology and belief.[7]

Latin American culture, however, is to a large extent European. Vargas Llosa argues the advantage of being a 'barbarian'. Borges, too, suggests that marginality is a definite advantage, and brings out the fertility of the 'irreverence' that this marginality allows. The Argentinian, he asserts, is in the same marginal position as the Jews towards European culture and the Irish towards English culture. 'I believe', he continues, 'that we Argentinians, South-Americans in general, are in a similar position; we can handle all European themes, and handle them without superstitions, with an irreverence which may produce, and already has produced, favourable results.'[8]

The concept of utopia is a European ideal which has been consubstantial with the idea of America since almost before its discovery.[9] But it has also been a hope cherished by many Latin Americans right up to the Carlos Fuentes of *Terra Nostra* that the possibilities thwarted in Europe might be finally realized in the New World. Martínez Estrada, in 'El nuevo mundo, la isla de Utopía y la isla de Cuba', presents the strongest form of this view of utopia, giving it a perfectly well defined geography and future. He argues at length that More based his 'imaginary' republic on what he had learned of the newly discovered island of Cuba, and, encouraged by the success of the Cuban revolution of 1959, he asserts in a wider context that 'Utopia in fact contains, whether in a messianic and prophetic or logical and deductive form, a prognosis of the natural development of the Latin American historical process'.[10]

The case of Alejo Carpentier is exemplary. In 'De lo real maravillosamente americano', where he reproduces and comments on his famous prologue to *El reino de este mundo* (1949), he recounts how, disappointed with the formula-ridden, 'bureaucratic' fantasy of European surrealists, he discovers, on returning to the Caribbean, a reality and mentality far more fantastic than literature. The Venus of Canova comes to life for him in Pauline Bonaparte in the Caribbean; Piranesi's *Carceri* in Henri Christophe's fortress La Ferrière; Amadís de Gaula in Bernal Díaz del Castillo's *Historia verdadera de la conquista de la Nueva España*. Latin American reality is very literally fabulous: 'But what is the history of the whole of America if not a chronicle of the fabulous-real (*lo real-maravilloso*)?'[11]

By the time of *Los pasos perdidos* (1955) disillusionment follows enthusiasm: reality does not fit the idea, 'reflexivity and *dédoublement* crack faith and show the void through the fissures'.[12] Magic realism gives way to the baroque, where any trajectory 'is divided by that same absence around which it moves. Neo-Baroque: the necessarily pulverized reflection of a knowledge which knows that it is no longer "calmly" closed in on itself.'[13] Faith gives way to masquerade, carnival, ironic inversion of king and clown.[14]

But the faith in utopia, and in the coincidence between literary ideals and reality, cannot be banished so easily. In *Consagración de la primavera* (1978), Carpentier still insists that in Cuba 'surrealism is present in its raw state'.[15] Cortázar's *Fantomas contra los vampiros multinacionales* is described in its subtitle as an 'utopía realizable', a 'feasible utopia'. Cortázar is pleased but hardly surprised when an episode from *Libro de Manuel* is repeated almost exactly in the streets of Lyons (*C* 33). 'Nature imitates art', he repeats in many of his works (e.g. *62* 153, *M* 351). His constant desire for a future state reflecting a lost paradise seems somehow less distant and metaphorical than it does in the words of the Europeans he quotes, such as the lines from Alberti's *Sobre los ángeles*, 'paraíso perdido, perdido por buscarte' (*R* 432). If not actually converted, the sceptical European cannot but be excited by the conviction of Cortázar's language. Cortázar has no naive belief in the magical nature of language, and insists like Sarduy and González Echevarría on the fragmentation and limits of rational knowledge and discourse. But his voids and 'black blots' are not empty. A negative image of paradise is registered in the perturbations of the conventional side of his double text. The carnivalesque inversion in his work is not mere parody, and his monsters are sensed to be real forces at least as recoverable as Eurydice.

It is this cluster of 'irreverence', eclecticism, congenital optimism and refusal or incapacity to be limited by theory, inherited and renewed by Cortázar, which allows him, with some measure of success, to face up to one of the limitations of modern writing: that it cannot (argues Barthes) express political commitment due to the polysemia inherent in it:

Comme créature de langage, l'écrivain est toujours pris dans la guerre des fictions (des parlers), mais il n'est jamais qu'un jouet, puisque le langage qui le constitue (l'écriture) est toujours hors-lieu (atopique); par le simple effet de la polisémie (stade rudimentaire de l'écriture), l'engagement guerrier d'une parole littéraire est douteux dès son origine.[16]

The Latin American tendencies discussed above in Cortázar's writing may be illustrated by a brief comparison of *62* and the *nouveau roman* of Robbe-Grillet, to which Barthes's comments seem most relevant.

Those who reject 'bourgeois' culture often fall into a parallel and equally exclusive and partial fetishism of the text. Robbe-Grillet, in an article on his *Projet pour une révolution à New York*, points out that a *nouveau roman* is often based on a set of what he calls 'thèmes générateurs', banal episodes taken from the 'matériau mythologique qui m'environne dans mon existence quotidienne',[17] which generate a whole network of similar episodes. The relation between the episodes is purely formal, created by formal means, 'selon un mode de développement comparable à ceux qui mettent en œuvre la musique sérielle ou les arts plastiques modernes'. He radically refuses to use, and thus be contaminated by, any conventional value system when faced with modern myths – the violence on the New York underground, sexual violence and perversion, secret societies. To condemn them, he argues, 'au nom des valeurs admises', bringing into play concepts of 'profondeur' and 'culpabilité', would constitute 'une attitude de fuite, un refuge dans le passé'. He prefers to play with these myths as images without relief or depth: 'Ou bien alors les assumer, et, tout en les laissant à leur platitude d'images de mode, [...] il me reste la possibilité de jouer avec elles.'

There seems to be a measure of ambiguity in this relationship with literary material. Whereas Robbe-Grillet believes that to play with myths is the 'seul espace de ma liberté', Barthes claims that it is the author himself who is the plaything of language, that 'l'écrivain est toujours pris dans la guerre des fictions (des parlers), mais qu'il n'est jamais qu'un jouet'. Politically, Robbe-Grillet justifies the gratu-itousness of his works in a slightly facile way, recalling the belief in 'mai '68' that 'la révolution elle-même est un jeu'. Though Cortázar shares this enthusiasm for the ludic, even in a revolutionary context, the attitude of the Latin American is less one-dimensional, and ultimately more responsible.

In *62* the *thèmes générateurs* are the elements of the European literary myths, the codes which go to form the *figuras* within the text. A basic scene of vampirism generates a net of episodes in a manner similar to the construction of Robbe-Grillet's novels. Cortázar's eclecticism, however, does not prevent him from introducing into the textual game elements which would be taboo to the purist Frenchman – psychological motivation, moral value systems, guilt. Textual means are used to investigate and denounce the insincerity and false naturalness of conventional attitudes, while the *profondeur* of existential psychology is used to highlight and bring alive the formal links between the various occurrences of one theme. When Juan and Tell, for example, play with the literary and existential material before them, 'invent' an episode, although the formal links between that episode and others are similar to those linking episodes in the *nouveau roman*, their reasons for introducing an episode, their good or bad faith regarding their situation and the theme, determine not only our reading of the novel, but its whole textual development. An enormously fertile ambiguity and flexi-bility of analysis is created by this overlaying of the formal laws of the text and language with the introduction of motive.

The psychology of Cortázar's characters, as was hinted earlier and should have emerged from the discussion of the novels, has highly ideological connotations. Such connotations are extended to the laws of writing and language, partly through the mediation of the author or authors within the novel. By the time of the writing of *Libro de Manuel*, a set of ideological readings within the categories of both writing and psychology has emerged and is sufficiently established to be fruitfully allied to a well-defined 'engagement guerrier' only latent in his earlier works. This *engagement* does not reduce the polysemia of the writing, and would not seem to be excessively relativized by it.[18]

Robbe-Grillet makes an important point about the modern myths that he employs in his novels. They have a dual status: at once the image that society likes to project of itself, as what it most fears, 'à la fois l'image qu'elle veut donner d'elle-même et le reflet des troubles qui la hantent'. Fuentes makes a parallel comment on literature in general: 'But there you are. The heroes of Antiquity invented literature because they forced the natural forces to hide and reappear in disguise.'[19] These two phrases together suggest that modern myths function in the same way as does classical literature, itself a more subtle and more official image of society, in that both propose to our attention the most explosive aspects of man in order to deform and defuse them. Cortázar, following Borges, finds it natural not to separate his interest in literature and thought (order, control, beauty) from his fascination with monsters (chaos, nature). He rejects the 'platitude d'images de mode' of his monsters. By exploring in depth the links between their creation and perpetuation and the laws of the literary and psychological processes involved, Cortázar's hope would seem to be that the two only apparently unrelated forces might serve to redeem each other: monsters from their monstrosity by a refusal of the conventions which create them; literature from its literariness.

Literature can do little more than offer images. Those of Cortázar assert with force and conviction that the utopia and new society opposed by Barthes to sophisticated literature is not a nowhere or an elsewhere, but that its possible elements lie precisely within the structures of our literature and culture. It is here that Cortázar seeks to confront the two divided sides of man, 'our own limits from which we are so distant face to face' (*R* 453). Like the surrealists, he believes that it is on this encounter that the possibility of any new future rests. The monstrous sailors of the *Malcolm*, who both block the way to the stern of personal and social liberation, and are the forces which will break the *escamoteo*, the 'sleight of hand' of the 'American world' (*P* 358–9), are purified and reincorporated into the world which had denied them in la Maga's reincarnation in Talita; in the shape of taboo, their final marrying with the world and logic of San Juan leads to a modest but real Verrières which perhaps suggests that schizophrenia is not the only possible direction of all societies and cultures.

Notes

Introduction

1. See E. Picon Garfield, *Julio Cortázar* (New York, 1975).
2. Summarized in *Casa de las Américas* 57 (November–December 1969), 136–8.
3. E. Sabato, *El escritor y sus fantasmas* (Buenos Aires, 1976), 59.
4. *El escritor*, 18.
5. 'El escritor argentino y la tradición', in *Discusión, Obras completas* (Buenos Aires, 1974), 272.
6. García Márquez. *Historia de un deicidio* (Barcelona, 1971), 208.
7. 'El barroco y el neobarroco', in *América Latina en su literatura*, ed. César Fernández Moreno (Mexico, 1969), 175.
8. *El recurso del método* (Madrid, 1974), 146.
9. *El escritor*, 194.
10. See Picon Garfield, 6.
11. 'Julio Cortázar: Una apuesta a lo imposible', an interview, in *Cosas de escritores*, by E. González Bermejo (Montevideo, 1971), 133.
12. See R. Reeve, 'Carlos Fuentes', in *Narrativa y crítica de Nuestra América*, edited by Joaquín Roy (Madrid, 1978), 310.
13. A full account of the affair is given in *Libre* 1 (September–November 1971), 95–145.
14. See Luis Harss, 'Julio Cortázar, o la bofetada metafísica', in *Los nuestros* (Buenos Aires, 1973), 292.

Los premios

1. This image is perhaps suggested by similar ones in *The Upanishads*, e.g. 'On life all things are resting, as spokes in the centre of a wheel' (*The Upanishads* (trans. Juan Mascaró; Harmondsworth, 1973), 69).
2. According to Breton, Valéry once declared that he would never use the phrase 'la marquise sortit à cinq heures'. See André Breton, *Les manifestes du surréalisme* (Paris, 1955), 10.
3. Cortázar, in Harss, 277.
4. Cortázar, in Harss, 278.
5. *Museo de la novela de la Eterna* (Buenos Aires, 1975), 129.
6. *Adán Buenosayres* (Buenos Aires, 1966), 144.
7. E. Mallea, *Historia de una pasión argentina* (Buenos Aires, 1944), 73.

8. *El mito gaucho* (Buenos Aires, 1964), 150.
9. *Radiografía de la pampa* (Buenos Aires, 1942), ii, 154.
10. *Los siete locos* (Buenos Aires, 1971), 142.
11. See Martínez Estrada, *Radiografía*, i, 131.
12. *De la barbarie a la imaginación* (Barcelona, 1976), 52.
13. Moreno Durán, *De la barbarie*, 52.
14. *L'écriture et la différence* (Paris, 1967), 414.
15. *L'écriture*, 410.
16. Alejo Carpentier, *Los pasos perdidos* (Barcelona, 1972), 201.
17. Mallea, *Historia*, 94.
18. *Hombres de maíz* (Buenos Aires, 1967), 239. This book is read by one of the characters of *Los premios*.
19. See Alfredo Lozada, *El monismo agónico de P. Neruda.*
20. Compare with Neruda's 'Let, then, what I am, be, / an established and assured and ardent witness, / carefully destroyed and preserved without end' (*Residencia en la tierra* (Buenos Aires, 1969), 70).
21. Compare with Neruda's 'Of hereditary hopes mingled with shadow, / of tearingly sweet presences, [...] / what is left in my scant termination, in my feeble product' (*Residencia*, 36).
22. For an analysis of the social classes in the novel, see José Amícola, *Sobre Cortázar* (Buenos Aires, 1969), 123–40.
23. Persio also believed the passages to be the dwelling-place of Goethe's 'Mothers', the original, semi-divine presences that Faust descended to rediscover: 'And nevertheless the Mothers were there' (402). More than any other, it is Helen of Troy that Faust seeks. The name of the heroine of *62*, Hélène, may be significant in this light.
24. In a letter to Dr Ann Duncan, 24 September 1976.
25. Borges, 'El espejo de los enigmas', in *Otras inquisiciones, Obras completas*, 722.
26. 'La esfera de Pascal', in *Otras inquisiciones, Obras completas*, 638.
27. 'Nueva refutación del tiempo', in *Otras inquisiciones, Obras completas*, 763.
28. See L. Lugones, *Las fuerzas extrañas* (Buenos Aires, 1966), 90–1.
29. *The World as Will and Representation* (trans. E. F. Payne; New York, 1969), i, 128. This work is specifically mentioned in monologue E.
30. Substitution is a basic element in the creation of doubles. In *Rayuela*, the superficial life of Traveler is a 'substitute' for the ontological centre sought by Oliveira.
31. See Alan Watts, *The Way of Zen* (Harmondsworth, 1962), 68.
32. *The Upanishads*, 85.
33. Suzuki, quoted by C. Humphreys in *Zen Buddhism* (London, 1949), 100.
34. There may be an echo here of Eliot's famous 'neither does the agent suffer, nor the patient act' (*Murder in the Cathedral*, in T. S. Eliot, *The Complete Poems and Plays* (London, 1969), 245).
35. In J. R. Jiménez, *Libros de poesía* (Madrid, 1967), ii, 433.
36. See M. Butor, 'Sur les procédés de Raymond Roussel', in *Répertoire*.

37. J. Ricardou, 'L'activité roussellienne', in *Pour une théorie du nouveau roman* (Paris, 1971), 105.
38. R. Barthes, *Le degré zéro de l'écriture* (Paris, 1971), 10.
39. Ricardou, 108.
40. *Les mots et les choses* (Paris, 1966), 397.

Rayuela

1. Pedro Ramírez Molas, *Tiempo y narración* (Madrid, 1978), 127.
2. Picon Garfield, *Julio Cortázar*, 106.
3. Borges, 'Examen de la obra de Herbert Quain', in *Ficciones, Obras completas*, 464.
4. *Œuvres poétiques* (Paris, 1967), 128.
5. The terms and oppositions discussed in this preliminary approach are also to be found in Roberto Arlt's *Los siete locos*, where an intuitively rejected, yet elusive 'wind of lies' is opposed to a necessary 'metaphysical lie': 'But life cannot be like this. A feeling inside tells me that life should not be like this. If I were to discover the actual reason why life cannot be like this, I would prick myself, and would be emptied of all that wind of lies like a punctured balloon' (90). But later on we have: 'Human happiness can only rest on a metaphysical lie' (141).
6. D. Viñas, *De Sarmiento a Cortázar* (Buenos Aires, 1970), 123.
7. *Los signos en rotación y otros ensayos* (Madrid, 1971), 73.
8. *Juan sin Tierra* (Barcelona, 1975), 20–3.
9. There is an excellent analysis of the Berthe Trépat episode in R. Echavarren's 'Berthe Trépat revisitada', in *Palabra de escándalo*, ed. Julio Ortega (Barcelona, 1974), 79–94.
10. There is a parallel reversal of the traditional values in Quevedo's 'Gracias y desgracias del ojo del culo'.
11. Viñas, 124.
12. In González Bermejo, 132-3.
13. Borges, 'Tlön, Uqbar Orbis Tertius', in *Ficciones, Obras completas*, 443.
14. *Ibid.*
15. Borges, 'Anotación al 23 de agosto de 1944', in *Otras inquisiciones, Obras completas*, 728.
16. *Ibid.*
17. Ants are also seen as a monstrous subterranean force in the short stories 'Bestiario' and 'El veneno'. In 'Todos los fuegos el fuego', they may be taken as the carriers of taboo from one historical period to another. Something similar is suggested in J. C. Curutchet's 'Julio Cortázar, cronista de las *eras imaginarias*: para una interpretación de "Todos los fuegos el fuego" ', in *Estudios sobre los cuentos de Julio Cortázar*, ed. D. Lagmanovich (Barcelona, 1975), 95–6.
18. See Rodríguez Monegal, 'Le fantôme de Lautréamont', in *Narradores de esta América* (Buenos Aires, 1974), vol. II.

19. Graciela de Sola, *Julio Cortázar y el hombre nuevo* (Buenos Aires, 1968), 51.
20. *El museo de la novela de la Eterna*, 202.
21. Other authors refer to this fear, e.g. Murena: 'She murmured that Achard was without doubt "fiercely closed away in his arrogance" and that behind his arrogance there had to be "a fear of something [. . .], a fear which he hadn't been willing to accept, that had made him puff out his chest [. . .]." She added that in this sense he was "very Argentinian" ' (H. A. Murena, *Las leyes de la noche* (Buenos Aires, 1963), 156).
22. Quoted in Hollingdale's notes to Nietzsche's *Beyond Good and Evil* (trans. R. J. Hollingdale; Harmondsworth, 1974), 209.
23. 'Mi ametralladora es la literatura', in *Crisis* 1, 2 (June 1973), 12. Astrada refers to the phrase 'no te metás' as a 'classical piece of *criollo* advice', and records the popular verses, 'cuando veas a otro ganar / a estorbarlo no te metás: / cada lechón en su teta / es el modo de mamar' (*El mito gaucho*, 116).
24. Part of the roles of these two writers is fulfilled in later novels by M. Ochs and Lonstein, though the latter are not writers.
25. *Gestes et opinions du docteur Faustroll, pataphysicien*, in A. Jarry, *Œuvres complètes* (Paris, 1972), 1, 668.
26. The problem faced by Persio, 'the enormity of the range of choice', is very similar.
27. J.-P. Sartre, *L'existentialisme est un humanisme* (Geneva, 1965), 47.
28. L. Wittgenstein, *Tractatus Logico-philosophicus* (London, 1961), 51.
29. *Ibid.*
30. *The Anti-Christ*, in *Twilight of the Idols and The Anti-Christ* (trans. R. J. Hollingdale; Harmondsworth, 1975), 119.
31. This irrationalism is also practised by Morelli: 'That violent irrationality seemed *natural* to him, in the sense that it abolished the structures that constitute the speciality of the West [. . .] discursive thought [. . .] its instrument of choice' (489).
32. *Beyond Good and Evil*, 16.
33. *Beyond Good and Evil*, 17–18.
34. In his prologue to the *Obras completas* of Onetti (Mexico, 1970), 19.
35. Contrasted with the constant heat of Buenos Aires.
36. Onetti, *Obras completas*, 1085.
37. Onetti, *Obras completas*, 1105.
38. This postponement will be of extreme importance in *62*.
39. 'Onetti o el vicio de escribir', in *Triunfo*, 17 August 1974, 43.
40. L. Cernuda, *La realidad y el deseo* (Mexico, 1970), 14.
41. A. Breton, *Nadja* (Paris, 1969), 176.
42. *Nadja*, 157.
43. R. Crevel, *Etes-vous fous?* (Paris, 1966), 169.
44. *Mon corps et moi* (Paris, 1925), 109.
45. Cortázar, in his review of the novel, in *Realidad* 5, 15 (March–April 1949), 349–50.

46. See *Adán Buenosayres*, 401.
47. *La voz a ti debida*, in *La voz a ti debida y Razón de amor* (Madrid, 1969), 51.
48. *La voz*, 83.
49. *La voz*, 68.
50. See C. Jung, *Los complejos y el inconsciente*, trans. J. López Pacheco from the French, *L'homme à la découverte de son âme* (Madrid, 1969), 395–6.
51. The transgression involved in Oliveira's attitude on the death of Rocamadour, described as 'a negative, a total inversion' (185), is seen as the vigil of a knight over his arms (186). Lonstein's discussion of masturbation in *Libro de Manuel*, also an 'ogre' or monster, is likewise seen as a 'knight's vigil before the night at Verrières' (219).
52. Might not the names Maga and Gekrepken be an echo of Margareta and Gretchen?
53. See R. Cook, *The Tree of Life: Symbol of the Centre* (London, 1974), 16–17.
54. I would stress the very active role of the writer in creating a 'space' for such a reading, and disagree with the following type of analysis of the concept of the 'reader accomplice': 'Secondly, the whole idea of the *lector-cómplice* suggests that the barriers dividing life and literature be destroyed or, at least, removed. If this situation were completely realized, would not the novelist's responsibility for his own creation be reduced considerably?' (R. Brody, *Julio Cortázar: Rayuela* (London, 1976), 35).
55. 'What *Rayuela* is saying [...] is that until we make a deep critique of the language of literature, we will not be able to attempt a deeper metaphysical critique of human nature. It must be a parallel and so to speak simultaneous process' (M. García Flores, 'Siete respuestas de Julio Cortázar', in *Revista de la Universidad de México* 21, 7 (March 1967), 11).
56. M. Eliade, *Le mythe de l'éternel retour: archétypes et répétition* (Paris, 1949), 63.
57. George Steiner draws an analogy between the chemical functioning of the brain and that of language, which would have similar consequences: 'In a manner we cannot as yet formulate with our blunt tools of introspection, it may be that human speech is in some way a counterpart to that decoding and translation of the neuro-chemical idiom which defines and perpetuates our biological existence. The next dimension of psychology, the step that may at last take us beyond a primitive mind/body empiricism, could well be semantic' ('The Language Animal', in *Extraterritorial* (Harmondsworth, 1972), 76).
58. *Bhagavad Gita* (trans. Juan Mascaró; Harmondsworth, 1975), 57.
59. *Bhagavad Gita*, 58.
60. *Bhagavad Gita*, 57.
61. *Bhagavad Gita*, 105.

62. St John of the Cross, *Obras escogidas* (Madrid, 1969), 34.
63. Borges, 'El idioma analítico de John Wilkins', in *Otras inquisiciones, Obras completas*, 708.
64. Traveler is familiarly called Manú. Manu, who, in Indian mythology reigned over the living, can be seen as a sort of Everyman. See G. A. Davies, 'Mondrian, abstract art, and theosophy in Cortázar's *Rayuela*', in *Proceedings of the Leeds Philosophical and Literary Society (Literary and Historical Section)*, 16, 6 (November 1976), 140.
65. In E. Auerbach, *Scenes from the Drama of European Literature: Six Essays* (New York, 1975).
66. The words *sombra* and *imagen* are constantly used with reference to Hélène in *62*.
67. G. Meyrink, *El golem* (Barcelona, 1975), 269.
68. See Humphreys, *Zen Buddhism*, 12 and 117.
69. See Breton, *L'amour fou* (Paris, 1957), 51.
70. Brody, 20.
71. L. Aronne Amestoy, *Cortázar: la novela mandala* (Buenos Aires, 1972), 93.
72. Harss, 285.
73. J. Roy, *Julio Cortázar ante su sociedad* (Madrid, 1974), 205.
74. Harss, 269.
75. Sosnowski, *Julio Cortázar: una búsqueda mítica* (Buenos Aires, 1973), 160.
76. Sola, 126.
77. N. García Canclini, *Cortázar: una antropología poética* (Buenos Aires, 1968), 50.
78. García Canclini, 57.
79. As in Samuel Beckett's *Murphy*. There are various coincidences between the two novels. Murphy, who works at the Magdalen Mental Mercyseat, is given out as mad by the director Bom (139); Mr Endon, like the madmen in *Rayuela*, switches lights on and off (139); Murphy identifies with the madness of the inmates (100–1); he has a mystical experience (138); there is a droll scene in the asylum morgue (ch. 12). Page references are to *Murphy* (London, 1978).
80. Harss, 286.
81. Watts, *The Way of Zen*, 172.
82. Watts, 147.

62. Modelo para armar

1. *La mise à mort* (Paris, 1965), 58.
2. For a similar refusal to 'construct' in recent Spanish literature, see Cela's declarations on his *Oficio de tinieblas 5*: 'I want to keep growing and, to this end, I refuse to construct' ('Abdico de mi maestría', in *Triunfo* 587 (December 1973), 45.
3. Paz, *Conjunciones y disyunciones* (Mexico, 1969), 132.

4. Paz, *El arco y la lira* (Mexico, 1973), 282.
5. Compare, for example, *62*, 76, and *Prosa del observatorio*, 12.
6. C. Fuentes, 'El tiempo de Octavio Paz', prologue to Paz's *Los signos en rotación y otros ensayos*, 11.
7. See J. Lacan, *Ecrits* 1 (Paris, 1971), 58.
8. 'Sur la phénoménologie du langage', in Merleau Ponty, *Signes* (Paris, 1960), 113.
9. See M. Foucault, *Les mots et les choses*, 397.
10. Merleau Ponty, 'Le langage indirect et les voix du silence', in *Signes*, 94.
11. Philippe Sollers, 'Le roman et l'expérience des limites', in *Logiques* (Paris, 1968), 243.
12. The name *paredros* is taken from 'the Egyptian concept of a guiding spirit, a fellow traveler'. See G. Rabassa, 'Lying to Athena: Cortázar and the art of fiction', in *The Final Island*, ed. J. Alazraki and I. Ivask (Norman, Oklahoma, 1978), 59–60.
13. M. Hernandez, *Obras completas*, vol. II (Montevideo, 1970), 49. This volume, and the fourth (Montevideo, 1967), will be referred to in the text as *OC* II and *OC* IV.
14. In 'El perseguidor', Johnny is seen to 'pawn' his life to his critic, Bruno; see *Las armas secretas*, 152–3.
15. The *and* is italicized by the author in the last three cases.
16. V. Nabokov, *Pale Fire* (Harmondsworth, 1973), 53. Juan's eternity is also based on something similar to a misprint: 'He had cheated, if it made sense to talk about cheating in that (ironic, automatic) acceptance that *saignant* and *sanglant* were synonyms' (10).
17. *Pale Fire*, 53.
18. This initial and basic expulsion is mirrored at other levels in concrete episodes of expulsion, invariably by some form of authority: Inspector Carruthers expels various characters from England, and the final consequences of Marrast's 'provocations' are not known; the SNCF inspector throws the group off the Paris train, and Osvaldo the snail's race against time is interrupted; the waiter Curro threatens to eject them from the Cluny; Boniface Perteuil dismisses Polanco from his job at the officially subsidized plantations for his experiments with the canoe. Conversely, the recovery of the lost presence is perhaps reflected in the 'rescue operations', significantly less successful: Feuille Morte is rescued from the train; Calac, Polanco and 'my paredros' from the island on the lagoon; Marrast from the town officials; Juan does *not* save Nicole or the English girl from Frau Marta, nor Hélène the 'dead lad'.
19. S. Freud, *Beyond the Pleasure Principle* (trans. J. Strachey; London, 1966), 4.
20. F. de Saussure, *Cours de linguistique générale* (Paris, 1965), 166.
21. 'La différance', in 'Tel Quel', *Théorie d'ensemble* (Paris, 1968), 58.
22. *Ecrits* 1, 53.
23. This work is referred to by M. Paley de Francescato in 'Julio Cortázar y un modelo para armar ya armado', in *Homenaje a Julio Cortázar:*

variaciones interpretativas en torno a su obra, ed. H. F. Giacoman (New York, 1972), 369. Giacoman's useful compilation of essays will be referred to hereafter as *Homenaje*.

24. The name Polidor is almost certainly an echo of John William Polidori, author of *The Vampyre*, one of the earliest novels of the genre.

25. There are possible Mallarmean connotations in Cortázar's use of the term constellation: the constellation which may be the herald of the 'compte total en formation' in *Un coup de dés*, in *Œuvres complètes* (Paris, 1970), 477.

26. 'A Review of the Complex Theory', in C. Jung, *The Structure and Dynamics of the Psyche* (trans. R. F. C. Hull; London, 1969), 94.

27. The relevance of this work is suggested in A. Dellepiane's '*62. Modelo para armar*: ¿Agresión, regresión o progresión?', in *Homenaje*, 163.

28. Archetypes could perhaps be described as the complexes of the collective unconscious. Jung asserts that 'the existence of complexes, of split-off psychic fragments, is a quite perceptible vestige of the primitive state of mind' (Jung, 'A Review of the Complex Theory', 104).

29. Jung, 'Synchronicity', trans. R. F. C. Hull, in Jung and Pauli, *The Interpretation of Nature and the Psyche* (London, 1969), 145.

30. 'Synchronicity', 14.

31. 'The meaningless dispersions due to chance are made meaningful by the activation of the psychoid archetype' (editor's note to 'Synchronicity', 34).

32. In the sense in which Butor uses and realizes this term, after Calder, in the series of novels beginning with *Mobile*.

33. Confirming Cortázar's threat that *62* would be a 'book with few readers' (in Harss, 288).

34. Marrast expresses the coincidence of heterogeneous elements in this *figura* in a paraphrase of the famous phrase by Lautréamont frequently quoted by Cortázar: 'The chance encounter of a Palladian villa and a woman who has suddenly discovered that she does not love me. At a first glance, the famous operating table is missing, but it's there as well [...], it's there all right' (74).

35. *Parsifal*, trans. H. L. and F. Corder (London, 1879), 15. Abbreviated in the text as *Pa*.

36. There is probably an echo in this phrase of the St Sebastian code.

37. O. Paz, *Apariencia desnuda: la obra de Marcel Duchamp* (Mexico, 1973), 122.

38. G. d'Annunzio, *Le martyre de Saint Sébastien*, in *Tragedie, sogni e misteri*, II (Verona, 1946), 517–18.

39. *Le martyre*, 539.

40. *Le martyre*, 572.

41. *Le martyre*, 526.

42. For a discussion of the basilisk symbolism and its meaning within the novel, see J. C. Curutchet, *Julio Cortázar o la crítica de la razón pragmática* (Madrid, 1972), 120.

43. Sheridan le Fanu, 'Carmilla' (or 'Vampire Lovers'), in *The Vampire Lovers and Other Stories* (London, 1970), 40.

44. Bram Stoker, *Dracula* (London, 1973), 55.

45. See *Dracula*, 216.

46. J. S. Hay, *The Amazing Emperor Heliogabalus* (London, 1911), 263.

47. Borges, 'La lotería en Babilonia', in *Ficciones, Obras completas*, 459.

48. P. J. B. Chaussard, *Héliogabale, ou esquisse morale de la dissolution romaine sous les empereurs* (Paris, 1802), 402.

49. Antonin Artaud, *Héliogabale ou l'anarchiste couronné*, in *Œuvres complètes* (Paris, 1970), VII, 104.

50. Artaud, *Héliogabale*, 128.

51. *Cambio de piel* (Barcelona, 1974), 158.

52. *Cambio de piel*, 482.

53. *Cambio de piel*, 479.

54. Compare with the final scene of Wedekind's *Pandora's Box*. There may be a connexion between Austin, described as 'more or less red-haired' (230), and Williams, the murderer in De Quincey's *On Murder Considered as One of the Fine Arts*, who has, as Cortázar notes, 'hair of an astonishing orangey yellow' (*V* 2 86).

55. Fuentes is, on his own admission, a frequent companion to Cortázar on visits to the cinema to see monster films.

56. *Cambio de piel*, 178.

57. *Cambio de piel*, 180.

58. Butor, *La modification* (Paris, 1970), 276–7. Abbreviated in the text as *Mo*.

Libro de Manuel

1. See, for example, 'Acerca de la situación del intelectual latino-americano', in *Ultimo round*.

2. M. Alascio Cortázar, *Viaje alrededor de una silla* (Buenos Aires, 1971), 29–30.

3. Alascio Cortázar, 22.

4. Alascio Cortázar, 34.

5. Alascio Cortázar, 45.

6. 'Documentos. El caso Padilla', in *Libre* 1 (September–November 1971), 131. Referred to henceforth as *CP*.

7. Carlos Díaz Sosa, 'Diálogo con Cortázar', in *Imagen* 101–2 (January–February 1975), 27.

8. Díaz Sosa, 'Diálogo', 27.

9. García Canclini, 29–30.

10. A. Breton, *Position politique du surréalisme* (Paris, 1972), 95.

11. A. Breton, *Les manifestes du surréalisme*, 8.

12. 'El boom entre dos libertades', in M. Benedetti, *Letras del continente mestizo* (Montevideo, 1969), 37.

13. Gabriel and Daniel Cohn-Bendit, *Obsolete Communism: The Left-Wing Alternative* (trans. A. Pomerans; Harmondsworth, 1969), 12.

14. Cohn-Bendit, *Obsolete Communism*, 31.
15. See Macedonio Fernández's 'Bobo de Buenos', in *Papeles de Recienvenido, poemas, cuentos, miscelánea* (Buenos Aires, 1967), 147, and *Museo de la novela de la Eterna*, 199ff.
16. See Juan Goytisolo, *Señas de identidad* (Mexico, 1973), 84.
17. Similar enterprises are recorded in Louis Pauwels and Jacques Bergier, *Le matin des magiciens* (Paris, 1972): the 'adjectifs à double face' of Charles Hoy Fort designed to express a 'nouvelle structure mentale', 'un troisième œil de l'intelligence' (202); an Austrian professor's 'refonte du langage occidental', where, for example, 'le retard sur l'avance que je souhaitais prendre' becomes 'l'atard' (203).
18. *L'Abbé C.*, in *Œuvres complètes*, III (Paris, 1971), 356.
19. *L'Abbé C.*, 339.
20. *L'Abbé C.*, 344.
21. This is also true of the literary code of verisimilitude which, as Sollers points out, is highly ideological: 'LE ROMAN EST LA MANIÈRE DONT CETTE SOCIÉTÉ SE PARLE, la manière dont l'individu DOIT SE VIVRE pour y être accepté' (*Logiques*, 228).
22. U. Eco, *Opera aperta: forma e indeterminazione nelle poetiche contemporanee* (Milan, 1971), 107.
23. *Opera aperta*, 105.
24. *Opera aperta*, 116.
25. Both women have in their names (Pola *París*, *Franc*ine) a reference to France, i.e. to culture and order.
26. *Bar Don Juan* (Rio de Janeiro, 1971), 137.
27. In an interview with F. Wagener, 'Marier Joyce et Mao', in *Le Monde*, 20 September 1974, 26.
28. St John of the Cross, *Obras escogidas*, 57.
29. *Obras escogidas*, 49.
30. Borges, 'El escritor argentino y la tradición', in *Discusión*, *Obras completas*, 274.
31. 'El escritor argentino', 270–1.
32. Borges makes a similar use of what is presumably the nightingale in 'Nueva refutación del tiempo' after the famous moment before the pink fence (*Otras inquisiciones*, *Obras completas*, 765).
33. Oliveira, after the syncretism of la Maga and Talita, 'emerged [. . .] into the world under his eyelids' (*R* 374).
34. *L'amour fou*, 106.
35. *Les manifestes du surréalisme*, 51.
36. W. Reich, *The Sexual Revolution* (London, 1969), 191.
37. In *Prosa del observatorio* (p. 67), we have the phrase, 'We have not yet learned to make love, [. . .] to strip death of its suit of guilt and debts.' For more discussion of transgression and death in Cortázar, see E. Rodríguez Monegal, 'Le fantôme de Lautréamont', in *Narradores de esta América*, II; S. Sarduy, 'Del Yin al Yang', in *Escrito sobre un cuerpo*; M. A. Safir, 'An Erotics of Liberation: Notes on Transgressive Behaviour in *Rayuela* and *Libro de Manuel*', in *The Final Island*.

38. Within this reading, the death of *el que te dije* would indicate the abolition of the duality between the two positions represented by himself and Andrés.

Conclusion

1. *Le plaisir du texte* (Paris, 1973), 63.
2. Carlos Fuentes similarly refuses to evade the issue, at the risk of his 'death': 'I feel I am very much straddling two orders and two cultures [...]. There is a culture I refuse. I am against it – but I love it in a way. I believe in a new hope, but I am terribly afraid that its realisation will signify my death, that it will murder me. And I think the only valid way you can fight something is by loving it – only then can a struggle be fruitful' ('The Hope that Murders', an interview with Robin Smyth, in *Observer Colour Supplement*, 26 June 1977, 37).
3. L. Pollmann, *La 'nueva novela' en Francia y en Iberoamérica* (Madrid, 1971), 273.
4. Pollmann, 103.
5. Pollmann, 357.
6. Pollmann, 215.
7. Pollmann, 105.
8. 'El escritor argentino y la tradición', in *Discusión, Obras completas*, 273.
9. See E. Núñez, 'Lo latinoamericano en otras literaturas', in *América Latina en su literatura*, ed. C. Fernández Moreno, 93–120; S. Zavala, *Sir Thomas More in New Spain: A Utopian Adventure of the Renaissance* (London, 1955); and J. Ortega, 'Prólogo', to *La utopía incaica*, by El Inca Garcilaso de la Vega (Madrid, 1972).
10. Martínez Estrada, *En torno a Kafka y otros ensayos* (Barcelona, 1967), 259.
11. A. Carpentier, *Tientos y diferencias* (Mexico, 1964), 135.
12. González Echevarría, 'Alejo Carpentier', in *Narrativa y crítica de Nuestra América*, ed. J. Roy, 155.
13. S. Sarduy, 'El barroco y el neobarroco', in *América Latina en su literatura*, 183.
14. Sarduy, 'El barroco y el neobarroco', 175.
15. *La consagración de la primavera* (Madrid, 1979), 336.
16. *Le plaisir du texte*, 57.
17. Part of this article, which first appeared in *Nouvel Observateur*, 26 June 1970, is reproduced in the first edition of *Projet*. Subsequent quotes from Robbe-Grillet are taken from this article.
18. Arguments concerning spontaneism and irrationalism, like those discussed in relation to *Rayuela* and *Libro de Manuel*, though answered intelligently by Cortázar, cannot be totally ignored.
19. Fuentes, *Cambio de piel*, 180.

Bibliography

A very complete bibliography of works by and on Cortázar, compiled by Marta Paley Francescato, is included in *The Final Island: The Fiction of Julio Cortázar*, ed. J. Alazraki and I. Ivask. This bibliography, therefore, limits itself to listing the works quoted in the present study, and a short selection of other important items.

Works by Cortázar (dates first published, and editions quoted from)

Los reyes, 1949 (Buenos Aires, 1970)
Bestiario, 1951 (Buenos Aires, 1969)
Las armas secretas, 1959 (Buenos Aires, 1966)
Los premios, 1960 (Buenos Aires, 1966)
Historias de cronopios y de famas, 1962 (Barcelona, 1970)
Rayuela, 1963 (Buenos Aires, 1969)
Final del juego, 1964
Todos los fuegos el fuego, 1966
La vuelta al día en ochenta mundos, 1967 (Madrid, 1970)
62. Modelo para armar, 1968 (Buenos Aires, 1968)
Ultimo round, 1969 (Mexico, 1969)
'Literatura en la revolución y revolución en la literatura: algunos malentendidos a liquidar', in *Literatura en la revolución y revolución en la literatura* (a collection of related articles by Collazos, Cortázar, and Vargas Llosa), 1970 (Mexico, 1971)
Viaje alrededor de una mesa, 1970 (Buenos Aires, 1970)
Prosa del observatorio, 1972 (Barcelona, 1974)
Libro de Manuel, 1973 (Buenos Aires, 1973)
'Corrección de pruebas en Alta Provenza', 1973, in *Convergencias/divergencias/incidencias*, ed. J. Ortega (Barcelona, 1973)
Octaedro, 1974
Fantomas contra los vampiros multinacionales: una utopía realizable, 1975 (Mexico, 1975)
Alguien que anda por ahí, 1977

Books and collections of essays on Cortázar

Alascio Cortázar, Miguel, *Viaje alrededor de una silla*, Buenos Aires, 1971
Alazraki, Jaime, and Ivask, Ivar (eds.), *The Final Island: The Fiction of Julio Cortázar*, Norman, Oklahoma, 1978

Amícola, José, *Sobre Cortázar*, Buenos Aires, 1969

Arellano González, Sonia, *Tres eslabones en la narrativa de Cortázar*, Santiago de Chile, 1972

Arriguci, Davi, Jr, *O Escorpião encalacrado. A poética de destruição em Julio Cortázar*, São Paulo, 1973

Blanco Campos, J., *La narrativa de Franz Kafka y Julio Cortázar*, San José, Costa Rica, 1974

Boletín de Literaturas Hispánicas, 6 (1966)

Brodin, B., *Criaturas ficticias y su mundo en 'Rayuela' de Julio Cortázar*, Lund, 1975

Brody, R., *Julio Cortázar: 'Rayuela'*, London, 1976

Curutchet, J. C., *Julio Cortázar o la crítica de la razón pragmática*, Madrid, 1972

Escamilla Molina, Roberto, *Julio Cortázar: visión de conjunto*, Mexico, 1970

Fernández Retamar, Roberto, et al., *Cinco miradas sobre Cortázar*, Buenos Aires, 1968

Filer, Malva, *Los mundos de Julio Cortázar*, New York, 1970

García Canclini, Néstor, *Cortázar: una antropología poética*, Buenos Aires, 1968

Garfield, Evelyn Picon, *¿Es Julio Cortázar un surrealista?*, Madrid, 1975
Julio Cortázar, New York, 1975

Genover, Kathleen, *Claves de una novelística existencial (en 'Rayuela' de Cortázar)*, Madrid, 1973

Giacoman, H. F. (ed.), *Homenaje a Julio Cortázar: variaciones interpretativas en torno a su obra*, New York, 1972

Lagmanovich, David (ed.), *Estudios sobre los cuentos de Julio Cortázar*, Barcelona, 1975

MacAdam, Alfred, *El individuo y el otro: crítica a los cuentos de Julio Cortázar*, Buenos Aires, 1971

Mastrángelo, Carlos, *Usted, yo, los cuentos de Julio Cortázar y su autor*, Córdoba, Argentina, 1971

Pereira, Teresinka, *El realismo mágico y otras herencias de Julio Cortázar*, Portugal–USA, 1976

Revista Iberoamericana, 84–5 (July–December 1973)

Rein, Mercedes, *Julio Cortázar: el escritor y sus máscaras*, Montevideo, 1969
Cortázar y Carpentier, Buenos Aires, 1974

Roy, Joaquín, *Julio Cortázar ante su sociedad*, Madrid, 1974

Scholz, Lásló, *El arte poética de Julio Cortázar*, Buenos Aires, 1977

Sola, Graciela de, *Julio Cortázar y el hombre nuevo*, Buenos Aires, 1968

Sosnowski, Saúl, *Julio Cortázar: una búsqueda mítica*, Buenos Aires, 1973

Tirri, Sara and Néstor (eds.), *La vuelta a Cortázar en nueve ensayos*, Buenos Aires, 1968

Viñas, David, *De Sarmiento a Cortázar: literatura argentina y realidad política*, Buenos Aires, 1971; not exclusively on Cortázar

Articles on, and interviews with, Cortázar

Barrenechea, Ana María, 'La estructura de *Rayuela* de Julio Cortázar', in *Nueva narrativa latinoamericana*, ed. J. Lafforgue (Buenos Aires, 1972), II, 222–47

Benedetti, Mario, 'Julio Cortázar, un escritor para lectores cómplices', in *Letras del continente mestizo* (Montevideo, 1970), 58–76

Callado, António, 'Stages in the Latin-American novel', in *Censorship and Other Problems of Latin-American Writers* (Centre of Latin American Studies, Cambridge, Working Papers no. 14, 1974), 34–47

Carbone, A., 'Mi ametralladora es la literatura', *Crisis* I, 2 (June 1973), 10–15

Collazos, Oscar, 'La encrucijada del lenguaje', in *Literatura en la revolución y revolución en la literatura* (Mexico, 1971), 7–37

Curutchet, J. C., 'Julio Cortázar, cronista de las *eras imaginarias*: para una interpretación de "Todos los fuegos el fuego" ', in *Estudios sobre los cuentos de Julio Cortázar*, ed. D. Lagmanovich (Barcelona, 1975), 156–73

Davies, Gareth, 'Mondrian, abstract art, and theosophy in Julio Cortázar's *Rayuela*', *Proceedings of the Leeds Philosophical and Literary Society* (*Literary and Historical Sections*) 16, 6 (November 1976), 124–47

Dellepiane, Angela, '*62. Modelo para armar*: ¿Agresión, regresión o progresión?', in *Homenaje*, ed. Giacoman, 151–80

Díaz Sosa, Carlos, 'Diálogo con Cortázar', *Imagen* 101–2 (January–February 1975), 19–42

Echavarren, Roberto, 'Berthe Trépat revisitada', in *Palabra de escándalo*, ed. J. Ortega (Barcelona, 1974), 79–94

Fuentes, Carlos, 'Cortázar: la caja de Pandora', in *La nueva novela hispanoamericana* (Mexico, 1972), 67–77

García Flores, Margarita, 'Siete respuestas de Julio Cortázar', *Revista de la Universidad de México* 21, 7 (March 1967), 10–13

González Bermejo, Ernesto, 'Julio Cortázar: una apuesta a lo imposible', in *Cosas de escritores* (Montevideo, 1971), 91–131

Harss, Luis, 'Julio Cortázar, o la bofetada metafísica', in *Los nuestros* (Buenos Aires, 1973), 252–300

Hernández, Ana María, 'Vampires and Vampiresses: A Reading of *62*', in *The Final Island*, ed. Alazraki and Ivask, 109–14

Lezama Lima, José, 'Cortázar y el comienzo de la otra novela', in *Homenaje*, ed. Giacoman, 13–29

Pereda, Rosa María, 'Cortázar: obra abierta y revolucionaria', *Camp de l'Arpa* 11 (May 1974), 8–12

Pollmann, Leo, '*Los premios*', and '*Rayuela* y el año 1963', in *La 'nueva novela' en Francia y en Iberoamérica* (Madrid, 1971), 267–74 and 297–303

Rabassa, Gregory, 'Lying to Athena: Cortázar and the Art of Fiction', in *The Final Island*, ed. Alazraki and Ivask, 57–62

Ramírez Molas, Pedro, 'Julio Cortázar, el perseguidor', in *Tiempo y narración: enfoques de la temporalidad en Borges, Carpentier, Cortázar y García Márquez* (Madrid, 1978), 116–66

Rodríguez Monegal, Emir, 'Le fantôme de Lautréamont', in *Narradores de esta América* (Buenos Aires, 1974), II, 156–73

Safir, Margery A., 'Notes on Transgressive Behaviour in *Hopscotch* and *Libro de Manuel*', in *The Final Island*, ed. Alazraki and Ivask, 84–96

Sarduy, Severo, 'Del Yin al Yang', in *Escrito sobre un cuerpo* (Buenos Aires, 1969), 9–30

Wagener, Françoise, 'Entretien avec Julio Cortázar: marier Joyce et Mao', *Le Monde* (20 September 1974), 26

Index

215